INTRUSION DETECTION

Rebecca Gurley Bace

MACMILLAN
TECHNICAL
PUBLISHING
U·S·A

Intrusion Detection

Rebecca Gurley Bace

Published by:
Macmillan Technical Publishing
201 West 103rd Street
Indianapolis, IN 46290 USA

International Standard Book Number: 1-57870-185-6

Library of Congress Catalog Card Number: 99-63273

03 02 01 00   7 6 5 4 3 2 1

Interpretation of the printing code: The rightmost double-digit number is the year of the book's printing; the rightmost single-digit number is the number of the book's printing. For example, the printing code 00-1 shows that the first printing of the book occurred in 2000.

Composed in Galliard and MCPdigital by Macmillan Technical Publishing

Printed in the United States of America

Trademark Acknowledgments

All terms mentioned in this book that are known to be trademarks or service marks have been appropriately capitalized. Macmillan Technical Publishing cannot attest to the accuracy of this information. Use of a term in this book should not be regarded as affecting the validity of any trademark or service mark.

Warning and Disclaimer

This book is designed to provide information about intrusion detection. Every effort has been made to make this book as complete and as accurate as possible, but no warranty or fitness is implied.

The information is provided on an as-is basis. The authors and Macmillan Technical Publishing shall have neither liability nor responsibility to any person or entity with respect to any loss or damages arising from th information contained in this book or from the use of the discs or programs that may accompany it.

Feedback Information

At Macmillan Technical Publishing, our goal is to create in-depth technical books of the highest quality and value. Each book is crafted with care and precision, undergoing rigorous development that involves the unique expertise of members from the professional technical community.

Readers' feedback is a natural continuation of this process. If you have any comments regarding how we could improve the quality of this book, or otherwise alter it to better suit your needs, you can contact us at networktech@mcp.com. Please make sure to include the book title and ISBN in your message.

We greatly appreciate your assistance.

PUBLISHER
David Dwyer

EXECUTIVE EDITOR
Linda Ratts Engelman

MANAGING EDITOR
Gina Brown

PRODUCT MARKETING MANAGER
Stephanie Layton

ACQUISITIONS EDITOR
Karen Wachs

DEVELOPMENT EDITOR
Katherine Pendergast

PROJECT EDITOR
Alissa Cayton

COPY EDITOR
June Waldman

INDEXER
Larry Sweazy

ACQUISITIONS COORDINATOR
Jennifer Garrett

MANUFACTURING COORDINATOR
Chris Moos

BOOK DESIGNER
Louisa Kluczink

COVER DESIGNER
Aren Howell

COMPOSITORS
Scan Communications Group, Inc.
Amy Parker

About the Author

Rebecca Gurley Bace is the president of Infidel, Inc., a consulting practice specializing in intrusion detection and network security technology and strategy.

Prior to founding Infidel, Ms. Bace spent 13 years in government, the first 12 as an employee of the National Security Agency (NSA). She led the Computer Misuse and Anomaly Detection (CMAD) Research program from 1989 through 1995, as a charter member of NSA's Office of Information Security (Infosec) Research and Technology (R2).

As the leader of CMAD research, Ms. Bace was responsible for championing much of the early research in intrusion detection, funding academic research at Purdue University (COAST project); University of California, Davis, (Security Lab); University of New Mexico; and Tulane University. She also served as the government's technical monitor for the Wisdom and Sense and STAR anomaly detection research projects at Los Alamos National Laboratory.

Ms. Bace's research collaborations with Dr. David Icove of the Federal Bureau of Investigation led to the commercial publication of a manual for computer crime investigation and a government study of convicted hackers. She and the CMAD workshop series she founded and sponsored were involved in the 1995 detection, traceback, and apprehension of Kevin Mitnick, at the time the FBI's most wanted computer criminal. She receives mention in Tsutomu Shimomura's book on the subject, *Takedown* (Hyperion Press, 1995). Ms. Bace received the NSA's Distinguished Leadership Award in 1995, in recognition of her work building the national CMAD community.

After leaving the NSA in 1996, Ms. Bace served as deputy security officer for the Computing, Information, and Communications Division of the Los Alamos National Laboratory. In this role, Ms. Bace was charged with determining protection strategies that allowed the Laboratory to balance needs for security with needs for availability and performance.

A native of Leeds, Alabama, Ms. Bace holds a bachelor of science degree from the University of the State of New York and a master of engineering science degree from Loyola College.

About the Technical Reviewers

These reviewers contributed their considerable practical, hands-on expertise to the entire development process for *Intrusion Detection*. As the book was being written, these folks reviewed all the material for technical content, organization, and flow. Their feedback was critical to ensuring that *Intrusion Detection* fits the reader's need for the highest quality technical information.

David Neilan has been working in the computer/network industry for more than eight years, the last five of which have been primarily devoted to network and Internet security. From 1991 to 1995, he worked at Intergraph, dealing with graphics systems and networking. David then spent four years working with DEC firewalls and network security at Digital Equipment. Since 1998, David has been working with Present Online Business Systems, LAN/WAN, and Internet security where he is designing network infrastructures to support secure LAN/WAN connectivity for various companies utilizing the Internet to create secure virtual private networks.

Robin Roberts has been in the information security industry for more than 10 years. Since 1997 she has been employed by BTG Inc., a technology integrator and services provider. At BTG she serves as an information security subject matter expert and manages an information and network security services group with particular focus on customers from the intelligence community. From 1986 to 1997, Robin worked for the Central Intelligence Agency, managing the Information Security R&D Program and providing subject matter expertise to a variety of agency projects.

Stephen E. Smaha was founder and CEO of Haystack Labs, Inc., which designed, implemented, and fielded software-based intrusion and misuse detection systems starting in 1989. Before launching their first commercial product in 1993, Haystack Labs did research and development work on intrusion detection systems for a variety of government agencies and their contractors, including the FBI, National Security Agency, Department of Energy, the U.S. Air Force, and some unmentionables. Haystack Labs, Inc., was acquired in October 1997 by Trusted Information Systems (TIS). At TIS, Smaha served as vice president for technology until that company's acquisition by Network Associates in April 1998. Since that time, he has served on several computer company boards of directors and technical advisory boards and is actively involved in mentoring startup companies. Prior to founding Haystack Labs, Smaha developed computer security systems for military customers at Tracor Applied Sciences, managed an artificial intelligence software group at Schlumberger, designed office automation workstations at Syntrex Corp., and wrote biostatistics software for Health Products Research. Smaha is a well-known speaker and contributor to Interop, COMDEX, Internet World, and a variety of security-related forums. He has served on federal and state-level expert panels on security and privacy. Smaha's undergraduate degree is from Princeton University in math and philosophy. He has a master's degree from the University of Pittsburgh in philosophy and a master's degree from Rutgers University in computer science.

Fred Chris Smith practices law in Santa Fe, New Mexico, where he has lived since 1978. Since 1985 he has also consulted from time to time with the Los Alamos National Laboratory about various digital evidence analysis tools and other computer forensic technologies developed by the national labs. He currently consults with the lab in an ongoing effort to make new computer forensic tools and techniques available to public law enforcement and to private computer security professionals. He served as the director of special prosecutions and investigations for four consecutive New Mexico attorneys general. Since 1989 he has worked with SEARCH and recently helped to develop the advanced Internet investigation course curriculum for state and local law enforcement officers, which he helps to teach in Sacramento, California. He currently serves on the National White Collar Crime Center Executive Director's Advisory Board in Richmond, Virginia. Over the past 10 years, Fred has developed training programs and spoken to numerous state and federal agencies about computer crime and new developments in theories of legal liability resulting from an increased use of networked software applications in commerce. He works as a consultant for groups and companies from the private sector on investigation and litigation strategies where electronic evidence is involved. His most recent publication is a manual for the National Coalition for the Prevention of Economic Crime, *Forming Partnerships for the Prosecution of Computer Network Intrusions,* which will be published sometime after Y2K. Fred attended the University of Michigan as an undergraduate and received his law degree from Stanford in 1972.

Christopher Wee has been a researcher in intrusion detection and network security since 1991. His research interests are in host-based audit monitoring, the exploitation of vulnerabilities in network protocols, and the specification of security policies. As a graduate student and postdoctoral researcher at University of California, Davis, he worked on the DIDS, LAFS, GrIDS, and IDIP intrusion detection systems. Chris is currently a senior Infosec analyst with Intel Online Services, Inc. He holds a bachelor of science degree in electrical engineering and a master's degree and doctorate in computer science from University of California, Davis.

Dedication

To the "Graybeards" and "Nobeards" of computer security—may we someday get it right.

In loving memory of Joey Bace,

(1985–1994)

who taught his mom what matters most.

Acknowledgments

During the writing of this book, as in the rest of my life, I've been blessed with an abundance of extraordinary people who have spun a web of support around me.

I am deeply indebted to Steve Smaha, who has been my intrusion detection muse for many years. He, Jessica, and Rebecca have been a source of support and inspiration to me through the past decade. It was at Steve's behest that I tackled writing this book, and he was the source of much entertaining and informative discussion throughout the process.

Jennifer Garrett, Katie Pendergast, Alissa Cayton, and Linda Engelman of Macmillan Technical Publishing have been a joy to work with, encouraging and guiding me through the totally alien landscape of the publishing business.

My colleagues in network and information security make up a wise, intelligent, and incredibly entertaining community. They have been generous with information and encouragement, responding to my requests for opinions and explanations with unfailing good humor, funny email, fresh gossip, and profound insight. Special thanks go to Jim Anderson, Dorothy Denning, Gene Spafford, Bob Abbott, Marv Schaefer, Ruth Nelson, Marcus Ranum, Kevin Ziese, Adam Shostack, Chris Wee, Fred Smith, Drew Gross, Carolyn Turbyfill, Robin Roberts, Stephanie Fohn, Gene Kim, Ron Gula, and Dave Icove.

My former colleagues in the National Security Agency are brilliant and dedicated professionals who perform a critical, though all too often thankless function in our society. I consider it an honor to have been part of that organization, and I salute them for their support of the nation.

Finally, my family has been a source of immense joy and enlightenment to me. This includes the family to which I was born as well as the family that has gathered around me in the form of close and steadfast friends. I'm fortunate to have so many who have opened their hearts and lives to me. I am especially indebted to Terri Gilbert and to Paul Bace for their love, support, and patience as I wrote this book.

OVERVIEW

CONTENTS

INTRODUCTION

Computer and networking technologies dominate much of our lives today. Many of us rely on these technologies in our everyday lives: Our work, leisure, community, transportation, and communications are enabled by these systems. The widespread panic associated with Y2K problems and the subsequent threat to public infrastructures demonstrates how dependent we are on support structures ultimately controlled by computers.

Even as we rely on these systems, we're painfully aware of the flaws and imperfections in them. System failures are blamed for catastrophes ranging from airliner crashes to medical equipment failures. Media coverage of hacker incidents and disastrous system failures capture our attention and elevate public concern about the dependence upon these all too fallible machines. However, this concern is tempered by the appeal of new technologies, which offer near-magical capabilities to us. Even commerce has been transformed by the vision of a society that purchases goods and services in a virtual marketplace, where storefronts are built of bytes and network packets, not brick and mortar.

Over time, the wide-scale adoption of new consumer technologies follows a rather predictable pattern. First the technology is introduced, and early adopters of the technology utilize it, becoming the leading edge for the rest of the populace. Depending on the nature of the technology as well as the circumstances of the society, this phase is followed by mainstream adoption of the technology. As access to the new technology increases, some users exploit its capabilities to drive progress. Unfortunately, others utilize the technology to cause injury and to facilitate criminal activity. Ultimately, in response to public concern, the legal and law enforcement communities institute statutory and enforcement measures to deal with these problems.

Our experience with computers and networks have been no different. Initially, the lack of access to computers and the high cost of building and maintaining them limited the problems associated with security breaches. As the amount of critical information entrusted to the systems increased along with the remote access capabilities, the security problems became apparent.

The advent and rapid growth of the ARPANET, born of a partnership between government and academia, served to accelerate this security exposure. ARPANET was designed to function in a small community in which members were trusted and information had little perceived value. "Handshake" agreements were the order of the day, the number of account holders was small, and many users of the network knew each other.

From the figure below, which shows the growth of the Internet over the last few years, it is apparent that those days of the early Internet are long gone. Gone with them is the high-trust culture that defined the network community of that era. Many business organizations use the Internet as a setting for their most critical business operations. Government organizations use the Internet as a means of providing public access to public records and information, with future plans to utilize the network as a staging ground for elections and referenda.

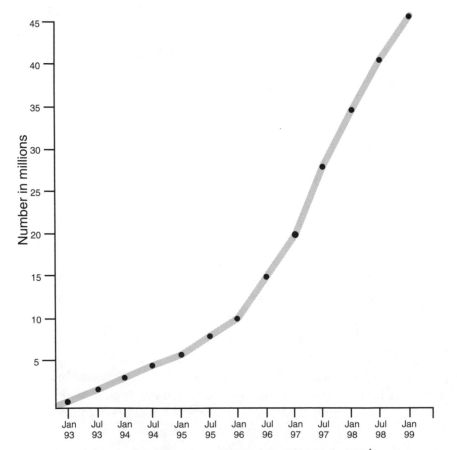

Internet Domain Survey, January 1999, Number of Hosts Advertised in the DNS[1]

In this network world, the needs for security and appropriate systems of control are apparent. The marching orders for those who would secure computer systems and networks are ambitious indeed. The security achieved must be reasonable yet sufficient, balancing needs for accountability with equally important needs for privacy. It must be flexible enough to accommodate a global range of statutes and regulations yet consistent enough to allow tracking of criminals across multiple jurisdictions.

The blend of management and technical measures necessary to meet these security requirements is rich and complex, a veritable smorgasbord of topics and issues for the interested researcher or developer. The area of security audit and intrusion detection has become an important part of computer and network security. The functions provided by these technologies serve the goals of security both directly, by providing traceback and detection capabilities, and indirectly, by monitoring the health and trustworthiness of other security mechanisms in the system.

Defining Intrusion Detection

Intrusion detection is the process of monitoring the events occurring in a computer system or network, analyzing them for signs of security problems. You can probably think of analogous monitoring systems in other areas, including burglar alarms and video-monitoring systems found in convenience stores and banks. On a grander scale, civil defense and military early-warning systems fall into this functional category. Although the monitoring strategies and targets differ, the general idea remains the same—these systems all provide sentinel functions, alarming and alerting responsible parties when activities of interest occur.

Note

The term intrusion detection is also used by the military to refer to systems that monitor physical entities (such as communications cables) for evidence of tampering or other physical alteration. Military standards describe system functions and benchmarks for this area. In this book *intrusion detection* refers to the monitoring, detection, and response functions that target activity in computer systems and networks.

Intrusion detection is a relatively young technology, as is noncryptologic computer security in general. The bulk of intrusion detection research and development has occurred since 1980. However, this research has produced a wide range of proposed solution strategies for accomplishing intrusion detection goals.

The youth (and subsequent immaturity) of intrusion detection brings other complications to bear. A gulf still exists between theoretical and practical aspects of intrusion detection. This situation creates all sorts of temptations for those researching and developing products in the area. For example, there are temptations to define terms on the fly and to develop proprietary solutions that aren't interoperable with other parts of the system security or management infrastructure. Another strong temptation is to claim that a favorite solution or approach solves all problems regardless of the validity of the claim.

These issues will eventually be resolved, driven by customer need and increased funding for research and development. The importance of intrusion detection in defensive information warfare is apparent, and the government has announced plans for additional expenditures in this area.

By Way of Introduction

I've spent the last 10 years immersed in the world of intrusion detection. In that time, I've seen a plethora of problem statements, proposed solution strategies, commercial products, and experts in the area come and go. I have directed government research for the area, attempting to marry research interests with operational needs. I've performed research of my own, exploring the techniques utilized by hackers to defeat security mechanisms. After years in the research community, I moved to a security management job and utilized some of the products in a challenging operational environment. And, coming full circle, I've devoted the last couple of years to working with security novices as they utilize existing commercial products and build new ones. Throughout this time, I've been delighted to see the successful transfer of many intrusion detection products to the commercial marketplace.

That delight, however, has been tempered with frustration. I see a commercial product market that utilizes but a fraction of the insight the last 15 years of research have produced. I see practitioners and developers who prescribe and build systems without ever asking end users what they really need and how best to integrate intrusion detection capabilities with their existing systems and practices. I see research and development initiatives that demonstrate no apparent understanding of the problems users face or of the work that has been already done. Finally, I see continuing resistance to the free and open discussion of intrusions and vulnerabilities with those who desperately need that information to protect their systems.

Despite these problems, I still believe in the value and future of intrusion detection as an integral part of computer security. Security, well done, can protect our privacy and the information that defines so much of who we are in this virtual universe. It also enables the formation of new and transformative communities by the users of the Internet, allowing us to collaborate in solving many of the pressing problems before us in the new millennium.

It is in this sprit that I wrote this book. It represents an opportunity to record the experiences of one blessed with the chance of a lifetime—to witness the growth of a technology from concept to commercial product. I hope that the information included enables you to include intrusion detection in your arsenal as you work toward achieving your system security goals.

Endnote

1. The survey data charted in the figure is provided by Network Wizard. The data is also available on the Internet at `http://www.nw.com/`.

The History of Intrusion Detection

"Life was simple before World War II. After that, we had systems."
- Admiral Grace Hopper

When I explain intrusion detection to those not familiar with network security, it's usually easy to describe what intrusion detection systems do: "It's a burglar alarm for computers and networks," or "It looks for criminals breaking into a computer system and lets someone know about it." Most people understand that when systems handle things that are considered valuable, the systems themselves are natural targets of attack.

Although the goals of intrusion detection systems may be intuitively obvious to both technical and nontechnical users, many people are not aware of the history of intrusion detection research and development. This lack of information results in repeating mistakes made in the past or needlessly settling for suboptimal approaches to critical functions.

Intrusion detection has merged traditional electronic data processing (EDP) and security audit with optimized pattern-matching and statistical techniques. Intrusion detection has become an integral part of modern network security technology. In this section, I describe the history of audit and intrusion detection from the perspective of the people who did the initial research and development and their projects.

1.1 Audit: Setting the Stage for Intrusion Detection

Before intrusion detection, there was audit. *Audit* is defined as the process of generating, recording, and reviewing a chronological record of system events. People audit systems to accomplish a variety of goals. These goals include the following:

- To assign and maintain personal accountability for system activities
- To reconstruct events
- To assess damage

- To monitor problem areas of the system

- To allow efficient damage recovery

- To deter improper use of the system

Figure 1.1 shows a simple diagram of an audit process. It includes the audit trail generator, logger, analyzer, and a reporting mechanism. Note that this audit process can apply to both manual as well as computer processes.

Figure 1.1   Basic Audit System

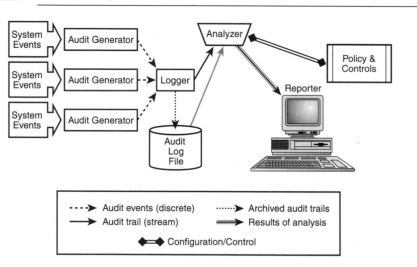

A premise that underlies all audit processes is that a set of rules governs the audit. The exact form and substance of this rule set varies, depending on the context of the audit process. In financial audit, the rule set may comprise generally accepted accounting principles, procedures, and practices. In management audit, the rule set comprises management controls, procedures, and practices meant to assure certain goals for the business. These business goals include items such as judicious use of resources, maximization of profits, minimization of costs, compliance with applicable laws and regulations, and appropriate control of risk.

In the special case of computer security audit, the rule set is usually articulated in a *security policy*. As you'll see in Chapter 3, "Information Sources," for intrusion detection to perform a complete and competent analysis of the audit data, additional rules that are not so clearly articulated in policy form are required. Note that the rules against which the system is checked affect the entire audit process. Consequently, we design the audit mechanism to collect the data elements necessary to detect noncompliance with the rules. In addition, the size and complexity of the rule set also drives decisions we make regarding the storage and analysis requirements of the audit analysis and archive systems.

1.1.1 Differences between Financial and Security Audit

Although the processes of traditional financial and management audit appear to be identical to computer security audit at the highest levels of abstraction, significant differences exist between the problems addressed. Financial audit addresses tracking transactions from cradle to grave; in other words, financial audit involves tracing the trail of evidence that links a chain of transactions to the summary figures in a financial statement. Another assumption for financial audit is that it reviews a *deterministic* process; in other words, a process that allows transactions to be traced both forward and backward in the system from any entry point within the chain of transactions that occurred within that system. The process is also assumed to be chronologically ordered in some consistent fashion.

Where these properties may still apply to accounting systems, they do not apply to the processes of many modern computer systems! Furthermore, there is no metric analogous to the summary balance in financial systems that can serve to confirm that the system is in a secure state at any given time. Finally, as the security audit is considered part of the *protection envelope* for the system it monitors, the security audit is likely to be a target for attack. Therefore, additional requirements exist for the protection of the audit mechanism, the system on which it runs, and the audit trail generated by the mechanism.

1.1.2 Audit as a Management Tool

In early computing environments, computers were large, novel, and expensive to acquire, operate, and maintain. Therefore, access to computing time was precious. Audit mechanisms in early operating systems were devoted to accounting for every microsecond of computing time (and, of course, billing users for the use of this time!).

As computers became more common and the number of business applications increased, someone noticed that the information collected in audit trails was useful for purposes other than billing. In particular, the information from audit trails could allow management to understand how the computer was being utilized, whether this use was appropriate to the organizational goals, and where resources might require modification.

Close on the heels of this discovery came the realization that these audit trails also supported the investigation of problems involving misuse of the systems. This area was of interest to organizations that used computers to conduct financial transactions. It was of even more interest to organizations that used computers to handle sensitive information. Hence came the earliest requirements for manual audit trail review. These requirements gave rise to the two major camps in computer audit. EDP audit served the objectives of the business-computing community. Security audit initially focused on needs in the military and government-computing world.

1.1.3   EDP Audits and Early Computer Security

Perhaps the first documented work defining a specialized EDP audit program was initiated in the mid-1950s. One of the earliest major corporate users of computing technology was the Bell Telephone System (which was the legally designated telephone monopoly for the United States at that time). A Bell Telephone Laboratory task force assembled in 1954 to analyze the future use of computers in the telephone business. This task force established the need for EDP auditing, differentiated it from the primarily paper-driven audit processes that marked system audit up to that point, and, by 1959, had an audit staff that was integrally involved in the design of the first large-scale computerized telephone-billing system.

The objectives of EDP audit mirror those of the manual business audit process that came before it. These objectives were to curb losses associated with error and fraud. Bell Telephone personnel noted, even in the 1950s, that to perform meaningful audits, auditors had to be able to evaluate software for the set of controls implemented by the programmers.

The concerns stated by the audit researchers were that auditors were attempting to audit "around the machine," not "through the machine." Auditing *around the machine* meant that auditors limited their audit examinations to the input and output of computer systems. Auditing *through the machine* meant that auditors had to understand what the system and its programs were doing and how they did it. Furthermore, the auditor needed to be able to use the computer itself to perform some of the audit checks, utilizing specialized audit programs to perform data sampling, seeding input data with test cases, and filtering transaction data for special cases.[1]

Many of the concerns articulated by EDP auditors are mirrored in the computer security world. Some computer security specialists have practiced within the EDP audit world for many years, with special interest communities that have functioned since the 1960s. An active software product market serves the specialized needs of EDP auditors, most of them facilitating searches and statistical checks of financial and other business process information.[2]

1.1.4 Audit and Military Models of Computer Security

The U.S. Department of Defense (DOD) backed an extensive research effort during the 1970s, which explored security policies, guidelines, and controls for operating "trusted systems," culminating in the DOD Security Initiative of 1977.

Trusted systems were defined as "systems that employ sufficient hardware and software assurance measures to allow their use for simultaneous processing of a range of sensitive or classified information."[3] Thus, trusted systems were designed from the ground up in a way that allowed military and intelligence organizations to place information of different sensitivity levels (typically corresponding to levels of classification) on the same computer system. The Trusted Systems Initiative provided a venue in which the computer security experts of the era explored the features and protections that were necessary for trusted systems to function. (Trusted systems are discussed in more depth in Chapter 3.)

During the initial explorations, researchers debated whether security audit mechanisms would contribute to the assurance level of a trusted system. Ultimately, the audit mechanism was indeed included as part of the *Trusted Computer System Evaluation Criteria*[4] ("Orange Book") requirements for systems evaluated at trust levels C2 and above. The series of documents that outlined the DOD's Trusted Systems Initiative are often referred to as the "Rainbow series," in a reference to the brightly colored covers of the documents.

A document, which addresses the issue of audit in trusted systems, is included in the Rainbow series. It is the "Tan Book," titled *A Guide to Understanding Audit in Trusted Systems.*

The Tan Book outlines five security goals for audit mechanisms:

- To allow the review of patterns of access (on a per-object and per-user basis) and the use of protection mechanisms of the system

- To allow the discovery of both insider and outsider attempts to bypass protection mechanisms

- To allow the discovery of a transition of a user from a lesser to a greater privilege level; for example, when a user moves from clerical to system administrator roles

- To serve as a deterrent to users' attempts to bypass system-protection mechanisms

- To serve as yet another form of user assurance that attempts to bypass the protection will be recorded and discovered, with sufficient information recorded to allow damage control

Although the Tan Book (as well as much of the Rainbow series) reflects a rather centralized mainframe view of computing, its principles of security audit still apply.[5]

1.2 The Birth of Intrusion Detection

As the speed, size, and number of computers increased over the 1970s, the need for computer security became increasingly apparent. The government, realizing that the traditional audit community had experience in dealing with tracking activities that took place on computers, made a decision to enlist its assistance. In 1977 and 1978, the National Bureau of Standards convened meetings of representatives of government and commercial EDP auditing organizations, which produced reports on the state of security, audit, and control at that time.

At the same time, the DOD, increasingly concerned about security issues associated with the proliferation of computer usage in military systems, increased its scrutiny of computer audit as a security mechanism. This task fell into the able hands of James P. Anderson.

1.2.1 Anderson and the Audit Reduction Problem

James P. Anderson is acknowledged as the first person to document the need for automated audit trail review to support security goals. Anderson, who published the Reference Monitor concept in a planning study for the U.S. Air Force, wrote a report in 1980 that is considered to be the seminal work on intrusion detection.[6] In this report, he proposed changes to computer audit mechanisms to provide information for use by computer security personnel when tracking problems. The goal of *audit reduction*, the elimination of redundant or irrelevant records from security audit trails, was first articulated in this report.

A major classified customer who handled sensitive data in mainframe environments featuring stringent security-management controls motivated Anderson's work. This customer had policies that required the auditing of all computer activity, supported by a security staff that manually reviewed audit trails and investigated problems uncovered in the audit trail review. The task of performing this manual review and investigation was becoming onerous as computing volume increased. Furthermore, the customer's security staff was discovering that its ability to detect some security problems in its audit review was jeopardized by missing or superfluous information in the audit trails.

Anderson proposes a taxonomy for classifying risks and threats to computer systems (see Figure 1.2) that differentiates between external and internal sources of problems on both a full system and per file/object basis. This articulation of concerns was helpful in structuring requirements for audit trail content.

Figure 1.2   Anderson's Threat Matrix

	Penetrator not Authorized to use Data/Program Resource	Penetrator Authorized to use Data/Program Resource
Penetrator not Authorized Use of Computer	CASE A: External Penetration	
Penetrator Authorized Use of Computer	CASE B: Internal Penetration	CASE C: Misfeasance

Anderson's report articulates several goals for security audit mechanisms:

- They should provide enough information for security personnel to be able to localize problems, but not so much that the audit trails themselves provide enough information to enable an attack.

- To optimize audit trail content to allow detection of problems, one must be able to collect information on a variety of system resources.

- To detect insider abuse of systems, the audit analysis mechanism should be able to discern some notion of "normal" activity for a given resource (where a user is considered to be a resource).

- The design of an audit mechanism should take the strategy of a system attacker into account.

Anderson points out that when a violation occurs in which the attacker attains the highest level of privilege, such as *root* or *superuser* in UNIX, there is no reliable remedy. For this worst-case scenario, one can instrument a system with embedded audit mechanisms that monitor CPU and other systems internals, but this defense is not particularly durable.

He devotes some time to the problem associated with *masqueraders*, those adversaries who access systems using purloined user IDs and passwords. To the system, masqueraders appear to be legitimate users. Anderson suggests that some sort of statistical analysis of user behavior, capable of determining unusual patterns of system use, might represent a way of detecting masqueraders.[7] This suggestion was tested in the next milestone in intrusion detection, the IDES project.

1.2.2 Denning, Neumann, and IDES

From 1984 to 1986, Dorothy Denning and Peter Neumann researched and developed a model for a real-time intrusion detection system, named the Intrusion Detection Expert System (IDES). This research, funded by the U.S. Navy's Space and Naval Warfare Systems Command (SPAWARS), proposed a correlation between anomalous activity and misuse. *Anomalous*, as defined in this project, meant "rare or unusual" in a statistical sense (in effect, outside of some statistical characterization of normal).

This assumption served as the basis for many intrusion detection research and system prototypes of the 1980s. Denning's 1987 paper on the topic is considered to be another seminal work in intrusion detection.[8]

The IDES model is based on *profiles*, data structures that use statistical metrics and models to describe the behavior of system subjects (primarily users) with respect to system objects. *Activity rules* specify actions to be taken at a given time (either the generation of an event record or the end of a time interval). The statistical metrics and models allow the system to evaluate behaviors against both fixed and dynamic measures of normality.

Denning and Neumann's model was instantiated in the landmark IDES prototype system, developed at SRI International from 1986 to 1992.

The IDES prototype system used a hybrid architecture, comprising an *anomaly detector* and an *expert system*.

The anomaly detector used statistical techniques to characterize abnormal behavior. The expert system used a rule-based approach to detect known security violations. The expert system was included to mitigate the risk that a patient intruder might gradually change his or her behavior over a period of time to defeat the anomaly detector. This situation was possible because the anomaly detector adapted to gradual changes in behavior to minimize false alarms.

The IDES prototype system was developed on a TOPS-20 system. Principal investigators and researchers of the IDES prototype included Peter Neumann, Harold Javitz, Teresa Lunt, R. Jagganathan, and Fred Gilham.[9]

1.2.3   A Flurry of Systems through the 1980s

The Anderson report and the work on IDES launched a cluster of research prototype systems over the next few years. We will mention several of these efforts, outlining the general assumptions, approaches, architectures, and results of each. Some will be covered in greater detail as we explore details of various approaches to analysis.

1.2.3.1   Audit Analysis Project

In 1984 to 1985, a research group at Sytek conducted a project funded by the U.S. Navy's SPAWARS Command. The Automated Audit Analysis project prototyped a system that utilized data collected at the shell level of a UNIX machine running in a research environment. The data was then analyzed by using database tools. This research demonstrated the capability to distinguish normal from abnormal system usage. Principal researchers for this effort were Lawrence Halme, Teresa Lunt, and John Van Horne.[10] Lunt went to SRI International, after the completion of this project, to lead the IDES project.

1.2.3.2   Discovery

Discovery is an expert system designed for detecting and deterring problems in TRW's online credit database. It was sponsored as an internal research and development project at TRW. This system was a bit different from the monitoring environment of the other systems from this era in that the database application, not the operating system, was monitored for intrusions and misuse. The goal for Discovery was to process daily inquiry activity in search of unauthorized inquiries. The processing load for the database system monitored by Discovery was estimated at approximately 400,000 inquiries per day, representing approximately 120,000 access codes. Audit trails were collected and the system was run against the data in batch mode.

Discovery used statistical inference to locate patterns in the input data. The system was designed to detect three types of abuse scenarios: unauthorized access, insider misuse, and invalid transactions. Discovery's statistical engine was written in COBOL, with an expert system written in an AI shell. Both parts of the system ran on an IBM 3090. The principal architect was William Tener.[11]

1.2.3.3 Haystack

Haystack is a system that was developed by Tracor Applied Sciences, Inc. (initially, from 1987 to 1989) and Haystack Labs (from 1989 to 1991) for the U.S. Air Force Cryptologic Support Center. Haystack was designed to help security officers detect insider abuse of Air Force Standard Base Level Computers (SBLC). These computers, Sperry 1100/60 mainframes running early 1970s vintage operating systems, were used to do traditional mainframe data processing tasks. The tasks (accounting, finance, inventory control, and personnel) handled data considered "unclassified but sensitive." The computers were running operating system software that was equivalent to a Trusted Systems evaluated level of B1, which included extensive audit mechanisms. The systems generated audit records reflecting more than a million events per week.

Haystack was implemented on an Oracle database management system running on an IBM-AT clone. Haystack's analysis engine was written in ANSI C and SQL and performed anomaly detection in batch mode, which meant that it periodically downloaded the audit trail file from the target SBLC system and then processed it.

Haystack characterized the information from system audit trails as sets of "features." Examples of features include session duration, number of files opened, number of pages printed, number of CPU resources consumed in the session, and number of sub-processes created in the session. Because there was no notion at the time of which features were most effective in detecting intrusions, the system included more than 30 features for each session. It used a two-stage statistical analysis to detect anomalies in system activity. The first stage, which checked each session for unusual activity, checked each feature against specified bounds and then performed a statistical test to determine whether the number of features that exceeded bounds was large enough to indicate unusual behavior. The second stage used a statistical test (the Wilcoxon-Mann-Whitney Ranks test) to detect trends in sessions. The combination of the two techniques was designed to allow detection of both "out-of-bounds" activities as well as activities that gradually deviated from normal over time. Haystack was fielded in 1992 and used on all U.S. Air Force SBLC systems for several years. The principal architect of Haystack was Steve Smaha.[12]

1.2.3.4 MIDAS

Multics Intrusion Detection and Alerting System (MIDAS) was developed by the National Computer Security Center (NCSC) to monitor the NCSC's Dockmaster system, a Honeywell DPS 8/70 running Multics, a highly secure operating system.

MIDAS was designed to take data from Dockmaster's answering system audit log. (On Multics, the answering system handled the user logins and password challenges, spawning user sessions.) Multics augmented the audit log data by collecting other information from the system. This data was organized, used to construct session profiles, and then compared to user profiles of normal behavior. MIDAS, like IDES and several other systems of the era, used a hybrid analysis strategy, combining statistical anomaly detection with expert system rule-based approaches.

MIDAS's expert system used a forward-chaining algorithm featuring four levels of rules. Figure 1.3 describes this heuristics structure in more detail. In addition to this rulebase, MIDAS kept user and system-wide statistical profiles in a statistical database, which was updated at the end of each user session. The statistical and rule-based analysis portion of MIDAS was coded in LISP and ran on a Symbolics workstation. MIDAS was placed online in 1989 and monitored Dockmaster through the mid-1990s.[13]

Figure 1.3   MIDAS Expert System Architecture

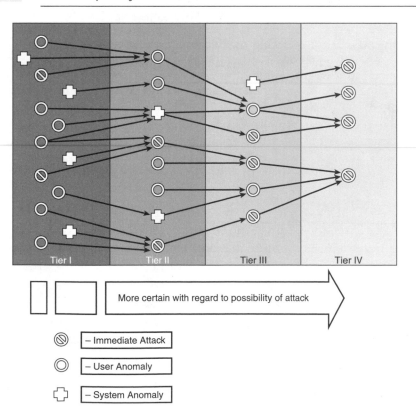

Note

MIDAS, one of the first intrusion detection systems that monitored an operational system connected to the Internet, gave a fascinating view of the Internet threat. Dockmaster was an attractive target for attack due to its affiliation with the Defense Department. Perhaps the most interesting insight that MIDAS gave us was a demonstration of the value of strong identification and authentication (I&A) mechanisms. In the late 1980s, after MIDAS came online, the NCSC decided to utilize token-based I&A as a replacement for weaker password mechanisms. In the scheme selected, users had a calculator-style token, protected by a PIN. When someone logged into Dockmaster, the system issued a multidigit challenge; this challenge was entered into the token, and the resulting multidigit response was sent back to Dockmaster, at which time the user session began.

MIDAS allowed the Dockmaster security staff to see the effects of enacting this stronger login mechanism. Doorknob-rattling and password-guessing incidents dropped dramatically after the token-based I&A system was in place. This effect emphasizes again the importance of thinking holistically when determining a protection strategy for systems.

The intrusion detection system could have continued to record attempts to hack into the system by password-guessing or other such attacks on weaker I&A mechanisms. Attackers might have been deterred, but only after a great deal of time and energy were spent on investigating the incident—tracking down the attacker, going through the phases of a criminal investigation and prosecution, and hoping for a sufficiently harsh sentence to discourage further attacks. The desired effect (to make external attackers stop) was much more quickly and easily accomplished by using a strong protection mechanism at the system access point.

Another even more important point is that, despite strengthening I&A to a point where external attackers were thwarted, the organization continued to run MIDAS to monitor for insider abuse.

1.2.3.5 *NADIR*

Network Audit Director and Intrusion Reporter[14] (NADIR) was developed by the Computing Division of Los Alamos National Laboratory to monitor user activities on the Integrated Computing Network (ICN) at Los Alamos. This network is Los Alamos's main computer network and serves more than 9,000 users—connecting supercomputers, local and remote terminals, workstations, network services machines, and data communications interfaces. NADIR monitors the network by processing audit trails generated by specialized network service nodes. It was designed to run on Sun UNIX workstations and, like many other systems of the time, it performs a combination of expert rule-based analysis and statistical profiling. NADIR is written in SQL and runs on a Sybase database management system, using some of Sybase's internal triggers and other features.

NADIR remains one of the most successful and durable intrusion detection systems of the 1980s and has been extended to monitor systems beyond the ICN at Los Alamos. NADIR continues to monitor the ICN at the time of this publication, and the team continues to modify the system to accommodate new threats and target systems. The principal architect for NADIR is Kathleen Jackson.

1.2.3.6 NSM

The Network System Monitor (NSM) was developed at the University of California at Davis to run on a Sun UNIX workstation. It represented the first foray into monitoring network traffic and using that traffic as the primary data source. Before this time, most intrusion detection systems consumed information from operating system audit trails or keystroke monitors. The general architecture of the NSM is still reflected in many commercial intrusion detection products at the time of this publication. The NSM functioned by doing the following:

- Placing the system's Ethernet network interface card into promiscuous mode (in which each network frame generates an interrupt, thereby allowing the monitoring system to listen to all traffic, not just those packets addressed to the system)

- Capturing network packets

- Parsing the protocol to allow extraction of pertinent features as shown in Figure 1.4

- Using a matrix-based approach to archive and analyze the features, both for statistical variances from normal behavior and for violations of pre-established rules

NSM was a significant milestone in intrusion detection research because it was the first attempt to extend intrusion detection to heterogeneous network environments. It was also one of the first intrusion detection systems to run on an operational system (the computer science department local area network at UC Davis). In a widely cited, two-month test of NSM, it monitored more than 111,000 connections on the network segment, correctly identifying more than 300 of them as intrusions. The system administrators for the network discovered less than one percent of these intrusions. This test emphasized the need for and the effectiveness of intrusion detection systems as part of the protection suite. Principal architects for NSM were Karl Levitt, Todd Heberlein, and Biswanath Mukherjee of the University of California at Davis.[15]

Figure 1.4   NSM Architecture

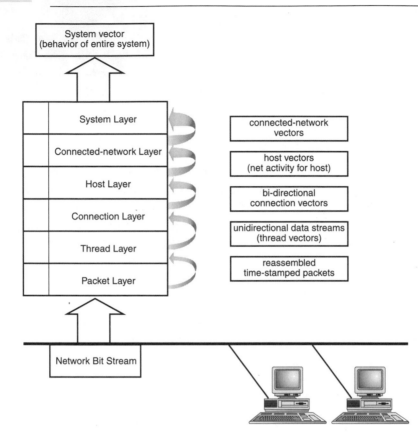

1.2.3.7   *Wisdom and Sense*

Wisdom and Sense[16] was an anomaly detection system developed by the Safeguards and Security Group at Los Alamos National Laboratory in partnership with Oak Ridge National Laboratory. Wisdom and Sense was the second pass at an intrusion detection system for mainframes (the initial system, called ALAP, was fielded by the U.S. Department of Energy in several of the department's facilities). Wisdom and Sense operated on a UNIX platform and analyzed audit data from Digital Equipment Corporation VAX/VMS systems. Wisdom and Sense performed statistical, rule-based analyses that were quite different from other systems of the time. The system used *nonparametric techniques* (which are statistical techniques that make no assumptions about the distribution of the data) to derive its own rulebase from archival audit data. Wisdom and Sense then compared subsequent activity to this rulebase, looking for exceptions. The rulebase was structured into arrays of tree structures (called "forests"), and because the rules were "human readable," they could be "pruned" and modified by humans. These rulebases defined normal behavior as observed from the historical audit data.

The approach used by Wisdom and Sense was originally developed for a process control environment to monitor the transfer of nuclear materials within a Department of Energy test facility. Problems observed in Wisdom and Sense were similar to those observed in many machine-learning approaches of this era:

- Generating reliable learning sets of audit data that were known *not* to contain intrusions was extremely difficult.

- False alarm rates were high.

- The memory required to accommodate the huge rulebases was difficult to manage, making the prototype systems unstable.

Principal investigators for Wisdom and Sense were Hank Vaccaro, of Los Alamos National Lab; and Gunar Liepins, of Oak Ridge National Lab.

1.2.4   *Integrating Host and Network-Based Intrusion Detection*

Until 1990, intrusion detection systems were largely host-based, confining their examination of activity to operating system audit trails or other host-centric information sources. As noted in the preceding section, the NSM extended intrusion detection to the network environment. At the same time, drastic increases in the interconnectivity of systems (due to the growth of the Internet and the increase in computing and communications bandwidth) resulted in equally drastic increases in computer security concerns. The Internet worm of 1988 brought this concern to a fevered pitch,[17] and funding increased for both commercial and academic research and development efforts. The first major initiative to integrate host and network-based monitoring approaches was the Distributed Intrusion Detection System (DIDS).

The DIDS effort was a large-scale collaboration between the United States Air Force Cryptologic Support Center; Lawrence Livermore National Laboratory; University of California, Davis; and Haystack Laboratories.[18] The research was funded by the U.S. Air Force, the National Security Agency, and the Department of Energy. It was the first attempt to integrate host and network intrusion detection capabilities so that a centralized security management group could track security violations and intrusions across networks. The primary architect for DIDS was Steve Smaha.

The initial concept of DIDS was to use techniques (previously demonstrated in Haystack and NSM at host and network level, respectively) that centralized control and reporting in a DIDS central controller. Figure 1.5 illustrates the DIDS architecture.

Figure 1.5   DIDS Architecture

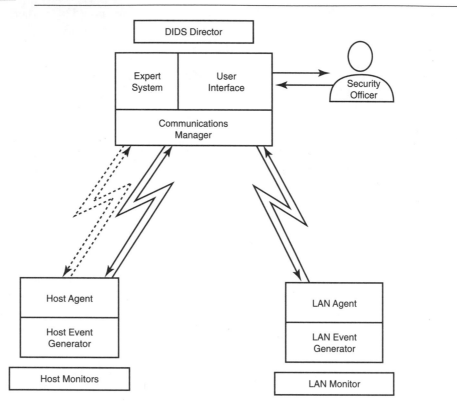

DIDS addressed several problems. One, a pressing issue in large network complexes, was tracking network users and files across the network environment. This function was especially critical, given two factors. First, network intruders typically use the interconnectivity of different computer systems to hide their true identity and location. Some intruders, in fact, mount distributed attacks, in which each stage of an attack is sent from a different system. Second, perhaps the most durable cure for a network attack is to discover the person responsible for the attack, collect evidence of the person's responsibility for the attack, and then use law enforcement and the legal process to prosecute the person. DIDS was the first system to allow customers to deal with this problem in this context by automating the tracking and correlation of user identities across the monitored network.

For example, suppose someone on my corporate system decides to "network hop" through my system, en route to attacking my payroll server. Fortunately, I'm running DIDS on my network. By tracking the attacker's identity as he assumes user identities of Smith on host1, Jones on host2, and Bace on host3 (at which point the intruder attacks the file server for the payroll system), DIDS allows investigators to see that the person they need to talk to is actually the person sitting at the terminal associated with Smith on host1, not me!

Another problem addressed in DIDS was how one could correlate data from events happening at various layers of abstraction in the system. Such information is required to "see" problems as they affect the entire network. DIDS correlates the data by using a six-layer intrusion detection model, with each layer representing the results of a transformation applied to the data.

1.2.5   The Advent of Commercial Products

In the late 1980s to 1990, several organizations built intrusion detection tools—some in an attempt to capture early interest in this new security technology, others to support higher levels of trusted systems evaluations by the NCSC. Three of the earliest of these systems are discussed here. Others are covered in more depth in chapters that discuss specific strategies and lessons learned.

1.2.5.1   ComputerWatch

ComputerWatch is an audit trail analysis tool that was developed by AT&T in the late 1980s to provide audit trail analysis and limited intrusion detection capability. Data reduction was supported with an examination mechanism that provided different views of the audit data. These views were specified based on information relationships. For instance, one could see the sequence of events associated with a particular user or group of users. Similarly, one could see all the events that occurred during a particular time interval. Finally, one could see all the events that involved a particular file or part of the system.

ComputerWatch supported a variety of queries and reporting features designed for a system security officer. An expert system was used to summarize system security-relevant events, and a statistical analyzer and query mechanism allowed statistical characterization of system-wide events. The system was designed to consume operating system audit trails generated by UNIX System V/MLS.[19]

After a brief period of availability as a commercial tool, AT&T withdrew ComputerWatch as a turnkey tool, using it as an internal resource in its consulting services group. Cherie Dowell was program lead for the ComputerWatch effort.

1.2.5.2   ISOA

The Information Security Officer's Assistant (ISOA) was developed by PRC, Inc. as a real-time security monitor. It was implemented on a UNIX workstation and supported automated as well as interactive audit trail reduction and analysis. ISOA used a set of thresholds and indicators to spot deviations from normal or expected behaviors, using a hierarchical scheme for correlating the indicators with levels of concern or suspicion. Detection was done both in-stream, in real time with discrete audit event checks; and at the end of sessions, with a threshold check of session statistics. The principal architect for ISOA was Vic Winkler.[20]

1.2.5.3   Clyde VAX Audit

Audit is a product that was developed by Clyde Digital (later RAXCO, and then Axent) to scan audit trails generated by Digital Equipment Corporation's VAX/VMS operating systems. Audit filters audit trails against 14 indications of possible security problems, including such things as dial-up sessions (indicating outsider access), sessions that occur after business hours, and sessions indicating file system browsing. Audit assigns weights and scores correlating to each of these indicators, and then provides summary reports that feature scores for each user on the system (where a high score indicates a high-risk user).[21]

Note

Allan Clyde, with sons Robert and Stephen, performed independent research and development in the mid-1980s on a surveillance-based security kernel for secure systems. These security kernels were built around surveillance gates (called *S-gates*), which were small software modules that monitored data paths within the operating system. The S-gates captured information from these data paths and processed it by using a weighted scoring analysis. The system then reported the results in a "suspicious event report."

The Clydes were notable for two reasons. First, they were building and fielding commercial products that were far ahead of most others in the security-monitoring field. Robert Clyde developed a product in 1977, called Control,[22] which allowed a system manager to monitor another user's terminal session for security reasons. He also wrote the first version of Audit, built on the S-Kernel model in 1983. Both of these products were developed for the Digital Equipment Corporation PDP-11 and VAX operating system environments. Second, the Clydes performed their research and development without government funding, building a commercially successful product organization that remains a major player in intrusion detection.

1.3   Conclusion

This chapter drew a timeline associated with audit, security audit, audit reduction, and intrusion detection. We outlined the concepts and strategies that are relevant to intrusion detection, and pointed out the seminal works for the area. It is important to note that the requirements and functions for these systems have changed significantly over the last 20 years as the nature of computing technologies and environments has changed.

The need for intrusion detection is even greater today than it was in the early 1980s when the seminal papers were written and initial research studies done. Developers of the next generation of intrusion detection products should be cognizant of the exploration done and the approaches tried in decades past. We'll revisit many of the systems cited in this chapter as we discuss the features and strategies for intrusion detection throughout this book.

Endnotes

1. Wasserman, Joseph J. "The Vanishing Trail." *Bell Telephone Magazine,* 47, no. 4, July/August 1968.

2. Abbott, Robert P. Personal communication, May 1999.

3. National Computer Security Center. *Glossary of Computer Security Terms.* Version 1, Rainbow Series, October 1988.

4. National Computer Security Center. *Department Of Defense Trusted Computer System Evaluation Criteria.* Orange Book, DOD 5200.28-std, December 1985.

5. National Computer Security Center. *A Guide to Understanding Audit in Trusted Systems.* Version 2, June 1988.

6. Anderson, James P. *Computer Security Technology Planning Study* 2. ESD-TR-73-51, Bedford, MA: Electronic Systems Division, Air Force Systems Command, Hanscom Field, October 1972.

7. Anderson, James P. *Computer Security Threat Monitoring and Surveillance.* Washington, PA: James P. Anderson Co., 1980.

8. Denning, Dorothy. "An Intrusion Detection Model." Proceedings of the Seventh IEEE Symposium on Security and Privacy, May 1986: 119–131.

9. Lunt, Teresa F. et al. "IDES: A Progress Report." Proceedings of the Sixth Annual Computer Security Applications Conference, Tucson, AZ, December 1990.

10. Halme, Lawrence, T. Lunt, and J. Van Horne. "Automated Analysis of Computer System Audit Trails for Security Purposes." Proceedings of the National Computer Security Conference, Washington, D.C., September 1986.

11. Tener, William T. "Discovery: An Expert System in the Commercial Data Security Environment." Proceedings of the IFIP Security Conference, Monte Carlo, 1986.

12. Smaha, Stephen E. "An Intrusion Detection System for the Air Force." Proceedings of the Fourth Aerospace Computer Security Applications Conference, Orlando, FL, December 1988.

13. Sebring, Michael M., E. Shellhouse, M. E. Hanna, and R. A. Whitehurst. "Expert Systems in Intrusion Detection: A Case Study." Proceedings of the Eleventh National Computer Security Conference, Washington, D.C., October 1988.

14. Hochberg, J. et al. "NADIR, An Automated System for Detecting Network Intrusion and Misuse." *Computers and Security* 12, no. 3, May 1993: 235–248.

15. Heberlein, L. T. "A Network Security Monitor." Proceedings of the 1990 IEEE Symposium on Research in Security and Privacy, Oakland, CA, May 1990: 296–304.

16. Vaccaro, H. S. and G. E. Liepins. "Detection of Anomalous Computer Session Activity." Proceedings of the 1989 IEEE Symposium on Research in Security and Privacy, Oakland, CA, May 1989: 280–289.

17. Spafford, Eugene H. *The Internal Worm: Crisis and Aftermath.* Communications of the ACM, 32(6), June 1989: 678–687.

18. Snapp, S. R. et al. "DIDS (Distributed Intrusion Detection System)—Motivation, Architecture, and An Early Prototype." Proceedings of the Fifteenth National Computer Security Conference, Baltimore, MD, October 1992.

19. Dowell, Cheri and P. Ramstedt. "The ComputerWatch Data Reduction Tool." Proceedings of the Thirteenth National Computer Security Conference, Washington, DC, October 1990.

20. Winkler, J. R. "A UNIX Prototype for Intrusion and Anomaly Detection in Secure Networks." Proceedings of the Thirteenth National Computer Security Conference, Washington, DC, October 1990: 115–124.

21. Clyde, Allan R. *Insider Threat Identification Systems.* Rockville, MD: A. R. Clyde Associates, September 1987.

22. Clyde, Robert. Personal communication, June 1999.

CHAPTER

2

Concepts and Definitions

2.1   An Introduction to Intrusion Detection

Intrusion detection is the process of monitoring computer networks and systems for violations of security policy. In the simplest terms, intrusion detection systems consist of three functional components:

- An information source that provides a stream of event records

- An analysis engine that finds signs of intrusions

- A response component that generates reactions based on the outcome of the analysis engine

We'll flesh out this model as we proceed through this chapter.

Intrusion detection is an incarnation of the traditional practice of system audit. *Audit* is defined as "the official systematic examination of accounts to ascertain their accuracy."[1] Intrusion detection augments the traditional audit, which was designed to occur at infrequent intervals, thus making it a continuous process.

To better understand the core process of intrusion detection, let's look at the historical process from which it evolved. In computer security circles, *auditing* systems meant manually reviewing audit trails generated by computer operating systems and other system-logging mechanisms. This security audit trail review was structured to allow responsible parties to ensure that the activities that occurred on the computer system were in compliance with some set of security policies. Where the activities were found not to be in compliance, there were additional goals:

- Accountability—Determine who was responsible for the breach

- Damage assessment—Determine what actions they took and what damage ensued

- Damage recovery—Determine what steps are required to repair the damage and restore the system to secure operation

These traditional audit principles and practices are discussed in more detail in Chapter 1, "The History of Intrusion Detection."

As computer systems became faster, more complex, and more numerous, the size and complexity of audit trails increased as well. The task of reviewing the data grew much more onerous and then simply became impossible. Automating the process of audit review was a logical remedy for this problem. The requirement for an automated audit trail reduction and review function was included as part of the National Computer Security Center's Trusted Systems Security Criteria of the 1980s. Research done in the course of satisfying this automated audit requirement yielded much of what we know about modern security audit and intrusion detection technology.

2.2 Security Concepts

Intrusion detection was initially proposed and is constantly evolving to meet a set of functional goals, all associated with improving the security of computers and networks. In this section, we'll define some of the fundamental terms and concepts of computer and network security. This information will allow you to look at current and future intrusion detection strategies, and to ask yourself the following questions, which remain constant, even as the technology changes:

What security goals do I need to support?

What assumptions should I make about the security goals of the target system?

Exactly what assets do I need to protect?

Answering these questions (and more important, by noting which questions remain unanswered) will allow you to make intelligent judgments about the value of a proposed intrusion detection approach.

2.2.1 A Cultural View of Computer and Network Security

So what do we mean by *security*? Security can be viewed from two general vantage points: theoretical and engineering. Some practitioners of computer and network security approach the problem from an abjectly theoretical point of view. These security experts explore the theoretical foundations of computing and consider security in that context. They are interested in characterizing security properties mathematically by forming security models that are provably correct. The precision and clarity of view that these experts bring to the area can be quite valuable.

Another faction in the computer security world approaches security from a more pragmatic, engineering point of view. These security experts, although often interested in the etiology of security problems, are much more concerned with the questions of securing operational systems so that they can survive in the here and now. One might argue that all practitioners should be as technically rigorous as the theoreticians; one could also argue that all theoreticians should be able to administer operational systems!

Both of these approaches to computer security are legitimate, although purists in each group profess disdain for the other. Let's consider the fundamentals from both vantage points because each has something to offer to those interested in securing systems.

2.2.2   Practical Definition of Computer Security

A practical definition of a *secure* computer system is "a system that can be depended upon to behave as it is expected to."[2] From this intuitive view of security, we can infer the fundamental concepts associated with security. For instance, the notion of depending on a system implies that we *trust* that system. Is this trust quantifiable? If so, how do we measure it? Do we trust the system to behave as it is expected to? Who determines the expectations for system behavior? How do we determine whether the actual behavior of the system in fact matches the expected behavior?

2.2.3   Formal Definition of Computer Security

A more precise definition of security is given in terms of the "security triad": confidentiality, integrity, and availability.

Confidentiality is the requirement that access to information be restricted to only those users authorized for that access. Much of the work done by the government in computer security focuses on confidentiality.

An example of a system with goals of confidentiality is a banking system. As the customer of a bank, you expect the bank to protect your account information. Would you continue to do business with a bank if you discovered that your account records were accessible to other account holders or to the general public?

Integrity is the requirement that information be protected from alteration. Integrity is especially critical in systems handling data such as medical records (imagine the impact of someone altering doctors' orders on a patient record) or financial accounts. Many publicized Web site attacks involve breaches of integrity, in which address tables or site content are modified.

Availability is the requirement that the information and system resources continue to work, and that authorized users be able to access resources when they need them, where they need them, and in the form in which they need them. Many network-based attacks, such as "teardrop" and "ping of death," crash servers by sending them network traffic fashioned to exploit vulnerabilities in the operating system software running on those servers. These intrusions, which violate availability requirements, are labeled *denial of service* attacks.

A secure computer system supports all three goals of the security triad. In other words, a secure system protects its information and computing resources from unauthorized access, tampering, and denial of service.

2.2.4 Trust

If any central concept is associated with security, that concept is trust. *Trust* is the confidence that what is expected of a system entity corresponds to actual behavior. The level of trust corresponds to the level of confidence in this association between expected and actual behavior. System elements that interoperate do so with some assumption about the trust with which the other element is imbued. In cases where these trust assumptions prove unwarranted, vulnerabilities exist, and threats often follow.

In assessing trust relationships, you limit the area of concern by drawing a security boundary or perimeter. This approach allows a systematic assessment of trust relationships at each juncture, which yields considerable insight into the trustworthiness of the system.

Note that the question of trust arises, regardless of where you draw the security boundary of the system. You must be able to trust the administrators and users of the system not to abuse their privileges. You must also trust the environment in which the system physically resides to protect the system from physical hazards.

2.2.5 Threat

What determines the content of a security policy? Most security programs are driven by a desire to address a threat. A *threat* is defined as any situation or event that has the potential to harm a system. This harm can be in the form of disclosure, destruction, or modification of data; or denial of access to data or to the system-processing resources. Major categories of threat include hackers, viruses, fire, flood, lightning strikes—the list goes on and on.

From this list, you may have noticed that threats can be either internal or external to the system and can be intentional or incidental. To achieve security goals, you must consider physical threats as well as computer threats. You might also want to require background investigations of personnel serving in critical roles (such as system administrators) when they have significant control over computing and information resources.

How are threats structured in the computer security world? There are several ways to classify threat, and some involve the source of the threat. An early model specified the following three categories[3]:

- External penetrators—Unauthorized users of the system

- Internal penetrators—Authorized users of the system who overstep their legitimate access rights. These internal threats are divided into the following:

  - Masqueraders—Those who appropriate the identification and authorization credentials of others

  - Clandestine users—Those who successfully evade audit and monitoring measures

- Misfeasors—Authorized users who exceed their privileges

In intrusion detection, we build on this model of threat, using the term *intrusion* to mean any intentional violation of the security policy of a system. This definition encompasses all the threats covered in Anderson's model, plus other threats to system security not covered in his model. These threats include the following:

- People who attempt to gain access to a system or data

- Programmatic threats (software attacks such as viruses, trojan horses, and malicious Java or ActiveX applets)

- People who probe or scan systems in search of vulnerabilities they can exploit in a later attack

2.2.6   Vulnerability

Security problems in computer systems result from vulnerabilities. *Vulnerabilities* are weaknesses in systems that can be exploited in ways that violate security policy. Vulnerabilities occur in a multitude of ways. For example, weaknesses occur in the design and implementation of the system software and hardware. These weaknesses are sometimes called *technical vulnerabilities*. Other weaknesses occur in security policy, procedures, controls, configuration, or other system management areas. These fall in the realm of *procedural* or *management vulnerabilities*.

Several rules of thumb govern the likelihood of vulnerabilities occurring in systems. The larger the system, the greater the likelihood of vulnerabilities. The more complex the system, the greater the likelihood of vulnerabilities. The more dynamic the system and its environment (for example, the more often a system is updated or replaced with a new system), the greater the likelihood of vulnerabilities.

Although threat and vulnerabilities are intrinsically related, they are not the same. Threat is the result of exploiting one or more vulnerabilities. Intrusion detection is designed to identify and respond to both.

2.2.7 Security Policy

Security policy is required in order to map the sometimes-arcane concepts of security to the real world. In our initial definition of security, we pointed out that it is based on some notion of what constitutes expected behavior for a system. Security policy documents these expectations.

2.2.7.1 Procedural

Security policy has two common definitions. The term most often refers to the set of management statements that document an organization's philosophy of protecting its computing and information assets. This *procedural* or *managerial security policy* outlines security goals and commits management resources to meeting these goals. It also assigns responsibilities, defines roles, and establishes management and security controls. Finally, the policy sets up procedures and practices for securing information and computing assets. Figure 2.1 outlines the structure for a procedural or managerial security policy. Note that while policy remains consistent, the procedures are more specific, but they rarely change, and the practices are quite dynamic, reflecting the particulars of the system at the current time.

Figure 2.1   An Example of Procedural System Policy, Procedures, and Practices

Policy	Procedure or Standard	Practice or Guideline
"We will protect corporate systems from unauthorized alteration of software."	"Where applicable, virus checkers shall be run on corporate systems."	"Norton Anti-Virus will be run on all Windows 95/98 systems at least once a week. The software will be updated by MIS staff at least once a month."
	"Integrity-checking tools shall be used on critical system files and executables."	"Tripwire® will be run at least once per quarter and upon any update or alteration on all UNIX server systems directories, Checksums will be saved on removable media stored in accordance with corporate policy."

The goal of security policy for a computer system is analogous to the goal of legal codes in a society. Both seek to protect legitimate users of system resources from ill effects due to the activities of miscreants. Procedural security policies are usually informal; that is, they are written in ordinary language, not as mathematical expressions.

2.2.7.2 Formal

A *formal security policy* usually consists of a mathematical model of the system as a collection of all its possible states and operations, accompanied by a set of constraints on when and how the states and operations may exist. The government's Trusted Systems Initiative defines the security policy of the system as the set of rules enforced by the system's security features.[4] Writing security policies that formally and precisely define which activities are not allowed is a difficult job. Note that according to this definition, *every* system enforces an implicit security policy!

Formal security policies have certain advantages for those interested in performing intrusion detection. Such policies are structured and precise in a way that makes it easier to translate their intent into detection patterns. These policies can also provide guidance with regard to what information the system audit mechanism should collect for analysis.

2.2.8 Other Elements of the System Security Infrastructure

It is important to understand that intrusion detection is not, nor was it ever meant to be, a silver bullet for computer security (an infallible and complete system security solution). Many are tempted to consider it as such. It is, however, an integral part of a system security suite that in totality protects a computer system from intrusion and internal abuse.

Consider intrusion detection in the context of physical security. Suppose you have a valuable asset, you use physical security techniques and measures to protect it. For instance, you'd put the asset inside a building, under a well-sealed roof, and shielded from weather-related damage. You'd make sure that the building walls were constructed of strong materials—say, concrete block, not cardboard. The building would be designed with few windows and doors. Those openings would be located to minimize the possibility of a burglar using them as entry points. The asset might be placed inside a safe or vault, with a strong lock on the door. You might place fences, moats, or other barriers around the building. If you were particularly paranoid about protecting the asset, you might hire armed security guards and charge them with monitoring the premises, logging any entry to the building, and patrolling the building and grounds on a given schedule. Finally, you might install sophisticated burglar alarms and surveillance systems to provide additional assurance that the asset is protected. You see this sort of protection scheme implemented every day in banks, military bases, and art museums.

Although the burglar alarm and surveillance systems undoubtedly offer a great deal of protection to the asset, can they replace everything else in the protection suite? Of course not! The combination of protective measures function in concert to protect your asset. Together, they yield much more robust and cost-effective protection than pouring all your resources into any one of them alone.

This applies to the computer and network world, as well. Many components and functions serve as part of a sound system protection strategy. Some of these protection mechanisms are discussed in the following sections.

2.2.8.1   Access Control

Access control mechanisms are responsible for restricting access to objects according to the access rights of the subject. Access control is divided into Mandatory Access Control (MAC), in which decisions about access rights are embedded in the system; and Discretionary Access Control (DAC), in which the owner of an object sets up and controls access rights for that object. In systems offering MAC, the access rights are determined by security labels on the objects. Some commercial products offer encryption-based solutions that allow customers to formulate and enforce DAC policies.

2.2.8.2   Identification and Authentication

Identification and authentication mechanisms (I&A) support the positive identification of subjects and objects to the system.

Authentication mechanisms can be divided into three categories, depending on what they require of you: what you know, what you have, and what you are. Each category involves the system challenging a user for a secret that is known only to the user and the system. If the secret presented by the user matches the secret held by the system, the system validates the user's identity and allows access to the system.

"What you know" is the basis for the traditional I&A mechanism, found in most operating systems, in which a user login and password challenge identifies and authenticates users. Unfortunately, this approach has proven to be vulnerable to a variety of attacks, such as password-cracking and trojan horse password-grabbers. These attacks result in the exposure of the secret (the password) to adversaries. This authentication technique is gradually being replaced by stronger, zero-knowledge techniques that avoid passing the secret itself.

Examples of authentication systems based on "what you have" include token-based systems, such as those in which the user is provided with a smart card, a key, or a special disk. Many of these tokens are designed to use cryptographic mechanisms and physical tamper-resistance mechanisms to prevent attackers from counterfeiting or spoofing them.

Examples of systems based on "what you are" include biometric schemes, which use the voice, fingerprints, or retina of the user to identify and authenticate the user to the system. Some systems use hybrid approaches; for example, one commercial smart-card token includes a fingerprint scanner.

The underlying challenge-response authentication process is sometimes used for security purposes other than commencing system access. The process can also be used in intrusion detection as a means of establishing whether suspicious behavior is originating from an intruder or a legitimate user. This topic is discussed further in Chapter 5, "Responses," in which we discuss system responses to detected problems.

2.2.8.3   Encryption

Perhaps the oldest information security mechanism, encryption, safeguards information by performing a variety of functions. It can effectively obscure the content of data files or transmissions, eliminating the possibility of surveillance by unauthorized parties. It can also detect accidental or intentional alterations in data. Encryption can provide verification that the author or originator of a document is the person you expect.

Encryption is the process of taking an unencrypted message (called *plaintext*), applying a mathematical function to it (*encryption algorithm*) with a key, and producing an encrypted message (called *ciphertext*). Although encryption provides powerful protection of information, it is not perfect. It cannot prevent intentional deletion of encrypted data, for example. It cannot protect data before it is encrypted nor after it is decrypted. And the encryption is dependent on the key being protected. Should the key be guessed or divulged, the value of the encryption is nullified.

2.2.8.4   Firewalls

Firewalls provide a security boundary between networks of differing trust or security levels by enforcing a network-level access control policy. The mechanisms used include proxy servers, network packet filters, and encrypted data tunnels (also called Virtual Private Networks). Firewalls filter network packets, making decisions to allow and disallow passage of packets according to a specified policy. Firewalls also allow an address translation for networks so that the configuration details of an internal network can be hidden from potential intruders.

2.2.9   How Security Problems Occur

When security problems occur, especially given the ramifications of the problems, you might wonder why they exist. Although the number of specific problems is huge, the etiologies of the vast majority of security problems fall into three categories: design/development, management, and trust.

2.2.9.1 Problems in Design/Development

The first problem consists of errors, flaws, and omissions that occur in the design and development of systems. These result in vulnerabilities in both software and hardware. For instance, researchers have discovered that cryptographic keys, burned into smart-card hardware to protect them from disclosure, can be extracted by a process in which faults are injected into the cards by varying the operating voltages or clock cycles. Another classic example is the problem of race conditions in system software. Race conditions result when an interval occurs between the time a value is checked for validity and the time the value is actually used; in the interval, an adversary can substitute an illicit value and dupe the software routine into performing a nonstandard operation. Yet another vulnerability, which accounts for many known UNIX attacks, is the failure to check the arguments that are passed to privileged programs from the command line. Attackers create problems by invoking these programs, passing them arguments that overflow the input buffers, and thereby crashing the program and allowing the attacker a privileged shell.

Many problems in this category can be prevented by rigorous application of sound engineering practice, including quality assurance.

2.2.9.2 Problems in Management

The second problem area that leads to security problems is that of managing fielded systems. This problem encompasses errors made when configuring the system itself or security systems that are meant to provide protections to the system. An example is using inappropriate privilege settings for system files (such as making password files for UNIX systems readable and writeable by "world"). This problem area also includes scenarios in which system administrators or users disable or circumvent security mechanisms. A problem that commonly occurs in large organizations is that of users who install unauthorized modems on internal systems—desktop PCs, for example. Because the modems provide a path into the organizational internal networks, they allow adversaries to circumvent the protection afforded by the firewall!

2.2.9.3 Problems in Trust

Perhaps the most pervasive problem is that of naivete concerning appropriate assumptions regarding trust. Many of these occur because of an unforeseen differential between the development environment and the operational environment. For example, UNIX was originally developed by programmers in a collegial environment. The information sharing was standard and threat levels were low. With the passage of time, however, UNIX was fielded in commercial settings, where the threat model is different. In this case, trust assumptions did not generalize to environments beyond the original development site.

In fact, some problems in design and development actually apply here, too. Designers and implementers of systems trust that the system will be used in a certain manner within a certain context. The designer trusts the customer to use a system in a particular fashion. The customer trusts the product to perform as promised. In extensive systems, the users trust all parts of the system to function as expected. This trust extends to the human portions of the system as well. Users trust that someone is administering the system in a competent, consistent fashion.

So, what happens when this trust is breached? This situation usually means that a security problem has occurred. In many cases, the problem is transparent to everyone but the person responsible for the problem unless, of course, someone is monitoring the operation of the system and notices this unusual system activity. This topic is covered in greater depth in Chapter 8, "Understanding the Real-World Challenge."

2.3   Intrusion Detection Concepts

As intrusion detection evolved over the past 20 years, so did strategies for tackling the issues associated with intelligently monitoring systems for problems. This section outlines these strategies and the respective rationale that underlies each one. In so doing, I hope to provide you with an understanding of key concepts. This information will allow you to assess the strengths and weaknesses of future intrusion detection approaches as they are proposed.

2.3.1   Architecture

When audit was proposed as a protection for sensitive systems, it was apparent that for audit information to be trusted, it must be stored and processed in an environment separate from the system that it protected. This requirement was inherited by most intrusion detection approaches. Separating audit information from the system that the audit is protecting is necessary for three reasons:

- To keep a successful intruder from disabling the intrusion detection system by deleting audit records

- To keep a successful intruder from modifying the results of the intrusion detector to hide the presence of the intrusion

- To lessen the performance load associated with running intrusion detection tasks on an operational system

In this architecture, the system running the intrusion detection system is called the *host*, and the system or network being monitored is called the *target*.

2.3.2 Monitoring Strategy

The first requirement for intrusion detection is a data source. This element can also be considered an event generator. Data sources can be categorized in a variety of ways. For intrusion detection purposes, we first categorize them by location. This classification scheme divides system-monitoring views into four categories: host, network, application, and target. We will use the term *monitoring* to describe the action of collecting data from a data source and passing it to an analysis engine.

- *Host-based monitors* collect data from sources internal to a computer, usually at the operating system level. These sources can include operating system audit trails and system logs.

- *Network-based monitors* collect network packets. This is usually done by using network devices that are set to promiscuous mode. (A network device operating in promiscuous mode captures all network traffic accessible to it, not just that addressed to it.)

- *Application-based monitors* collect data from running applications. The data sources include application event logs and other data stores internal to the application.

- *Target-based monitors* function a bit differently from the other monitors listed in this section because target-based monitors generate their own data. Target-based monitors use cryptographic hash functions to detect alterations to system objects and then compare these alterations to a policy. Because the state of the target object is monitored versus the activity taking place on the system housing the object, this monitoring strategy can be efficient for some systems that cannot be monitored using other approaches.

2.3.3 Analysis Type

In the intrusion detection process, after information sources are defined and locations are established, the next requirement is an analysis engine. This system component takes information from the data source and examines the data for symptoms of attack or other policy violations.

In intrusion detection, most analysis approaches involve misuse detection, anomaly detection, or some mix of the two.

- *Misuse detection*—Engines look for something defined to be "bad." To do this, they filter event streams, searching for activity patterns that match a known attack or other violation of security policy. Misuse detection uses pattern-matching techniques, matching against patterns of activity known to indicate problems. Most current, commercial intrusion detection systems utilize misuse detection techniques.

- *Anomaly detection*—Engines look for something rare or unusual. They analyze system event streams, using statistical techniques to find patterns of activity that appear to be abnormal. This approach reflects the view of some intrusion detection researchers that intrusions are some subset of anomalous activity.

Significant advantages are associated with combining the two analysis schemes. The anomaly detection engine allows the system to detect new or unknown attacks, or other scenarios of concern. The misuse detection engine protects the integrity of the anomaly detection engine by ensuring that a patient adversary cannot gradually change behavior patterns to retrain the anomaly detector to accept attack behavior as normal.

Figure 2.2 shows a diagram of a typical intrusion detection system that uses both anomaly detection and misuse detection analysis approaches.

Figure 2.2   A Generic Intrusion Detection System

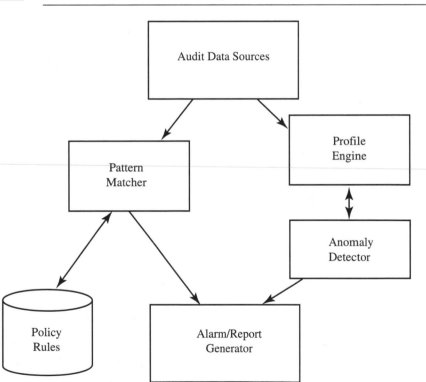

2.3.4 Timing

Another differential in analysis is the timing of the analysis of the data. Analysis can be done in a batch mode (known by some as "interval based" mode) or in real time.

2.3.4.1 Interval/Batch

Batch mode analysis means that the information source is conveyed to the analyzer in a file and that the information for a particular period of time is processed, with the results returned to the user after an intrusion takes place. Batch mode was the prevalent model for early intrusion detection because the communications and processing bandwidth of early systems did not support real-time monitoring or detection.

2.3.4.2 Real Time

As system speed and communications bandwidth grew, more intrusion detection systems moved to real-time analysis. In real-time analysis, the information source is conveyed to the analysis engine as the event happens (or with miniscule delay), and the information is processed immediately. We use the term *real-time* in the process control context, referring to a process that is fast enough to allow the results of the intrusion detection system to affect the progress or outcome of any intrusion it sees.

Note

For many years, the intrusion detection community engaged in a lively debate, in which the term *near real time* was coined to refer to intrusion detection that involved processing a continuous stream of events but not at blinding speed. In many analysis approaches, modern machine speeds have rendered that debate moot.

Real-time analysis approaches have enabled automated responses to intrusions. This development has considerable appeal to many customers.

2.3.5 Goals of Detection

Another factor in intrusion detection analysis is the goal the detector supports. The two traditional goals driving intrusion detection are accountability and active response.

The goals for intrusion detection affect a number of design and implementation decisions. For instance, if the goal is to establish user accountability for detected intrusions, one might need to maintain raw audit data to support legal requirements for prosecution. Suppose, on the other hand, one doesn't care about the identity of the intruder but is more interested in blocking the attack and then correcting the vulnerability that allowed it. In this case, after the data is analyzed and the intrusion is detected, the audit data can be discarded.

2.3.5.1   Accountability

Accountability is the capability to map a given activity or event back to the responsible party. Because the ultimate goal of establishing accountability is to extract some compensation or pursue some legal remedy against that responsible party, it helps if that responsible party is a human (not a machine name). Furthermore it is even more helpful if a physical address or other link to the physical world can be associated with that party.

Maintaining accountability on networks presents one of the major challenges in intrusion detection. Given current network schemes, when an attack utilizes programs and daemons running on separate machines, separate sets of identities are associated with each host involved. In general, the greater the number of hosts involved in a network attack path, the lower the probability of successfully detecting an attack and establishing accountability.

One of the earliest attempts to integrate host-based and network-based intrusion detection capabilities, the Distributed Intrusion Detection System (DIDS) was designed to enable a major customer to maintain user accountability on its large internal network complex. The customer also wanted DIDS to allow the tracking of related events across the network as a whole. The DIDS team approached this problem by creating a user network identifier (called a NID) the first time a user entered the environment monitored by DIDS and then mapping all subsequent activities of that user to that NID.[4]

2.3.5.2   Response

In intrusion detection, *response* occurs when analysis yields an actionable result. Response is not limited to taking action against a suspected attacker, although this option captures the imagination of many in the network security world.

Perhaps the most common response is to record the results of the analysis in a log file, using that file to generate a report. This information is helpful to a variety of people in the corporate management structure. Some report features allow automatic report generation, with options for providing findings at different levels of detail for different reporting audiences. For example, the report that goes to the CIO might list the numbers of intrusions detected and the severity of those intrusions. The report that goes to the system manager would have information about the intrusion, the files that the intruder touched, the vulnerability probably exploited, and whether any fixes are available for it.

A more immediate response option is to trigger alarms of a variety of predetermined types. These might include an alarm flag on a network manager's console, a message to a security manager's pager, or, in certain instances, an email message sent to a system administrator.

Another response is to modify the intrusion detection system or the target system. Modifying the intrusion detection system can involve changing the information collected by the monitors or changing the character of the analysis performed on the information stream. Modifying the target system can include changing configuration settings for critical files to block the progress of a known attack. This ability to adapt the system in response to a suspicion level is quite valuable.

The remaining response option receives a great deal of attention from the press, the military, and the science fiction writing community. This is the strike-back response in which one blocks the intrusion, sometimes mirroring the attack back to its ostensible source. More benign active responses are also available, such as sending messages to firewalls or routers, which direct them to block subsequent network accesses from the source of the attack.

2.3.6   Control Issues

Another aspect of intrusion detection is controlling the system. There are two major approaches to controlling intrusion detection systems when the system monitors multiple hosts or networks.

2.3.6.1   Centralization

The first approach is a centralized reporting and control architecture. In this approach, a central node controls all the intrusion detection elements of a system. Centralization carries some requirements with it. For example, there must be a way to secure messages between system components. There must also be a way to determine whether an element of the system has been tampered with or disabled at a given time. In addition, centralization requires a way to gracefully start and stop system components. Finally, the centralized approach requires a way of consolidating status information and presenting it to end users in a form that is meaningful to them.

2.3.6.2   Integration with Network Management Tools

One way of addressing some of the issues associated with the centralized control of intrusion detection is to simply regard intrusion detection as a function of network management. Some system information streams collected by network management packages can be used as information sources for intrusion detection. In addition, some alarms raised by intrusion detection systems affect network availability and performance. Therefore, integrating the two functions can be of value to customer organizations. Many commercial intrusion detection packages offer the option of spawning Simple Network Management Protocol (SNMP) messages for network management tool capture.

2.3.7 Determining Strategies for Intrusion Detection

Given the multiple options associated with each process component, many possible strategies are available for tackling the problem of detecting attacks and other activities of interest. The optimal strategy often depends on factors such as the following:

- The criticality or sensitivity of the system being protected

- The nature of the system (for example, the complexity of the system hardware and software platforms)

- The nature of the organizational security policy

- The threat level of the environment in which the system operates

2.4 Conclusion

Intrusion detection systems have, from their outset, generated a great deal of attention in the security world. To many, they present a vision of an ever-vigilant system sentinel, equipped with the capability to assimilate great quantities of information generated by complex systems, infallibly finding security problems, tracing them back to the responsible parties, and then taking action to isolate and heal any damage that occurred.

The current promise of intrusion detection is all this, and more. The growth of the Internet and the subsequent push to place more and more critical information on network-connected systems creates a scenario in which security is of critical importance.

Traditional approaches to computer security (such as the National Computer Security Center's Trusted Systems Evaluation program) espouse an approach to security based strictly on the mathematically rigorous secure design of systems. The alternative to the secure design approach is an approach called (often derisively) "penetrate and patch."

Intrusion detection systems allow users to optimize the penetrate-and-patch process by sharing penetration knowledge between sites. Many users readily acknowledge that penetrate and patch is not an optimal solution to system security problems. However, it is often the only available option to users who must depend on the operating systems and software developed by commercial entities that have neither the capability nor the inclination to perform secure design. Given this state of affairs, intrusion detection systems, by augmenting the commercial exchange of attack information, may represent the only way of avoiding a descent into security chaos.

In addition, the event monitoring and attack recognition capabilities of intrusion detection systems enhance the security of a system in other ways. First, these capabilities have a significant deterrent effect on attackers, who run a greater risk of discovery and subsequent prosecution for their attacks. Furthermore, intrusion detection systems can deal with insider threat, a significant problem in system security. Second, automated responses can disrupt some attacks at the outset, making subsequent attacks more difficult to stage. Third, monitoring the operation of the rest of the security infrastructure allows system security managers to see when security protections are not functioning properly and to rectify the situation before an attacker exploits it. And fourth, the information gained by monitoring the system can sometimes make it easier to manage the system in other ways, resulting in greater system reliability.

Endnotes

1. *Oxford English Dictionary, Second Edition.*

2. Garfinkel, S. and E. H. Spafford. *Practical UNIX and Internet Security, Second Edition.* O'Reilly and Associates, 1996.

3. Anderson, "Computer Security Threat Monitoring and Surveillance." J.P. Anderson Co., 1980.

4. Ko, C., D. Frincke, T. Goan, L. T. Heberlein, K. Levitt, B. Mukherjee, and C. Wee. "Analysis of an Algoritham for Distributed Recognition and Accountability." Proceedings of the First ACM Conference on Computer and Communication Security, Fairfax, VA, November 1993: 154–164.

3

Information Sources

"A computer, to print out a fact,
Will divide, multiply, and subtract.
But this output can be
No more than debris,
If the input was short of exact."
- Gigo

The first requirement for intrusion detection or any such data-driven processing task, is a set of input data. For intrusion detection, that input data comes from a variety of sources. In this chapter, I cover the data sources commonly used in intrusion detection and describe how they influence the capabilities of the intrusion detection system. I also discuss the issues associated with each of these data sources and identify possible strategies for dealing with them.

3.1   The Organization of this Chapter

This chapter covers three data categories: data derived from sources internal to individual systems (*host-based sources*), data derived from sources associated with the network (*network-based sources*), and data derived from other sources (out-of-band sources, such as telephone switches or physical security systems). I cover these sources in this order for several reasons. First, this sequence mirrors the path that computer technology in general, and intrusion detection specifically, has traveled over time: host-based centralized architectures, then network-based distributed models, and finally ubiquitous point products—each optimized to perform a particular function. Second, this approach moves from lower- to higher-level abstractions of the systems from which the data is collected.

> **Note**
>
> In this chapter, the generic term *monitor* refers to any information collection mechanism used by an intrusion detection system. The term *protection domain* refers to the area of the system that the intrusion detection system is meant to monitor and protect.

3.1.1 Which Source Is the Right Source?

So, your next question might be the following: Which of these sources is the best source for intrusion detection? The correct answer is that it depends on what you're interested in detecting. To detect an attack, the intrusion detection system must be able to "see" the evidence of that attack. Perhaps a subtler point is that to detect and then deal with the attack, the intrusion detection system must also be able to see the *right* data about the attack (for instance, the outcome of the attack).

For instance, suppose that an intrusion detection system detects an attack carried out by sending malformed network packets to a particular host. (This type of intrusion is a common form of network-based denial-of-service attack; a vulnerable target system responds to the attack by crashing.) A network-level monitor might capture the malformed packets and the fact that they were sent from a particular IP address to a particular host inside the protection domain. However, the addition of a host-level monitor can allow the intrusion detection system to see whether that malformed packet caused the system to crash. Furthermore, the addition of a network monitor on every network segment in the protection domain allows the intrusion detection system to see that 840 identical malformed packet attacks were launched against other hosts in the domain over the last six hours, and 300 of the attacks appear to have been launched from a single dial-up connection.

3.1.2 Enduring Questions

Several questions have persisted over the course of intrusion detection history. These include the following:

- How much information is enough to allow you to accurately diagnose security problems without crippling the systems you're trying to protect?

- How do you select the right information to collect, and from where should you collect it?

- How do you manage the information collected to support any legal remedies you might want to pursue against attackers?

- How do you honor your responsibility to handle the information collected about users so that you stay within legal, regulatory, and ethical policy limits?

• How can you format this data so that you can organize and make sense of a wide variety of system platforms? Being able to understand various platforms becomes the key to performing intrusion detection over complex systems of interest.

Keep these questions in mind as we explore the nature of information sources. There is more discussion in Chapter 7, "Technical Issues," in which we explore current technical issues; and in Chapter 9, "Legal Issues," in which we discuss the legal issues associated with intrusion detection.

3.2 Host-Based Information Sources

The intrusion detection product community is divided into several factions. Some define intrusion detection systems as strictly network-based systems. Others define intrusion detection systems as strictly host-based or as specific applications-based systems. Still others advocate integrated approaches to intrusion detection in which both host-based and network-based approaches are combined to improve detection performance.

These approaches are based on the *monitoring approach* of the system, that is, the point at which information is collected. This section considers host-based information sources and looks at the mechanisms that produce the information.

Host-based information sources consist of *operating system audit trails*—that is, records of system events generated by a specialized operating system mechanism—and *system logs*—files of system and application events, which are usually text files written a line at a time by system programs.

3.2.1 Operating System Audit Trails

The first host-based information source considered to be of security significance was the operating system audit trail. Operating system audit trails are generated by a specialized auditing subsystem included as part of the operating system software. These audit trails are a collection of information about system activities, which are placed in chronological order and then organized into one or more *audit files*. Each audit file is composed of *audit records*, each of which describes a single system event. These records are generated by user actions and by processes invoked on behalf of users, whenever either makes system calls or executes commands. The commands can be local or remote. Each audit record is composed of a series of *audit tokens*, each of which describes the fields within the record.

Many operating system audit trails were originally designed and developed to meet the requirements of the Trusted Product Evaluation Program. This U. S. government initiative produced evaluation criteria—most notably the Trusted Computer System Evaluation Criteria (TCSEC)—also known as the "Orange Book"—that outlined the features and assurances required of commercial operating systems and applications software that was to contain and process classified information. The evaluation process was structured to rate the operating systems according to "trust levels" that corresponded to the perceived trustworthiness of the system.

The audit requirements of the Orange Book represented a conundrum to the vendor and user community because there were extensive requirements for audit capabilities but no directions for actual audit utilization. The criteria outlined extensive lists of events that audit systems should be capable of monitoring, but offered no guidance for selecting those events. The requirements also neglected to define how to structure, store, and use the audit information that was generated.[1]

Consequently, vendors provided a crazy quilt of audit capabilities in an attempt to meet the letter of the C2 audit requirements. In extreme cases, intrusion detection developers who were adept at dealing with the audit trails generated by one operating system vendor would not be able to comprehend the audit trails produced by another. Furthermore, some implementations produced audit mechanisms that were not useful in operational environments, thanks to storage or performance costs. Indeed, some early intrusion detection research efforts in which I was involved found massive flaws in several C2-evaluated audit mechanisms that suggested that the mechanisms had not been tested before they were fielded.

3.2.2 Approaches to Structuring Audit Trails

Operating system vendors use at least two design approaches in their audit systems. One approach creates *self-contained* audit records, which do not require other records for interpretation. The other chooses to eliminate redundant information in audit trails by distributing the information about an event over multiple records. The former is easier to process and comprehend, but the latter is helpful when conserving storage space allocated to audit trails.

3.2.3 Problems with Commercial Audit Systems

Despite the fact that the intrusion detection community appears to be the major consumer of operating system audit trails, a recent study found that no major operating system vendor actually provides audit trails that support the needs of intrusion detection systems! Vendor documentation for audit subsystems is often missing. When the documentation exists, it rarely corresponds to the audit system, as built. Many audit trails generate irrelevant or insufficient information. These deficiencies have resulted in people suggesting significant amendments to audit systems. For instance, some have proposed that effective host-based intrusion detection may require the developer to amend operating system kernel code to generate event information. This approach extracts a cost in system performance, which might be unacceptable for customers running computationally greedy applications. Furthermore, appreciable costs are associated with the maintenance of these operating system software alterations.[2]

3.2.4   Pros and Cons of Operating System Audit Trails

Despite the problems outlined here, many intrusion detection experts consider operating system audit trails preferable to other common host-level information sources for intrusion detection purposes. The primary reason is that the operating system is often structured to provide substantive protection for the audit subsystem and the audit trails that the subsystem generates. This protection is of obvious interest, given the security goals of intrusion detection.

Another motivation for prizing operating system audit trails as a data source for intrusion detection is that they reveal system events at a finer-grained level of detail. This information allows the intrusion detection system to spot subtle patterns of misuse that would not be visible from a higher level of abstraction. This finer-grained level of detail also makes it more difficult for an adversary to successfully corrupt the audit process by inserting false audit records.

As one might expect, this finer level of detail comes at a price. Both the volume as well as the complexity of the audit data rise with greater detail. Ironically, as we already noted, although the level of detail makes it more difficult for an adversary to circumvent the audit process entirely, the greater volume and complexity of the data make it easier in practice for intruders to hide their footprints.

Collecting data at too coarse a level of detail presents problems, as well. In particular, this lack of detail makes it impossible to differentiate between system activity invoked directly by a user and activity invoked by a program that has taken on the user's identity.

This deficiency is significant. The concept that a system program can act as a user's agent without that user's permission represents a case for the *"on behalf of "* semantics implemented in UNIX and Windows NT operating systems. An entire class of system attack exploits the capability of programs to assume the identity of a user or other subject possessing greater privilege than the actual user. This behavior applies particularly to attacks that target SUID root processes in UNIX systems. To detect this class of attack, the data source for an intrusion detection system must provide data at a fine enough level of granularity to allow the intrusion detector to differentiate between user and process.

Another advantage of monitoring activity at a greater level of detail is that it highlights abnormal patterns of process execution. This monitoring detail enables the intrusion detection system to recognize the execution of trojan horses and other malicious code.

3.2.5   Content of Audit Trails

Most commercial operating systems record events at kernel level (reflecting system calls) and at user level (reflecting application events). Audit records contain information about subjects responsible for the event and any objects involved in the event. Most records also include information about the process that initiated the event, the userID associated with the event, which sometimes includes the current userID as well as the original userID (in case the user identity changes). Kernel-level entries contain system call arguments and return values, whereas user-level entries contain high-level descriptions of the event or application-specific data.

This section covers the audit trail structure and content of two major operating systems: Basic Security Module (BSM) from Sun and Windows NT from Microsoft.

3.2.5.1 Operating System Example 1: Sun Solaris BSM

Sun's BSM security package is provided to bring Sun's UNIX operating systems into compliance with the TCSEC C2 trusted system rating. Although we focus on the auditing features of the package, it also provides device allocation mechanisms that meet C2 requirements for object reuse.

BSM Auditing Subsystem Structure

The BSM auditing subsystem, pictured in Figure 3.1, consists of an audit log, audit files, audit records, and audit tokens.

Figure 3.1   Structure of Sun BSM Audit Data

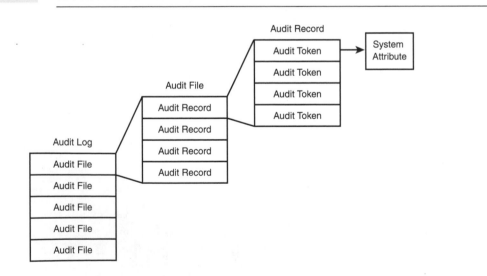

A BSM *audit log* consists of a sequence of *audit files*, which are in turn composed of *audit records*. Each audit record consists of a sequence of *audit tokens*, each of which describes a system attribute. Structures defining audit files have special file tokens to mark the beginning and end of files; header and trailer tokens delineate each audit record.

Audit records are described as either kernel-level or user-level generated records, depending on the nature of the event described in the record. As you might guess, kernel-level audit records are generated by kernel-level system calls; user-level records are generated by all other system calls.

BSM includes translation functions that help trace accountability for particular audit events. An event-to-system call translation translates each audit event to the kernel or user event that generated it, and an event-to-command translation translates each audit event to the application or command that generated it. These translations can be helpful in interpreting the contents of audit data.

BSM audit records are generated and managed in binary form. Predetermined byte orders and data sizes facilitate cross-platform compatibility.

Events are grouped into *audit event classes* for audit management purposes. *Preselection* (selecting the system events for which audit records are generated) and *postselection* (selecting the audit records to extract from an audit log file) of audit events is done by specifying the applicable audit event classes.

BSM Audit Record Structure

Figure 3.2 shows the structure of a typical BSM audit record. Each auditable event in the system produces a particular type of audit record. Each audit record begins with a header token, which marks the beginning of the audit record in the audit trail. Most audit records contain a subject token, which refers to the process that caused the event. Finally, depending on audit policy, the record may end with a trailer token. For user-level and kernel events, the tokens describe the process that performed the event, the objects on which it was performed, and the objects' tokens, such as the owner or mode.

Figure 3.2   Structure of Typical Sun BSM Audit Record

Audit Record

Header Token

Argument Token

Data Token

Subject Token

Return Token

Each user-level and kernel-level event has header, subject, and return tokens. In addition, many events also include a trailer token, but it is optional. Other optional tokens include the group and sequence tokens. Use of these tokens depends on current audit policy.

Each token begins with a 1-byte token type, followed by one or more data elements. The order of these data elements is determined by the record type. Event type and tokens within the record characterize different audit records. Some tokens consist of a single data element. (The text token is such a case.) Other tokens contain several data elements, as in the case of the process token, which contains the audit userID, the real userID, and the effective userID. For user-level and kernel-level events, tokens specify the process performing the event, any objects on which the event is performed, and tokens associated with the objects (including owner or mode).

BSM User-Level Audit Record Content

As previously noted, user-level generated audit records are created by applications that operate outside the kernel. The records are sorted alphabetically by program. The description of each record includes the following items:

- Name of the program

- Manual page reference (if appropriate)

- Audit event number

- Audit event name

- Audit record structure

BSM Kernel-Level Audit Record Content

Kernel-level-generated audit records are created by system calls used by the kernel and are sorted alphabetically by system call. The description of each record includes:

- Name of the system call

- Manual page reference (if appropriate)

- Audit event number

- Audit event name

- Audit event class

- Mask for the event class

- Audit record structure

System Audit Management Tools

Solaris BSM provides integrated audit trail management commands that allow the auditor or system administrator to perform a variety of audit trail functions. `Auditreduce` allows the auditor to perform post-selection of events, keying on attributes such as time intervals, specific user identifiers, and specific event identifiers. `Praudit` translates the audit records from their native binary format into a user-selected format. Humans can read these formats, but they are not otherwise interpreted and can serve as input for very basic reporting mechanisms.[3]

3.2.5.2 Operating System Example 2: Windows NT

Microsoft Windows NT Server operating system provides data sources in the form of its event-logging mechanisms. These mechanisms consolidate the information gathered from operating system and other system sources.

NT Event Logging Mechanism Structure

Windows NT event-logging mechanisms collect three types of system events: operating system events, security events, and application events. Each type of event is recorded in a separate log.

The system log consists of events generated by the Windows NT operating system components. These events include such events as driver or other component failures, application software crashes, and errors associated with data loss. The event types recorded in the system log are predetermined by the Windows NT operating system.

The application log consists of events recorded by applications. For instance, a database program might send an information event to the application log when the program successfully completes a backup operation. Event types recorded in the application log are determined by the application developers, and software toolkits are provided to help them use this logging feature.

The security log consists of events that are defined as security-relevant. These events were derived from the TCSEC C2 definitions of auditable events. They include valid and invalid logins and logoffs, and events related to system resource use, especially those having to do with the creation, deletion, and alteration of system files and other objects. Unlike system and application logs, security logs are accessible only to system administrators.

Although all events are of interest to those attempting to reconstruct system activities, the security log events are the primary focus of intrusion detection systems.

Event Log and Record Formats

Event logs are composed of sets of *event records*. Each event record is divided into three functional parts: the header, a description of the event, and an optional additional data field. Figure 3.3 shows the structure of an event record. Security log entries usually consist of the header and a description of the event.

Figure 3.3   Format of Windows NT Event Record

Header	Date	Time	User Name	Computer Name
	Event ID	Source	Type	Category

Description	Variable content, depending on event. Can be text explanation of problem and recommendation of corrective measures.

Additional Data	Optional field. If used, contains binary data which can be displayed in bytes or words. Information generated by source application for event record.

The event record header consists of the following fields:

- **Date** Identifies the date of the event.

- **Time** Identifies the time of the event.

- **User Name** Identifies on whose behalf the event occurred. This identifier can be the primary userID, a client ID, or both, depending on whether the Windows NT impersonation function is invoked. Impersonation happens when the operating system allows one process to inherit the security attributes of another. The security-event-logging mechanism reflects both the userID and the impersonation ID when impersonation has occurred.

- **Computer name** The name of the computer on which the event took place. This information simplifies the audit review when users centralize security administration functions across enterprises.

- **Event ID** A numerical identifier for the event type. This field is usually mapped to a text identifier (event name) in the description field of the event record.

- **Source** The software responsible for generating the event record. The source can be an application, a system service, or a device driver.

- **Type** An indicator of the event's severity. The available types depend on the type of log. In the system and application logs, the type can be error, warning, or information, in descending levels of severity. In the security log, the types can be success audit or failure audit.

- **Category** The triggering event type, used primarily in the security log to indicate the event type for which success or failure auditing has been enabled.

NT Event Log Management Features

Windows NT provides numerous features to allow system administrators to manage the operating system event log mechanisms. For instance, administrators can limit the size of the event logs and specify how to deal with the files as they approach this upper limit. The options include overwriting the oldest log records with new, in effect creating a circular queue; overwriting the oldest log records only if they are of a certain age; and halting the system until the event log file is manually cleared.

System and application event logging start automatically when the system is started. Logging stops when the log files are full and the system configuration specifies that they must be manually cleared. Security event logging, on the other hand, must be enabled by someone acting in an administrator capacity.

Security Logging and the Audit Policy

Security logging is governed by an audit policy, which is set up by using an auditing policy dialog box. The audit policy specifies the types of events to log and can be specified in terms of actions, users, and objects. The security event record shows the time and date of the action, the action performed, and the user responsible for performing it. Log entries can be generated for both successful and failed actions, recording evidence of actions that took place as well as attempts to perform actions that may have been prohibited by policy.

To audit specific files or folders, two separate steps are required. First, the audit policy is set to enable file and object auditing for the entire system. In TCSEC terms, this step renders these access events *auditable*. Next, the file property settings are accessed for each file, in order to turn on auditing for that file. This step corresponds to the TCSEC concept of making these events *audited*. Figure 3.4 shows the types of directory and file-access actions that can be audited under Windows NT, specifying permission settings that correspond to each event selection.

Figure 3.4   Audit Event Settings for Files and Directories

	File						Directory					
	Read	Write	Execute	Delete	Change permissions	Take ownership	Read	Write	Execute	Delete	Change permissions	Take ownership
Changing ownership						X						X
Changing permissions					X						X	
Changing Attributes		X						X				
Displaying owner and permissions	X	X	X				X	X	X			
Displaying Attributes												
Displaying names of files	X		X				X		X			
Displaying file data							X					
Altering contents	X											
Creating subdirectories and files												
Going to subdirectories									X			
Running file									X			
Deletion			X									

Tuning NT Audit

Balancing the performance loss associated with NT file audit with the benefit of additional detection capabilities still remains an art. Although you can simply set up audit for all system directories and subdirectories with a few keystrokes, this approach has the undesirable effect of slowing down system performance. On the other hand, auditing selectively at fine grain allows you to detect significant security problems (such as the execution of macro viruses and trojan horses). Performing this balancing act may be intuitively obvious only to the most experienced security administrators.

Audit-management features, which are provided as part of some commercial intrusion detection systems, can help system administrators fine-tune audit features, thus optimizing the audit to meet security and performance goals. This can be of great value to those charged with protecting an enterprise running Windows NT.[4]

3.2.6 Audit Reduction

Audit reduction is the process of filtering audit logs, identifying and removing information that is redundant or irrelevant. This process represents the classic problem of finding a needle in a haystack. Historically, there have been several significant impediments to designing and implementing a data reduction operation. Key to the reduction process is the capability to introduce some determinism to an inherently nondeterministic process. In other words, given the capability to state facts such as "Event X will always trigger events Y, Z, and K under conditions A and B," we can reduce the event stream consisting of (X [under conditions A and B] followed by Y, Z, K) to event X.

The problem with this approach is that (especially in multiprocessing, multitasking systems) this level of determinism is simply not present. Furthermore, the complexity of modern operating systems leads to scenarios in which a single high-level command triggers the generation of thousands of audit records. Worse yet, the order in which the records are recorded in the audit log is not consistent. For instance, a Sun OS UNIX `ls` command executed on a desktop workstation can generate more than 1,500 audit records. Repeating the command even seconds later often results in a different number of audit records, in a different order.

Research from the mid-1990s suggests that significant audit reduction can be done on records generated by trusted processes.

Note

In this context, *trusted processes* refer to those processes certified as supporting a security goal. Trusted systems most often refer to systems developed in compliance with the Department of Defense's TCSEC. In practical terms, trusted processes are those considered free of security problems.[1]

In this work, the assertion is made that when a user command spawns a process that is trusted (and that generates only trusted subprocesses), it is sufficient to record only the audit record corresponding to the user command, and to discard all the subsequent audit records for that process. When the process generated by the user command is untrusted, we record all the audit records for the untrusted processes and subprocesses spawned by the command. Again, if the untrusted process spawns trusted subprocesses, we can discard the event records associated with the trusted subprocesses. An event that fails is assumed to be a potential attempt to violate security protections. Thus, all records for the transaction from the time of failure until the completion of the transaction are recorded in chronological order.[5]

3.2.7 System Logs

A system log is a file that reflects various system events and settings. UNIX operating systems provide a rich assortment of system logs, along with a common service, syslog, which supports generating and updating event logs via the syslogd daemon. Although a rich lexicon of standard formats and definitions can be used in generating and interpreting syslog entries, the security of the logs so generated is considered to be weaker than that of kernel-generated operating system audit trails.

This perception of system logs as less trustworthy than operating system audit trails exists for several reasons. The log-generation software is usually running as an application and is thereby easier to subvert or otherwise modify than is the audit subsystem. Furthermore, the logs are usually stored in unprotected directories on the system. This convention makes it easy for an attacker to locate and destroy or alter the files. Finally, the logging operation is a simple text write, one line of input per log entry. Operating system audit logs are usually more cryptic, with many providing schemes for detecting alteration.

Several ways of mitigating some of the security problems associated with system logs have been suggested. For instance, Spafford and Garfinkel[6] propose that a secure logging host be established by connecting a dedicated microcomputer (perhaps one that has been retired from service due to obsolescence) to the host being monitored by using a serial connection. In this scheme, all system logs would be periodically redirected to this system.

3.2.7.1 Why Collect Data from System Logs?

Despite their weaker protection levels, system logs are usually easier to review than operating system audit logs. If generating operating system audit trails is not feasible in a particular situation or if intrusion detection tools are not available to interpret those operating system audit trails, system logs are a valuable source of information for system security managers. Furthermore, as discussed later in this chapter as well as in Chapter 9, if you need to use system information sources for evidence in a court of law, multiple independent data sources, all indicating that the same chain of events occurred, are considered much stronger evidence than a single source.

3.2.7.2 Typical Content of Logs

UNIX provides a rich variety of system logs that are suitable for security review. Table 3.1 lists the Sun Solaris system logs that are sometimes used for intrusion detection, the files to which they are written, and the information they contain.

Table 3.1   Sun Solaris System Logs

Log Name	Content	File Written/Used
pacct	Commands run by users plus resource usage	/var/adm/pacct
lastlog	Most recent successful/ unsuccessful login for each user	/var/adm/wtmp
loginlog	All login failures	/var/adm/acct/sum/loginlog
sulog	All use of su command	/var/adm/sulog
utmp(x)	Lists each user currently logged in; utmpx is a more current extended version of log	/var/adm/utmp(x)
wtmp(x)	Time-stamped list of all user logins/logouts and system startups and shutdowns; wtmpx is a more current extended version of log	/var/adm/wtmp(x)
nis.trans	List of all changes in NIS namespace	/var/nis/trans.log

In addition to these system logs, UNIX provides a `syslogd` daemon that logs system information in a special log file. In situations that call for a great deal of custom software to run in a critical installation, this gives the software developer options. By including logging commands in the custom software that write event records using `syslogd`, the developer can extend intrusion detection capabilities to nonstandard system processes.[3]

3.2.7.3 Consolidation of Log Information

For intrusion detection purposes, system logs can provide information that can be combined with the other system information sources to more accurately determine the events occurring on a system at a given time.

Multiple logging mechanisms can serve as a valuable "sanity check" to those interested in finding security problems on a system. Using information in system logs as additional views of the system activities increases the likelihood of discovering intruders. Discrepancies between events recorded from different vantage points help to identify situations in which an intruder was only partially successful in making the evidence of an attack.

One of the most widely publicized network security incidents of the 1980s occurred at Lawrence Berkeley Laboratories. A system administrator, Cliff Stoll, was assigned the task of resolving a $0.74 discrepancy between two accounting logs generated by separate logging mechanisms on the same computer system. Stoll's investigation led him to a foreign agent who had hacked LBL's systems in an attempt to gain access to sensitive information about critical weapons systems. Stoll's account of the investigation, *The Cuckoo's Egg*, remains a classic in computer and network security circles.[7] Several strategies are available for consolidating logs in a fashion suitable for use in intrusion detection. One that is still widely used involves storing the raw logs in a database and then constructing queries that present the data from a variety of perspectives. In some cases, when external evidence indicates that a problem took place during a particular time interval, it can be very helpful to simply isolate the logs that correspond to that interval. You can then sort them according to user, system object, and order of occurrence. Some commercial intrusion detection systems provide this capability.

In other cases, an administrator or intrusion detection system may be able to tell from operating system audit trails or network traffic that something is amiss, but may not be able to confirm or dispel that suspicion. In this situation, synchronizing events reflected in low-level kernel audit records with coarser-grained log events can sometimes help determine whether further investigation and/or responses are required. In Chapter 4, "Analysis Schemes," the discussion of the consolidation of multiple data sources will continue.

3.2.8 Applications Information

So far, we have focused on collecting data for intrusion detection at the system level. This approach reflects a rather traditional belief of computer security: The only trustworthy data is data collected in the bowels of the system, out of reach of all but the most expert intruders. Although this perception can still be true, as systems and operating systems evolve, so do security threats and protection models.

In a world in which the speed and complexity of systems seems to grow without bounds, those trying to protect their systems naturally look first for signs of trouble that are comprehensible to mere mortals. In modern systems, application logs often represent the only available user-level abstractions of system activity. As such, these logs may well be the only places in which administrative security policies can be traced and noncompliance with those policies shown.

Many members of the intrusion detection community assert that in the future all event information of interest will be generated at the application level. This effect is likely due to multiple factors. Perhaps the most powerful force driving monitoring toward the application level is the advent of object-oriented and distributed systems. We already note this trend in current versions of Microsoft Windows NT, as many events formerly recorded at the operating system event log level have migrated to application data stores.

Almost all commercial operating system audit mechanisms support the generation of application-level audit entries, but few include audit features in their own applications. Those that do compensate by automatically turning off operating system kernel audit for processes invoked by the application. This measure can be risky because it is difficult to guarantee that the application is completely trustworthy, but this feature makes audit logs somewhat easier to comprehend.[2]

3.2.8.1 Applications Data Sources Example 1: Database Systems

One example of an application environment in which the need for audit trails and intrusion detection is apparent is the database management system. In many large organizations, the most critical information resources are housed and accessed strictly via the database management system. For example, many health care institutions store patient records and other sensitive data on large database systems. Government agencies maintain large databases of tax and voter registration records.

Early in the Trusted Systems Initiative, the U.S. Department of Defense chartered research to explore the issues associated with application-level auditing of trusted database management systems. This research isolated several issues associated with audit and intrusion detection on these systems—some are similar to those challenges associated with operating system audit (for instance, performance issues); some are not.

Issues Associated with Data Volume

One such issue concerns audit data volume. In databases, as in operating systems, gigabytes of audit data can be generated in a matter of hours. This factor suggests several considerations when designing intrusion detection systems: suitable compression/archival techniques for audit data, policies and techniques for performing audit data reduction, and granularity of audit control. *Granularity of audit control* refers to whether the audit mechanism can be directed to record audit records for each event type; or whether the audit records must be switched on or off for an entire group of events, not just one. The latter approach is more apt to lead to problems with audit data volume because it forces the audit mechanism to record an entire group of events just to capture the needed one.

Temporal Issues

Another issue involves the time of audit data generation. Depending on where a software developer places a call to the audit subroutine to generate an audit event, a discrepancy can develop between a system event and the recording of an audit record reporting that event.

If you generate an audit record at the beginning of the execution of the transaction, you run the risk of having the time of execution off by fractions of a second to minutes or even hours, depending on the time it takes the execution of the transaction to complete. Worse yet, you also run the risk of the transaction crashing or aborting after the audit record is generated, resulting in a discrepancy between what the audit trail indicates happened and what actually happened.

If, on the other hand, you generate an audit record at the end of the execution of the transaction, you eliminate the possibility of directing the operating system or application to take corrective action in response to a detected problem. (An example is blocking access or commands upon evidence that something is amiss.)

Issues Associated with Level of Abstraction

Similar tradeoffs occur in both database systems and operating systems between the granularity of audit records and the ability of the user to make sense of the audit data. The lower the level of abstraction reflected by the data, the subtler the attack that the system can reveal. The higher the level of abstraction, the more intuitively obvious the reported events are to the reviewer. For this reason, in database systems (as in UNIX systems) many advocate the use of database transaction logs when performing intrusion detection. The use of these transaction logs and UNIX system logs present some of the same problems. For instance, they are not as well-protected as system audit trails are. If the database software itself is corrupted by an adversary, the transaction log can lie to you about what really happened, showing that a transaction occurred when operating system audit trails indicate that another operation was substituted for the purported transaction. Because many of the critical information resources that customers want to protect reside in large databases, database management system audit mechanisms comprise an important information source for intrusion detection systems. This remains an extremely important area of research.[8]

3.2.8.2 Applications Data Sources Example 2: WWW Servers

Because the current explosion in electronic commerce is built upon the World Wide Web, the Web server application is a common source of application-level information. Most Web servers support access log mechanisms that can be a rich source of information.

Access Log Formats

Current Web servers support at least two standard formats for log files. The first is the Common Log Format (CLF), derived from the early versions of the NCSA Web server.

(The National Center for Supercomputing Alliances was the source of the first widely deployed Web browser.) The second is an extended log format that depends on the specific Web server.

CLF logs contain the information displayed in Table 3.2.

Table 3.2	CLF Log
Field	**Format**
The host name of the visitor accessing the site	"Host.subnet.domain.net"
rfc931	information returned by identd for this user; otherwise "-"
The username if a userID was sent for authentication	userID
The date and time of the request plus time zone information	[DD/MMM/YYYY]:HH:MM:SS +TZO]
The name of the page requested and the protocol used by the server to communicate the page	"GET xxx.host.subnet.domain.net"
The status code for the request (200 indicates success)	NNN, "-" if not available
The number of bytes returned by the request	NNNNN, "-" if not available

A typical CLF access log entry would appear as follows:

```
duh.infidel.net-bbace[5/May/1999:02:00:03 +0600]"GET/~sret1/HTTP/1.0" 200 1893
```
[9]

An extended log file might include the data fields included in CLF plus additional information. This extended format is displayed in Table 3.3.

Table 3.3	Extended Common Log File Format Description
Field	**Format**
The host name of the computer accessing the site	"Host.subnet.domain.net"
rfc931	information returned by identd for this user; otherwise "-"
The username if a userID was sent for authentication	userID

continues

Table 3.3	Continued

Field	Format
The date and time of the request plus time zone information	[DD/MMM/YYYY]:HH:MM:SS +TZO]
The name of the page requested and the protocol used by the server to communicate the page	"GET xxx.host.subnet.domain.net"
The status code for the request (200 indicates success)	NNN, "-" if not available
The number of bytes returned by the request	NNNNN, "-" if not available
The address of the referring URL to this page (if visitor utilized) a hot link to access site	http://www.refsite.com/pagedir/page
The browser name and version used by the visitor	"browsername/versionnumber" (OS details)

Therefore, the preceding access results in this log entry:

```
duh.infidel.net-bbace[5/May/1999:02:00:03 +0600]"GET/~sret1/HTTP/1.0" 200 1893
"http://www.yahoo.com/security/anomalies" "Mozilla/2.0(X11;I;SUNOS A 06.07.8000/725)[10]
```

On the Microsoft front, Internet Information Server offers logs in either the CLF or a customized extended format. In addition, the server offers the administrator the option to log entries to a text file or to an open database connectivity (ODBC) database for later queries.

Because Web server logs are used as a basis for measuring Web site statistics that affect revenue generation in commerce sites, we can expect Web server vendors to continue to provide both embedded application log generators and some modicum of protection to these logs.

3.2.8.3 Issues Associated with Application Audits

The issues associated with application audits mirror many of the fundamental challenges of intrusion detection. The first of these is the temporal ordering of audit events. Any time you attempt to make sense of a chain of events based on information collected from more than one point of view, you need a way of organizing the information. In intrusion detection, information is usually organized by recording or assigning a time to each event and then placing the event stream in order according to this time stamp. If the time stamp is missing, then you are limited to seeing things that occur in a particular instant of time.

The second class of issues concerning application audits involves combining the audit trails so that users can make sense of them. The term *composition* is sometimes used to describe the combining of data streams; when the event streams involve information at a higher level of abstraction, some people use the artificial intelligence term *fusion* for this process. Composition and fusion both present significant challenges for a number of reasons. We explore these reasons in more depth when we discuss current issues in Chapter 7.

3.2.9 Target-Based Monitoring

Target-based monitoring is a variation on standard host-based monitoring. The premise of target-based monitoring is that in systems in which resource constraints prevent comprehensive kernel-level auditing, the partial logging of system activities is still possible. To determine where to perform logging, we first assess the most critical or valuable objects within the system, and then construct monitoring mechanisms designed to collect stale information of the object. The state transitions of the object are compared to a security policy and any discrepancies recorded.

3.2.9.1 Definition of Target-Based Monitoring Approaches

The most common target-based monitoring approach uses cryptographic integrity checkers to monitor state changes in system objects, such as critical files. Although this approach to monitoring is static (unlike the dynamic approaches represented by audit and logging mechanisms), it is still a powerful addition to the intrusion detection arsenal. The difference between the static target-based approach and dynamic approaches can be described as follows: Target-based monitoring is analogous to snapshots; dynamic approaches are analogous to video images. Consider the difference between the two when they are used to record the security status of a file cabinet. Although the snapshot might not inform us immediately of a problem, if the camera is set to take snapshots at one-minute intervals, it can provide valuable information at a very low cost. Video monitoring, on the other hand, displays a problem as it happens. However, a video camera costs more than a film camera, and if no one is present to react to the information, the speed of detection may be irrelevant to the organization.

An integrity checker computes a cryptographic checksum for every guarded system object and stores the result in a protected location. The checker computes the checksum using a specialized algorithm called a *message digest algorithm*. (Such algorithms are also known as *cryptographic hash codes* or *hash functions.*) Message digest algorithms are designed with two goals in mind. The first goal is to make the algorithm "cryptographically strong," meaning that the possibility of the algorithm computing the same result for two different inputs is small enough to be considered nonexistent. The second goal is to have a small change in the input to the algorithm produce a large change in the output. Thus, even the tiniest change in the protected object will be apparent at the second stage of integrity checking, when the cryptographic checksum is recomputed and the result compared to the stored value.

3.2.9.2 *Rationale for Target-Based Approaches*

One justification for target-based monitoring approaches is the following: In UNIX-based operating systems, all items of interest to users—including network connections, devices, and processes—can be represented as files. These items are represented by structures called *inodes.* Figure 3.5 shows the structure of an inode.

Figure 3.5   Contents of a UNIX File System Inode[6]

Item	Location	Type	Size in Bytes
Time	Inode Modified *CTime*	Contents Modified *Mtime*	File Accessed *Atime*
	Reference Count	Location of Data (Disk Address)	

Integrity checkers were designed to augment a traditional feature in some file systems. The primary checksum mechanism provided in UNIX systems (sum) is a cyclic redundancy check (CRC). However, this checksum is generated by a well-known polynomial. Furthermore, because the original purpose of CRC polynomials was to detect errors in data communications over noisy channels, the polynomials were designed to detect random changes, not deliberate modification of file contents. Analysis of early hacker attacks discovered a common use of tools that allowed you to nullify the CRC's capability to detect changes in a modified file. Therefore, stronger mechanisms were clearly required.

The Tripwire® integrity assurance tool was developed by Gene Spafford and Gene Kim of the COAST project at Purdue University. Tripwire®[11] was written in the early 1990s to optimize the process of utilizing cryptographic hash codes to protect critical files and objects in UNIX systems. The strength of the cryptographic mechanisms and the numerous options allowed security personnel to focus on critical files, generating information that constitutes a powerful data source for any detection mechanism. The system is now available as a commercial product, with versions for Solaris, Windows NT, and Linux.[12]

3.3 Network-Based Information Sources

Network traffic is the most common information source in current commercial intrusion-detection products. In network-based approaches, information is collected from the network traffic stream as it travels on the network segment. In this section we consider network data as an information source for intrusion detection.

3.3.1 Why Network Sources?

Network-based information sources are popular for many reasons. Primary among them is the fact that the information gained by network monitoring is considered to come at low or no performance cost because the monitor simply reads packets as they cross its network segment. Therefore, running the monitor does not affect the performance of other systems on the network.

Another advantage offered by network-based information sources is that the monitor can be transparent to users on the network, thereby decreasing the likelihood that an adversary will be able to locate it and nullify its capabilities without significant effort. Because the primary resource required of the monitoring system is storage space, organizations can sometimes use older, slower systems to perform monitoring on a network segment.

Finally, network monitors can see evidence of certain classes of attacks that are not easily visible to host-based systems. These attacks include network attacks based on malformed packets and various denial-of-service attacks, including packet storms.

3.3.2 Network Packets

A network-based ID system views packet traffic on its network segment as a data source. This is usually accomplished by placing the network interface card in *promiscuous mode*. Promiscuous mode is a network interface setting that generates interrupts for all network traffic that crosses the segment. Although simple and powerful, this approach does not always work on modern network systems. For instance, in the case of switched networks the network switch acts to isolate network connections between hosts so that a host can see only the traffic that is addressed to it. Also, data that travels via other communications media (such as dial-up phone lines) cannot be monitored using this approach.

An interesting approach to providing network-based monitoring and data collection is provided by Network Flight Recorder (NFR). Developed by Marcus Ranum, whose prior accomplishments included the design and development of several of the earliest network firewalls, NFR is not actually a network-based intrusion detection tool, but a generic network monitor with APIs suitable for supporting add-on intrusion analyzers. The packet capture and reassembly features of NFR are a real boon to customers who want to build customized, network-based, intrusion-detection systems.

3.3.3 TCP/IP Networks

The Internet and the Transmission Control Protocol/Internet Protocol (TCP/IP) protocol that enables it represent the staging area for much of the behavior that is of security interest today. As the protocol standards dictate the steps required to use network packet traffic as a data source, it is helpful to understand how TCP/IP works, and how it structures and packages data.

3.3.3.1 A Brief History of TCP/IP

TCP/IP was created in the 1960s under the ARPANET initiative. Funded by the (Defense) Advanced Research Products Agency (ARPA), the goal of TCP/IP was to enable the military to use computer networks that were robust enough to withstand any kind of disruption, up to and including nuclear war. TCP/IP networks are packet-based, shared communications networks in which communications between systems on the network take place as sequences of discrete packets. The packets travel a series of segments, interconnected by devices called gateways and routers, which are designed to make intelligent decisions about the optimal paths that packets should take en route to their destinations.

3.3.3.2 Structure of the Protocol Stack

The TCP/IP stack contains four protocol layers, which are pictured in Figure 3.6. The four layers are stacked so that each one uses the services of the layer below it. They are organized this way:

- **Applications** Applications such as mail, video server, login, and file transfer are on top.

- **Transport** Next is a protocol layer, such as TCP, which supports the applications by providing a reliable "virtual circuit" between the endpoints of the network connection. The overhead associated with this function includes splitting the data flow into packets, performing error correction, and calculating sequence numbers in order to reconstruct packets in proper order at the destination.

- **Internet** Next is the IP protocol, which serves as a packet multiplexer. It affixes an IP header to each packet from the higher-level protocols, and then sends it to the appropriate device driver for transmission to the specified destination. The nature of IP layer service is that each packet stands alone; this is a datagram service, not a virtual circuit.

- **Network interface** Finally, the bottom layer consists of device drivers that manage the physical communications medium, such as an ethernet local area network or Fiber Distributed Data Interface (FDDI).

Figure 3.6   Simplified TCP/IP Protocol Stack[13]

APPLICATION	Telnet	FTP	Gopher	SMTP	HTTP	BGP	Finger	POP	DNS	SNMP	RIP		Ping	
TRANSPORT	TCP							UDP					ICMP	OSPF
INTERNET	IP													ARP
NETWORK INTERFACE	Ethernet	Token Ring	FDDI	X.25		Frame Relay		SMDS	ISDN		ATM		SLIP	PPP

3.3.3.3   IP Address Structure

In TCP/IP, IP addresses are constructed of a 32-bit number that is divided into two parts: a network portion and a host portion. The host portion of the address is usually divided into a subnet and host address, where subnets are used to perform routing internal to an organization.

The number of bits used for the network is variable; many environments divide a single Class B network into 254 subnets. IP addresses are also characterized as a set of four octets. In the address, each octet is delimited by a period, yielding an address that looks like this: 125.30.254.1. Another scheme for addressing hosts on the Internet is to use a specialized distributed database called the Domain Name System (DNS). DNS translates the IP address into a textual address (for example, fw3.infidel.net).

3.3.3.4   Packet Structures

The TCP layer adds header information to packets, as shown in Figure 3.7.

Figure 3.7   IP Packet (Datagram) Header Format[13]

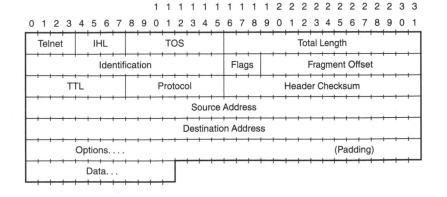

The packet with TCP header information is then forwarded to the Internet layer, where the IP datagram header is attached. The content of IP packet headers is shown in Figure 3.8.

Figure 3.8   TCP Segment Form[13]

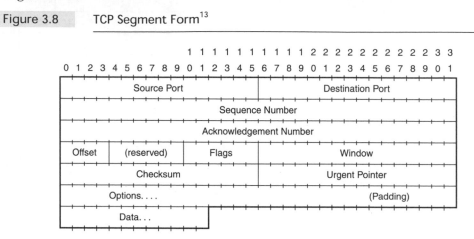

Finally, the packet is passed to the network interface and sent on to the intended destination, where the TCP layer strips off the header information and reconstructs the data stream from the source machine.

3.3.4   Packet Capture

Given this background information about the protocol stack and packet structures, we next turn to the following question: How do you actually grab packets from the network? We consider the two prevailing environments in which this step is performed, UNIX and Windows, and attempt to highlight the options available in each.

3.3.4.1   Windows/NT Packet Capture Options

Prior to the release of Windows NT, many of the packet-capture options available for Microsoft platforms were in the form of tools that captured raw data from ethernet network adapters. Examples of these tools included Gobbler, Ethdump, and Ethload.

Starting with early versions of Microsoft Systems Management Server (SMS), Microsoft provided the Microsoft Network Monitor, a packet sniffer designed to run under Windows NT. Effective with the release of Windows NT Server 4.0, Microsoft fielded the Network Monitor Tool as a standard feature in the operating system. It offered ethernet frame capture with a variety of protocol parsers, a filter language, and a Windows-standard user interface.

Microsoft also provides an interface that allows a remote machine to connect and capture local data. This password-protected feature has generated some interest within the security community because at least one hacker group has broken the authentication mechanism!

3.3.4.2 UNIX Packet Capture Options

The body of packet capture utilities in UNIX is far richer than in Windows environments. One reason is that most network technologies have evolved within the UNIX environment, and UNIX's popularity has in no small part been driven by this support of networking. In general, Windows also appears to have been developed with the assumption that most administrators in Windows environments have little to no interest in tinkering with the low-level operating system code.

That observation aside, let's take a look at the approaches to network packet capture under UNIX. This survey starts "in the olden days" to accommodate the fact that many users have not, for various reasons, chosen to run the most current operating system versions. This approach is also helpful for understanding how changes in the low-level packet-handling schemes have driven requirements for packet capture and analysis.

Early Packet Capture Approaches

The requirement for packet capture facilities in UNIX is rooted in the need for network managers and engineers to have diagnostic and analysis tools. As enterprises have become more reliant on networked systems, the importance of isolation and correction of network problems has grown.

The earliest work in the packet capture and filtering area resulted in the Xerox Alto packet filter. This packet filter was adapted to UNIX by a team from CMU and Stanford in the late 1970s/early 1980s. The CMU/Stanford Packet Filter (CSPF) was designed to run on a DEC PDP-11 computer. The CSPF design was carried forward into standard packet filter mechanisms that are included in more modern UNIX operating systems: NIT (SunOS), UPF (Ultrix), and Snoop (IRIX).

The CSPF used a memory-stack-based filter mechanism, optimized to the older system architectures that were common at the time. It used an expression tree to perform filtering operations, which led to some redundant computations and subsequent losses in performance. The package was restricted to parsing fixed-length packet headers and was furthermore restricted to 16-bit data types (a problem, considering that Internet addresses and TCP sequence numbers are 32-bit data!). Despite its problems, CSPF had significant strengths as well, notably a packet-handling scheme that allowed CSPF to be protocol independent and an abstraction scheme that allowed users to more easily describe and implement the filtering mechanism.

Berkeley Packet Filter

Realizing that there was a mismatch between the CSPF design and more modern RISC-based CPUs, researchers from Lawrence Berkeley Laboratory developed a new kernel architecture for packet capture in the early 1990s, called Berkeley Packet Filter (BPF). BPF implemented two architectural improvements over CSPF. First, BPF switched from a memory-stack-based filter to a register-based filter (a better match with the register-based RISC processors prevalent in modern systems); second, it used the massive increases in memory address space by relying on a nonshared memory model. The performance improvement over CSPF-based mechanisms was impressive, showing up to 150 times greater performance tested against the same hardware and traffic combinations.

BPF has two primary components: a network tap and a packet filter. The network tap takes packet information from network device drivers and carries it to listening applications. After the packet reaches the listening applications, the filter grabs the data and, based on the filtering operation, decides whether the data should be delivered to the listening application. If so, it decides how many bytes of data should be passed. (For instance, a return value of zero indicates that the packet should be completely dropped.)

Two widely used network-monitoring applications use BPF, tcpdump, and arpwatch. Tcpdump is a network monitoring and data acquisition tool that performs filter translation, packet acquisition, and packet display. The filter translation function provides a high-level language for characterizing filters, along with a user-transparent compiler and optimizer that yields BPF programs. Tcpdump is available in versions for SunOS, AIX, Ultrix, and BSD versions of UNIX. Arpwatch is a monitoring program that tracks ethernet to IP address mappings, and notifies administrators when new bindings are made or abnormal activity is observed.[14]

3.3.4.3 Libpcap

Some intrusion detection vendors (notably Network Flight Recorder) use libpcap, the packet-capture library used by tcpdump. Libpcap is a system-independent interface that provides a portable framework for low-level network monitoring. The portability across system platforms provided by libpcap is of considerable value to those who function in heterogeneous system environments. Other advantages associated with the use of libpcap include the capability to download any first-cut packet filtering into kernel memory, which presents significant improvement in performance. In addition, libpcap is supported in Linux, which is growing in popularity as a platform for network monitoring and intrusion detection applications.[15]

3.3.4.4 STREAMS-Based Packet Capture

STREAMS is a system programming model for writing device drivers. Originating in AT&T versions of UNIX and supported in a variety of major UNIX operating systems (including Sun Solaris, HPUX, SCO UNIX, and IBM's AIX), STREAMS provides an extensive collection of system calls, kernel resources, and kernel utility routines that create, use, and dismantle a data stream. A *stream* is defined as a full-duplex processing and data transfer path between a kernel-resident driver and a process in user space. A stream is designed as a pipe structure, with data passing between a driver and the stream head via messages ("upstream" or "downstream," depending on whether the messages are traveling from the driver to the stream head or vice versa).

Packet capture and buffering is offered as part of the standard STREAMS libraries (pfmod and bufmod, respectively, in Solaris), although the architecture of STREAMS makes the performance suboptimal when compared to the BPF-based approaches. The data link provider interface (DLPI), a sniffing interface, is also widely used on systems that use STREAMS.[16]

3.3.5 Network Devices

In addition to packet sniffers, various other network devices can yield information that affects the detection of problems. For example, a network management system can provide performance and utilization statistics that are extremely helpful for determining whether a detected problem is likely to be security-related or due to other system factors. Because an important design goal is to perform monitoring and detection in a fashion that optimizes the performance of the system being protected, investigating and using existing information sources is always preferable to custom building or duplicating the data-collection process.

3.3.6 Out-of-Band Information Sources

A category of data sources that is often neglected by those researching or designing intrusion detection systems is "out-of-band" sources. This category encompasses information that comes to the system by nonsystem, sometimes manual means. Although the notion of a human operator assisting and directing the system as it analyzes information for signs of problems is not as glamorous as a sophisticated artificial intelligence approach, relying on human assistance is still an effective way to perform this function.

Human input can be in the form of information that is manually generated, recorded, or reported. An example of this type of input is the manual logging of events that occur in the system environment. These manual logs can include entries documenting hardware failures, power interruption, failures of systems not within site control (such as telephone service), or anomalous events (threats or natural disasters) that might affect the outcome of an event analysis.

An additional human input comes in the form of user interaction with intrusion detection control components. This type of input can consist of system configuration or policy entry at the time of system installation and setup. It can also take the form of active interaction with the system console, responding to detected problems by directing the system to take additional action. Several generations of intrusion detection systems are likely to be required before detection schemes are mature and reliable enough to allow unsupervised operation. For some environments, the total automation of intrusion detection analysis functions may never be appropriate. In the meantime, you should consider intrusion detection systems as diagnostic tools that allow you to "see" system activity through a security-savvy prism, using this higher-level view to gain additional expertise in recognizing and dealing with security problems.

3.4   Information from Other Security Products

In general, the more event information that is considered in performing intrusion detection analysis, the more accurate and sensitive the results. This relationship is especially true in performing intrusion detection on networks, where stand-alone security products are common.

Many firewalls, I&A systems, access control systems, and other security devices and subsystems generate their own activity logs. These logs contain information that is, by definition, of security significance; they are therefore of particular value to the intrusion detection process. Including these logs as information sources is an obvious way to improve the quality of the intrusion detection process.

The process of integrating and analyzing event logs from other components of the system security infrastructure represents a significant and enduring role that intrusion detection systems can play. This role continues to be relevant, even as strong encryption or other measures address those threats we consider of greatest concern today. Although technical environments change, the attack strategies of adversaries remain relatively stable. Because an elementary step in attacking a system is to locate, investigate, and then nullify the existing system protections, monitoring security products will remain a stable requirement.

3.4.1   An Example of a Security Product Data Source

Table 3.4 presents a format diagram of the firewall log file generated by Firewall-1, a CheckPoint Technologies product. It allows you to see the transactions processed by the firewall, including mappings of ostensible sources and destinations of connections, the names of system objects associated with the transactions, and other information that was selected for inclusion.

Table 3.4   Firewall-1 Log File[17]

Field No.	Name of Field	Contents
1	Number	Transaction identifier
2	Date	Date of event—D(D)MMMYY
3	Time	Time of event—HH:MM:SS
4	Action	Accept or deny
5	Type	
6	Origination	
7	Alert	
8	Interface name	MAC address of ethernet card
9	Interface direction	Inbound/outbound
10	Protocol type	TCP or UDP
11	Src host	IP address of source
12	Dst host	IP address of destination
13	Type of service	Network service type
14	Port number for the source	Port number addressed by packet
15	"Rule"	Firewall rule tripped
16	Elapsed time	Time since session started
17	Packets for this session	Number of packets associated with session
18	Number of bytes	
19	Authenticated username	
20	Messages	

3.4.2   Organization of Information Prior to Analysis

As we noted when we discussed application-level data sources, issues arise when integrating data sources coming from different points in the network, especially when the sources are collected from different levels of abstraction. Security product data sources are no different in this regard.

Perhaps the best rule of thumb to apply in this case is to first temporally order the data according to a standard time reference. Network Time Protocol can be helpful in this regard; so can other forms of trusted network time service. After the data is sorted in chronological order, correlate log events to threat scenarios of interest. Alternatively, correlate log events to security policy noncompliance. Because security products are often the first heralds of attack, log events that correspond to attacks targeting the security products are usually reliable attack signatures in themselves.

As before, this binding of events to a time source, followed by correlation to a threat model, can be done either manually or with the assistance of a system. No system currently performs this correlation with enough reliability to eliminate the "man in the loop." For certain systems and environments, a human will remain a part of the process for some time to come.

3.4.3 Other System Components as Data Sources

Other system components also provide information that can be of value in intrusion detection. Many of these components are not often considered as legitimate data sources because they are not considered to be legitimate parts of the systems. Let's consider an example.

Early intrusion detection systems relied on a great many rules and detection algorithms to detect *masqueraders,* intruders who gained access to systems by using userIDs and passwords purloined from legitimate users. A variety of system audit trail approaches, ranging from statistical profiling of user activity (establishing patterns of "normal" behavior) to extensive rule trees (outlining the specific behaviors that a masquerader might exhibit) were proposed.

These approaches had a high false-alarm rate, and the amount of time devoted to investigating alleged masquerader attacks was appreciable.

In this case, information from physical access control systems can help determine whether a questionable access to the computer system is an attack. In this situation, if the intrusion detection system detects a suspected masquerade on the internal network, it can then query the physical access control system. If the physical access system indicates that the user in question is not on the premises, the implication is that the diagnosis of a masquerader attack is correct.

In another example of an out-of-band information source, consider a case in which a hacker attacks the network from a dial-up connection. After the specific modem used by the hacker is identified, the telephone switch caller ID channel might provide information that is useful to investigators who hope to identify the hacker. Telephone system traps and traces have also been used for this purpose.

3.5 Conclusion

In this chapter, we took a look at the plethora of data sources available for intrusion detection. We considered sources from different points within the system at different levels of detail and different levels of abstraction. In the next chapter, we begin to analyze the information drawn from these sources.

Endnotes

1. National Computer Security Center. "Department of Defense Trusted Computer System Evaluation Criteria." Orange Book, DOD 5200.28-std, December 1985.

2. Price, K. E. "Host-Based Misuse Detection and Conventional Operating Systems' Audit Data Collection." Master thesis, Purdue University, December 1997.

3. *Solaris Reference Manual Answerbook.* Sun Microsystems, Inc. Mountain View, CA, 1994–1998.

4. *Windows NT Reference Manual.* Microsoft Technet, Microsoft Corporation, Redmond, WA, 1999.

5. Lichtman, Z. L. and J. F. Kimmins. "An Audit Trail Reduction Paradigm Based on Trusted Processes." Proceedings of the National Computer Security Conference, October 1990.

6. Garfinkel, S. and E. H. Spafford. *Practical UNIX and Internet Security, Second Edition.* O'Reilly and Associates, 1996: 290.

7. Stoll, Clifford. *The Cuckoo's Egg: Tracking a Spy Through the Maze of Computer Espionage.* New York, NY: Doubleday, 1989.

8. Schaefer, M., B. Hubbard, D. Sterne, T. K. Haley, J. N. McAuliffe, and D. Woolcott. "Auditing A Relevant Contribution to Trusted Database Management Systems." Proceedings of the Fifth Annual Computer Security Applications Conference, Tucson, AZ, December 1989.

9. World Wide Web Consortium. "Logging Control in W3C httpd." in httpd documentation: User's Guide `http://www.w3c.org/daemon/user/logging.html`.

10. Hallam-Baker, Phillip and B. Behlendorf. "Extended Log File Format." World Wide Web Consortium Working Draft, WD-logfile 960523, *WWW Journal*, issue 3, March 1996.

11. Tripwire® is a registered trademark of the Purdue Research Foundation.

12. Kim, G. H. and E. H. Spafford. "Tripwire: A Case Study in Integrity Monitoring." *Internet Besieged: Countering Cyberspace Scofflaws*, edited by Dorothy and Peter Denning, Addison-Wesley, 1997.

13. Kessler Hill Associates, Inc. C. Gary. "An Overview of TCP/IP Protocols and the Internet." April 23, 1999: `http://www.hill.com/library/tcpip.html`.

14. McCanne, S. and V. Jacobson. *The BSD Packet Filter: A New Architecture for User-Level Packet Capture.* 1993 Winter USENIX Conference, San Diego, CA, January 1993.

15. Ranum, M.J., K. Landfield, M. Stolarchuk, M. Sienkiewicz, A. Lambeth, and E. Wall. *Implementing a Generalized Tool for Network Monitoring.* Proceedings of the Eleventh Systems Administration Conference (LISA '97), San Diego, CA, October 1997.

16. *Streams Driver Overview.* Driver Development for SCO Systems, The Santa Cruz Operation, Santa Cruz, CA, 1999.

17. Sundstrom, Peter. "Firewalls-1 Report Summariser (fwlogsum version 3.6.0)." www.ginini.com.au/tools/fw1, August 1999.

CHAPTER

4

Analysis Schemes

"Is there any other point to which you would wish to draw my attention?"
"To the curious incident of the dog in the nighttime."
"The dog did nothing in the nighttime."
"That was the curious incident," remarked Sherlock Holmes.
- Sir Arthur Conan Doyle

Given a variety of rich information sources about the system activities you're charged with monitoring, the next stop on the intrusion detection circuit is analysis. With analysis, you're faced with the core issue of intrusion detection: What is going on here, and should I be interested in or concerned about it?

Within the analysis function, information is synchronized, classified, and subjected to scrutiny of various types to identify activity patterns of security significance. This chapter covers the vast area of analysis, considers the various goals of analysis, and discusses the issues you must take into account when devising an analysis scheme for a particular goal or system. It also explores the variables that affect the quality of the analysis.

4.1 Thinking About Intrusions

In considering the analysis functions of intrusion detection, let's start by articulating the detection process in intuitive terms. This definition will lend structure to the subsequent discussion of the fundamental issues and functions of analysis.

4.1.1 Defining Analysis

Analysis, in the context of intrusion detection, is organizing and characterizing data about user and system activity to identify activity of interest. This activity can be isolated either as it happens or after the fact. In some cases, further analysis is needed to establish account-ability for the activity. Depending on the type of analysis, additional evaluation may be performed to tune or otherwise improve the outcome of subsequent analysis.

Intrusion detection is the second step in a general system security management process model, pictured in Figure 4.1. This model is helpful because certain analysis functions serve the needs of the investigative and resolution steps of the management process.

Figure 4.1   A General Model of Security Management

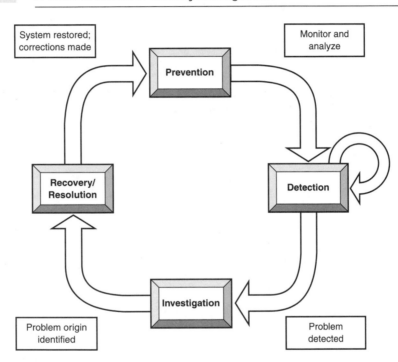

4.1.2 Goals

Security managers hope to gain several benefits by performing intrusion detection analysis. The overarching assumption is that people use intrusion detection systems to improve the security of their information systems.

- **Significant deterrence**   One benefit a security manager seeks is to deter problem behaviors. The knowledge that analysis is being performed and the credible threat of discovery and punishment serve as a deterrent to intruders.

- **Quality control for security design and administration**   Problems that are discov-ered in the course of analysis can indicate flaws in the design and management of security for the system. The security manager, so notified, can then correct these problems before an adversary utilizes them to damage or steal information.

- **Useful information on actual intrusions**   This information should be relevant, detailed, and trustworthy so that it can support criminal or civil legal remedies. It can also be used to identify needed corrections in the organization's security configuration, policy, or strategy.

4.1.3   Supporting Goals

Now that the goals of the analysis process are outlined, it's time to consider how each one drives specific functional requirements for an intrusion detection system. Structuring the requirements as sets of prioritized goals and subgoals helps to optimize the system.

4.1.3.1   Requirements

Intrusion detection analysis supports two basic requirements. One is, as we've mentioned before, *accountability*, which refers to the ability to link an activity with the person or entity responsible for it. Accountability requires you to be able to consistently and reliably identify and authenticate each user of the system. Furthermore, you must also be able to reliably associate each user with the audit or other event records of her activities.

Although the concepts of accountability are straightforward and common in business environments, they are difficult to implement in network environments. Unless you're in an environment featuring a single *sign-on system*, which centralizes identification and authentication for a large network, a user may have different user identities on different systems within the network. Because host-level audit trails reflect user activity in terms of the user's local identity, keeping track of user identity in activities that involve multiple hosts and user accounts requires additional processing.

The second requirement for intrusion detection analysis is *real-time detection and response*. This requirement includes the ability to quickly recognize the chain of events associated with an attack, and the ability to then block the attack (for instance, by terminating the network connection used by the attacker) or to shield the system from the impact of the attack (for instance, by tracing the commands sent by the attacker and restoring any altered files or objects to their pre-attack state).

4.1.3.2   Subgoals

Analysis also has subgoals. For instance, you might need to retain information in a form that supports system and network forensic analysis. Another subgoal might involve retaining some knowledge about the system performance or identifying problems that affect system performance. Yet another might involve archiving and protecting the integrity of event logs required by regulators or law enforcement entities.

4.1.3.3 Prioritizing Goals

After goals and requirements are articulated, they should be prioritized. Prioritization is necessary to determine the structure of the analysis subsystem. The priorities can be ranked by schedule (for instance, "this requirement will be serviced before that one"), by system (for example, "all requirements associated with system X will be serviced before those associated with other systems"), or by other attributes.

4.1.3.4 Trade-offs

At times, the goals and requirements of analysis may conflict. For example, one goal of analysis is to minimize the impact of analysis on the performance and resource consumption of the target system. However, the requirement to maintain logs for legal purposes often conflicts with this goal. In another example, the system overhead required to maintain accountability may affect the analyzer's ability to identify intrusions quickly enough to support active response.

4.1.4 Detecting Intrusions

To understand the nature of intrusion detection analysis, you should consider the full range of intrusion analysis available to customers, starting with those used in older systems. Although the focus here is on techniques suitable for automation, consider the full spectrum of discovery techniques for security intrusions and other violations of policy.

4.1.4.1 The Human Detector

Humans ("wetware" or "carbon units") are the most obvious and traditionally the most common source of intrusion information. A system manager may report that a machine is acting funny, or a user may report finding evidence of unauthorized activity on a system. Unfortunately, this approach is of extremely limited value because most incidents go unnoticed at sites where no intrusion detection systems are in place. For instance, one early study showed that over a period of time in which a prototype intrusion detection system detected several hundred intrusions, only 2% of those were detected by the humans charged with performing manual intrusion detection.

4.1.4.2 External Events

Events external to the computer system often trigger suspicion of potential intrusion. These events include hiring and firing (especially of key personnel), reports of anomalies (such as sudden unexplained affluence of employees who work on critical systems), results of security penetration tests, and discovery of missing goods or information. These events are some-times tracked as part of a traditional corporate fraud detection or loss control program.

News coverage or warnings posted to the Internet about particular classes of attacks also trigger suspicion of potential intrusion. This information appears to encourage the installation or use of antivirus tools.

4.1.4.3   Precursors to Intrusion

Next are the signs of intrusion that come from the victim systems. The first sign is evidence of an intruder having primed the system for future attack, which includes signs of trojan horse placement (that is, tampered system files) and unauthorized account additions to password files or trusted host configuration files (such as /etc/.rhosts in UNIX systems). These examples were the first symptoms of security problems targeted by early security tools such as COPS.

4.1.4.4   Artifacts of Intrusion

As precursors to intrusion alert customers to likely incidents, so do those indicators left in the wake of intrusions. These *artifacts*, evidence of past intrusions, can be reliable indica-tors of attack for both intrusion detection and vulnerability analysis. They can be discovered in real time (immediately upon the completion of the first step of an intrusion) or after the fact (during batch mode analysis of log files). Artifacts that are discovered immediately can be used by intrusion detection systems functioning in real time. Examples of artifacts of intrusions include password sniffer log files, unexplained system failures, and damaged files. Note that some artifacts are incidental to the intrusion (that is, they are not an intended goal of the intrusion) but excellent indicators, nevertheless, for detection pur-poses. Examples of such incidental outcomes include abnormal patterns of system resource use, discrepancies in accounting records (due to intruders deleting some, but not all, evidence of their activities), and unusual network traffic levels.

4.1.4.5   Observing Attack in Real Time

The final scenario for detecting misuse became possible with the advent and availability of intrusion detection systems—recognizing attacks by monitoring systems in real time. The ability to detect attacks by using these systems has opened the door to attack-blocking and other adaptive system responses to detected problems.

4.2   A Model for Intrusion Analysis

Analysis is the core function of intrusion detection. It can be as simple as an ad hoc deci-sion table constructed by someone who has manually reviewed transaction logs, or as complex as a nonparametric system trained with millions of transactions.

We can look at the process of intrusion detection analysis from several perspectives. In this section, I define a model that covers all approaches to finding evidence of intrusions in system event records. It divides the process of intrusion detection analysis into three phases: constructing the analyzer, actually performing analysis of live data, and feedback or refinement of the process. Each of the first two phases has three functions: data preprocessing, data classification (classifying data as either indicative of intrusion, indicative of no intrusion, or "not sure"), and postprocessing.

Figure 4.2 depicts a view of the activity space, reflecting the view of misuse detectors, anomaly detectors, and possible gaps between the two. The fundamental debate between proponents of anomaly detection and proponents of misuse detection centers on the overlap of the regions representing "normal," "misuse," and "not normal" activities. Denning's initial assertion was that the region of "misuse" activity falls far enough outside the region of "normal" activity to use normality measures as the basis for finding misuse. Therefore, her assertion is that the intersection between the two regions is minimal. Proponents of misuse detection assert that the intersection is quite large, to the point that given observed errors in characterizing "normal" activity, it is pointless to use anomaly detection as anything but a crude alarm flagging activities that require closer scrutiny. The debate will continue for awhile yet, and this remains an open research area.

Figure 4.2   Misuse versus Anomaly Detection

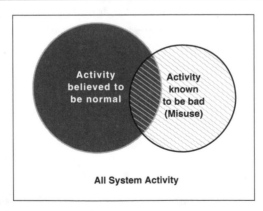

4.2.1   Constructing the Analyzer

In the analysis model, the first phase is the construction of the analysis engine. The analysis engine performs the core functions of preprocessing, classification, and postprocessing. For the engine to function properly, regardless of analysis approach, it must be tailored to the environment in which it is to operate; hence this phase is necessary even in rudimentary systems when it is performed solely as part of system development.

4.2.1.1 Collect and/or Generate Event Information

The first step of constructing the analyzer is collecting event information. Depending on the analysis approach, this phase might involve collecting event information generated by a system functioning in an operational environment, or collecting event information in a laboratory environment. In some cases, the event information may be handcrafted by a developer working from a set of formal specifications.

- **Misuse detection** For misuse detection, this part of the process involves gathering information about intrusions, including information about vulnerabilities, attacks, threats, specific attack tools, and observed scenarios of interest. At this time, information is also gathered about typical discretionary policies, procedures, and practices so that the behavioral model can accommodate organization-specific policy violations as well as problems associated with external attack.

- **Anomaly detection** For anomaly detection, event information is collected from the live system itself or from a system designated as similar. This information is needed to build baseline profiles indicating "normal" user behavior.

4.2.1.2 Preprocess the Information

After event information is collected, it goes through a variety of transformations in preparation for use in the analysis engine. It may be placed into a *canonical* or common format. This format is usually specified as part of the analyzer design. In some systems, the data is also structured (by placing it in a database or indexing it), some feature selection is performed (that is, the most relevant pieces of the data are identified and set apart), or other processing is performed.

- **Misuse detection** In misuse detection, the preprocessing of data usually involves transforming the event information collected into some sort of common form that corresponds to the data to be filtered when the intrusion detection system is placed into operation. For instance, the attack symptoms and policy violation information may be converted into state transition–based signatures or some sort of production system rules. In the case of a network-based intrusion detection system, the packets may be cached and Transmission Control Protocol (TCP) sessions reconstructed.

- **Anomaly detection** In anomaly detection, event data may be translated into arrays or tables, with some categorical data (for instance a system name), converted to numeric form (such as an Internet Protocol [IP] address). As in misuse data, different information may be converted into some canonical format.

Note

Canonical formats were originally used to allow a single analysis engine to monitor multiple operating systems, each of which usually had its own native format for event data. Intrusion detection developers could then leverage a common analysis engine to analyze data from many different operating systems. Because this practice allowed the developers to target new operating systems by translating the new event data to the canonical format, significant economic benefits were associated with this design approach. The utility of canonical formats still applies to situations in which one wishes to perform common analysis across a heterogeneous operating system environment. Some intrusion detection experts assert that enough organizations have converged on a common operating system for their entire enterprise so that canonical formats are no longer warranted.

At least one operational system accumulates user session data and then condenses it into numeric profile vectors. This reduces the event data to a form that takes up less space in memory and in storage. It also allows aggregation of certain data fields so that the analysis engine can easily recognize certain user activity patterns.

4.2.1.3   Build a Behavior Classification Engine or Model

The system developer, working from the design specification, then constructs a data classifier. This classifier separates event data corresponding to intrusive behavior from event data that appears not to indicate intrusions. The composition of this engine depends on the analysis approach.

Misuse Detection

In misuse detection, the data classification engine is built on behaviors described in terms of rules or other pattern descriptors. These rules or descriptors can be divided into single part (sometimes called *atomic*) signatures or multipart (sometimes called *composite*) signatures. An example of an atomic signature is one that detects a badly formed IP packet (with inconsistencies between the packet content and headers). An example of a composite signature is one that detects a UNIX `sendmail` attack (where the attack is a series of carefully timed steps).

One structure for a misuse detector classification engine is a *production* or expert system. *Expert systems* consist of a *knowledge base* containing descriptions of suspicious behavior based on knowledge of past intrusions (for instance, those gathered in the previous step of this process) and *rules* that allow matching to be done against the knowledge base. These rules are usually structured as if-then-else statements.

Another structure for a misuse detector classification engine is a pattern-matching engine that represents intrusions as attack signatures (patterns) to be matched against audit data.

Because many systems built on this model are extremely efficient and reliable, it represents the most common approach to intrusion detection in commercial products.

Anomaly Detection

In anomaly detection, the classification model usually consists of statistical profiles of user behavior over time. These profiles can also be used to characterize the behavior of system processes, an important consideration given the widespread use of automated attack scripts. These statistical profiles may be calculated with various algorithms, using schemes that make allowances for gradual change in user behavior patterns. The profiles may be amended on either a fixed or variable schedule.

An example of an anomaly detection-based classification model is the Intrusion Detection Expert System (IDES), an instantiation of Dorothy Denning's seminal intrusion detection system model.

IDES defines its behavior classification model in terms of *measures*, single aspects of a user or subject's behavior on the monitored system. Figure 4.3 shows the classification of IDES measures (first distinguishing ordinal measures from categorical measures and then binary from linear). *Ordinal* or *continuous* measures are expressed in terms of a numeric count or quantification of the measure. *Categorical* or *discrete* measures are expressed in terms of identity and of frequency of occurrence.

Categorical measures are divided into two additional classifications, *binary* and *linear*. *Binary categorical* measures are characterized in terms of whether the measure occurred or not (a true/false switch), whereas *linear categorical* measures are characterized in terms of a score indicating the number of times a particular behavior occurs (a counter). The majority of measures utilized by IDES fall into the linear categorical group.[1]

Figure 4.3   IDES Measure Categories and Examples

	Ordinal (Continuous)	Categorical (Discrete)
Binary	CPU time used Number of audit records produced	Whether a directory was used Whether a file was accessed Whether audit records indicated use for day/week/month
Linear		# of times each command was used # of system-related errors # of login failures in last hour # of audit events recorded # of files modified

4.2.1.4 Populate It with Event Data

After the model is built, it is populated with the collected and preprocessed event data. This instantiation of the model constitutes the analysis engine for the target system.

- **Misuse detection**   Misuse detectors are populated with the preprocessed event data or contents of an attack knowledge base, a collection of information about attacks expressed in terms meaningful to the analysis engine.

- **Anomaly detection**   Anomaly detectors are populated by running them against the collected reference event data (*training sets*), allowing the system to calculate user profiles based on this data. The fact that the historical data used to populate the anomaly detector is devoid of intrusions is often assumed without any corroborating evidence. Finding "clean" training sets for anomaly detectors remains a major issue.

4.2.1.5 Store the Populated Model in a Knowledge Base

Regardless of approach, the populated model is then stored in a predefined location, ready for operational use. At this point, the populated model contains all of the criteria for analysis, and in fact comprises the actual core of the analysis engine.

4.2.2 Performing Analysis

The second of the three phases in the analyzer is the operational analysis of a live event stream. In this phase, the analyzer is applied to live data to spot intrusions and other activity of interest.

- **Input new event record**   The first step of performing analysis is taking an event record as generated by one of the information sources. Such information sources might be network packet traces, operating system audit trails, or application log files, and it is assumed that they have not been compromised.

- **Preprocessing**   As in the construction of the analyzer, some preprocessing of the event data may be performed. The exact nature of this preprocessing depends on the nature of the analysis. Examples include threading together various TCP messages into a higher-level abstraction (a "session") and structuring process identifiers from operating system audit trails into high-integrity process trees.

  - **Misuse detection**   For misuse detectors, the event data is usually converted to some canonical form. This form corresponds to the structure of the attack signatures. In some approaches, the event data is aggregated (collected to make up some minimum interval of interest, such as a user session, a network connection, or other high-level event). In other approaches, the data is *reduced* by combining some attributes, eliminating others entirely, and performing calculations on others to create new, more compact data records.

- **Anomaly detection** In anomaly detection the event data is usually reduced to a profile vector with behavior attributes expressed as scores and flags.

- **Compare the event record to the knowledge base** The formatted event record is compared to the contents of the knowledge base. The next step of the process depends on the results of this comparison and on the analysis scheme in question. If the record indicates an intrusion, it may be logged. If the record does not indicate an intrusion, the analyzer simply accepts the next event record and repeats the formatting and comparison.

  - **Misuse detection** In the misuse detector, the preprocessed event record is submitted to a pattern-matching engine. If the pattern matcher finds a match between an attack signature and the event data, it returns an alert. In some misuse detectors, if a partial match is found (if a pattern indicating a possible preamble to attack is matched), that fact may be recorded or the record cached in memory, awaiting further event information that can be appended to it to make a more definitive decision. Detection engines that can "remember" sequences of events are called *stateful* detectors.

  - **Anomaly detection** In anomaly detection, the contents of the user behavior profile for the session are compared to the historical profile for that user. Depending on the analysis scheme, a judgment is made as to whether the user behavior is close enough to the historical profile to be considered "normal" and therefore not indicative of attack. If the user behavior is determined to be abnormal, an alert is returned. Many anomaly detection–based intrusion detection engines also perform misuse-detection in parallel with this process, so some cross-pollination may occur between these different analysis schemes.

- **Generate a response** If the event record corresponds to an intrusion or other behavior of interest, a response is returned. Again, the nature of the response depends on the specific nature of the analysis approach. The response can be an alarm, a log entry, an automated response, or some other action specified by the operator of the intrusion detection system.

4.2.3 Feedback and Refinement

Certain analysis approaches have a third stage of analysis, one that runs in parallel with the main analysis function. The functions associated with this third phase are either maintenance of the analysis engine or other adaptive functions (refinement of rule sets or other system attributes).

4.2.3.1   Misuse Detection

In misuse detection systems, the primary activity that occurs in this stage is the update of signature databases to reflect information regarding new attacks. Given the almost daily reports of new attacks, this function is important. Many optimized signature engines accommodate this update activity "on the fly." (In other words, the system operator can update the signature database while the system is monitoring event data without interrupting the analysis process.)

Some misuse detection engines use this phase to combine and otherwise optimize the state-retention portions of the system, periodically eliminating records that have not been resolved.

Most misuse-detection-based analysis schemes have some notion of a maximum time interval over which matching of an attack signature occurs. This interval is known as an *event horizon*. For some, the event horizon might be from user login to logout (a session). Other schemes make this determination in terms of elapsed time since login or the last recorded event for that user.

In any event, because a significant amount of memory is necessary to retain this state information (especially when multiplied by the number of users, processes, and network connections active on busy systems), aggressive management of this state information is critical to the stability of a system. You see this effect in network-based intrusion detection systems in which "up the stack" reassembly of TCP sessions is performed.

In early misuse-detection efforts, the incomplete session records used to maintain state were labeled *orphans.* Performing the memory management was called (somewhat tongue-in-cheek) *running the orphanage* and was a frequent topic of discussion in some research and development circles.[2]

4.2.3.2   Anomaly Detection

Depending on the type of anomaly detection performed, the historical statistical profiles are updated periodically. For example, in IDES, the first statistical intrusion detection system, the profiles were updated daily. At that time, the summary statistics for each user were added to the knowledge base, and the oldest day's statistics (30 days old) were deleted.

The rest of the statistics (for day 1 through day 29) were multiplied by an aging factor. In this way, more recent behaviors had more effect on the determination of normal activity than older ones had. This practice is motivated by the need to accommodate changes in user behaviors associated with work schedules (for instance, accounting duties that may change over the course of a month) and user learning curves.[1]

4.3   Techniques

Now that I have explained the hows and whys of analysis and have outlined a general process for performing analysis, it's time to outline the specific approaches. As mentioned in Chapter 2, "Concepts and Definitions," analysis is divided into two parts.

Intrusion detection is composed of *misuse detection*, which searches event data for predefined patterns of misuse, and *anomaly detection*, which characterizes data in mathematical terms, searching event data for patterns of abnormality.

4.3.1   Misuse Detection

Misuse detection asks the following question about system events: Is this activity bad? Misuse detection involves encoding information about specific behaviors known to be indicators of intrusion and then filtering event data for these indicators.

To perform misuse detection, you need the following:

- A good understanding of what constitutes a misuse behavior

- A reliable record of user activity

- A reliable technique for analyzing that record of activity

In a nutshell, misuse detection is best suited for reliably detecting known use patterns. It suffers the deficiency that you can detect only what you know about, although if you're clever, you can leverage the knowledge you have (for instance, of outcomes of attacks) to spot new exploits of old problems.

4.3.1.1   Production/Expert Systems

One of the earliest schemes for performing misuse detection was the use of production/expert systems. This approach was utilized in systems such as MIDAS, IDES, Next Generation IDES (NIDES), DIDS, and CMDS. In the case of MIDAS, IDES, and NIDES, the production system employed was P-BEST, designed by Alan Whitehurst. For DIDS and CMDS, the CLIPS system, a public domain system developed by the National Aeronautics and Space Administration (NASA), was used.

The advantage associated with using production systems is that the control reasoning of the systems is separated from the statement of the problem solution. This feature allows users to enter knowledge about attacks as if-then rules and then enter facts (in the form of audit events); the system evaluates those facts according to the knowledge entered. This process can occur without the user ever affecting (or understanding) the internal function of the production system; before production systems, users had to hard code the decision engine and rules in custom software, a difficult, time-consuming task.

The attack knowledge is entered using an if-then syntax. Conditions indicative of an intrusion are specified on the left side (the "if" part) of the rule. When they are satisfied, the rule performs the actions on the right side (the "then" part) of the rule.

Some practical problems are associated with the use of production systems in intrusion detection.

- They are ill-equipped to handle large volumes of data. This is true because the declarative representations used by production systems are generally implemented as interpreted systems and interpreters are slower than compiled engines.

- They do not provide any natural handling of sequentially ordered data.

- The expertise reflected by the production system is only as good as the person on whose skills the system is modeled (the standard "garbage in, garbage out" effect endemic to computer systems).

- They can detect only known intrusions.

- They cannot handle uncertainty.

Maintaining the rule base can be problematic, as one must make changes to the rules considering the impact of the changes on the rest of the rules in the knowledge base.[3]

4.3.1.2   State Transition Approaches

State transition approaches to performing misuse detection structure the problem of misuse detection in a way that allows the use of optimized pattern-matching techniques. Their speed and flexibility make them among the most powerful intrusion detection capabilities at this time.

State transition approaches use expressions of system state and state transitions to describe and detect known intrusions. Several approaches are available for implementing state transition approaches to intrusion detection. The three major approaches are language or Application Programming Interface (API), characterization of state transitions, Colored Petri Nets (CP-Nets), and state transition analysis. In this section, I explore these processes, outlining the strategies each uses to characterize misuse patterns and then filter event data against them.

State Transition Analysis

State transition analysis is an approach to misuse detection using high-level state transition diagrams to represent and detect known penetration scenarios. This approach was first explored in the STAT system and its extension to UNIX network environments, USTAT.

Both systems were developed at the University of California, Santa Barbara. Phillip Porras and Richard Kemmerer developed STAT; Koral Ilgun and Kemmerer developed USTAT.

A state transition diagram is a graphical representation of a penetration scenario. Figure 4.4 shows the components of a state transition diagram, as well as how they are used to represent a sequence. Nodes represent the states, and arcs represent the transitions. The concept of expressing intrusions in state transition form is rooted in the understanding that all intruders start with limited privileges and exploit system vulnerabilities to gain some outcome. Both the limited privilege starting point and the successful intrusion outcome can be expressed as system states.

In using state transition diagrams to characterize the intrusion sequences, the system can limit itself to expressing those key activities that result in a state change. The path between initial and intrusion state can be rather subjective; hence two persons can come up with different state transition diagrams that represent the same attack scenario. Each state consists of one or more state assertions (also shown in Figure 4.4).

Figure 4.4   State Transition Diagrams

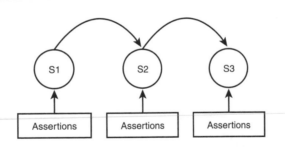

State transition analysis systems utilize finite state machine graphs (finite automata) to model intrusions. The intrusion is composed of a sequence of actions that lead from some initial system state to an intrusion state. The initial state represents the state of the system before the intrusion is executed, and the intrusion state represents the state of the system upon the completion of the intrusion. The system state is described in terms of system attributes and/or user privileges. The transition is driven by a user action. The state transition engine maintains a set of state transition diagrams, each representing a penetration scenario. At a given time, it's assumed that some sequence of actions have driven the system to a particular state in each diagram. When a new action takes place, the engine checks it against each state transition diagram to see whether the action drives the scenario to the next state. If the action nullifies the assertions of the current state, the inference engine moves the state transition back to the nearest state for which the assertions still hold. If the action drives the scenario to the end state, indicating an intrusion, the previous transition information is sent to the decision engine, which alerts the security officer to the presence of the intrusion.

The advantages of the STAT approach follow:

- State transition diagrams provide an intuitive, high-level, and audit-record-independent representation of penetration scenarios.

- The transitions allow one to represent partial order of signature actions constituting an attack scenario.

- A state transition diagram uses the smallest possible subset of signature actions that must occur for the penetration to be successful. Thus, the detector can generalize over variants of the same penetration.

- The hard-link information maintained by the system makes it easier to express penetration scenarios.

- The system can detect coordinated and slow attacks.[4]

Deficiencies of the STAT approach include the following:

- The list of state assertions and signature actions are hand coded.

- The state assertions and signatures may not be powerful enough for expressing more elaborate penetration scenarios.

- The evaluation of certain state assertions may require the inference engine to get additional information from the target system. This process could cause performance degradation.

- The system cannot detect many common attacks, so it must be combined with other detectors for operational use.

- The prototyped system is slow compared to other state transition–based approaches.[5]

Colored Petri-Net and IDIOT

Another state-transition-based approach to optimizing misuse detection is the Colored Petri (CP)-Net approach developed by Sandeep Kumar and Gene Spafford at Purdue University. This approach was implemented in the IDIOT system.

Note

The name IDIOT originated as a joke between Gene Spafford and the author; it stands for Intrusion Detection In Our Time, a wry commentary on the delays many members of the intrusion detection research community experienced in transferring research results to operational systems!

IDIOT uses a variation of CP-Nets to represent and detect intrusion patterns. Under this model, an intrusion is represented as a CP-Net in which the color of tokens in each state serves to model the context of the event. The signature matching is driven by the audit trail and takes place by moving tokens progressively from initial states to the final state (indicating an intrusion or attack). *Guards* define the context in which signatures are considered matched, and *post actions* are performed when the pattern is successfully matched.

At first glance, this approach might appear to be almost identical to the state transition approach of STAT. However, there are significant differences between the approaches. First, in STAT the intrusion is detected by the effect it has on the system state, that is, the *outcome* of the intrusion. In IDIOT the intrusion is detected by pattern-matching the signature that constitutes the penetration. In STAT guards are placed in the state, whereas in IDIOT the guards are incorporated in the transitions.

In IDIOT each intrusion signature is expressed as a pattern that represents the relationship among events and their context. This relationship pattern precisely represents a successful intrusion or its attempt. Vertices in the CP-Net graph represent system states. Intrusion patterns have preceding conditions and following actions associated with them. The scheme is independent of any underlying computational framework of matching and provides a model in which all categories in the classification are represented and matched.

This pattern-matching model consists of the following:

- A context representation that allows the matching to correlate various events that constitute the intrusion signature

- Semantics that accommodate the possibility of several intrusion patterns (possibly belonging to multiple event sources) being intermixed in the same event stream

- An action specification that provides for the execution of certain actions when the pattern is matched[2]

Figure 4.5 shows the CP-Net pattern for a TCP/IP connection (for a network connection not involving retransmissions).

Figure 4.5   CP-Net Pattern for TCP/IP Connection

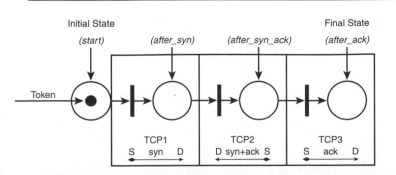

The following are significant and numerous advantages associated with this approach to misuse detection:

- It is extremely fast. In experiments involving a nonoptimized version of IDIOT, for every hour of intense activity (generating C2 audit records), the detector required about 135 seconds to match about 100 intrusion patterns. This result represents a processing load of less than 5% for a Sun SPARCstation 5 generating about 6MB of audit data per hour.

- The pattern-matching engine is independent of audit format, so you can apply it to IP packet streams and other detection problems.

- The signatures are portable across audit trails so that they can be moved among different systems without having to rewrite them to accommodate vendor audit trail differences.

- The patterns can be specified according to what needs to be matched, not how it is to be matched.

- The sequencing and other ordering constraints on events can be represented directly.

- The system provides a fine-grained specification of a successful pattern match (that is, it tells you why an intrusion was detected).

- IDIOT provides a front-end language for encoding the graphical representation of the net.

- The system allows you to specify an action that is executed upon the matching of the signature, thereby supporting automated responses.

The limitations of IDIOT are those of all misuse detection systems. Although the capability to characterize intrusions in terms of outcomes allows you to generalize some detection signatures, the system still cannot detect new attacks that it doesn't know about.[6]

Language/API-Based Approaches

A common strategy for optimizing commercial misuse detection tools is to devise a means for describing intrusions in a form that a detection engine can use. Although, as we discussed before, some production expert system languages (such as P-BEST and CLIPS) are available, they were designed for other uses. Three approaches to expressing intrusions for misuse detection purposes are the RUSSEL language developed by Mounji at Faculties Universitaires Notre-Dame de la Paix (in Namur, Belgium), the STALKER system, patented by Smaha and Snapp of Haystack Laboratories, and the N packet filtering language developed by Marcus Ranum and provided as part of the Network Flight Recorder.

RUSSEL

RUSSEL is a rule-based language that is designed to optimize the processing of unstructured data streams, specifically operating system audit trails. It is optimized for heterogeneous system environments. The goal of RUSSEL is to enable users to correlate events across multiple hosts and to support multiple levels of abstraction for events. RUSSEL is utilized in ASAX, a misuse detection system optimized for heterogeneous network systems. ASAX features the use of a common audit data format (called the Normalized Audit Data Format [NADF]) and provides a component that supports adaptive rules.

Event patterns are expressed in RUSSEL as guarded actions of the form **Condition — > Action**. This action can be specified at a level of abstraction that allows the intrusion detection user to specify responses to a given detection scenario.

The language is structured as bottom up. It starts by asserting audit records as basic facts and then, based on these facts, tries to find audit record patterns that can be viewed as derived facts. The bottom-up structure is utilized because the audit records are not known at the time analysis starts and because it is more efficient than top-down strategies when dealing with large audit trails.[7]

STALKER

Another approach to characterizing intrusion for misuse detection purposes is the approach utilized in the STALKER system, a commercial misuse detection product.[8] This patented approach utilizes a common audit data format (the SVR 4++ standard outlined in Chapter 7, "Technical Issues") and a state-based data structure for attack signatures.

The detector is implemented as a finite state machine (the underlying technology for compilers), which is optimized to pattern-matching tasks such as misuse detection.

The misuse detector operates by passing audit records to the misuse detection engine. The engine maintains a set of detection signatures in the form of state transitions. The signature expression consists of a data structure that contains an initial state, an end state, and one or more sets of transition functions for each misuse. Figure 4.6 shows the structure and operation of the STALKER misuse detector.

This approach was successfully implemented and fielded in a series of commercial products, which supported a variety of operating systems and applications environments. The STALKER product was withdrawn from the market when Network Associates acquired Haystack Laboratories in 1997, but the design has recently been returned to the market in the Cybercop Monitor.[9]

Network Flight Recorder—N-Code

A language-based optimization of network monitoring and analysis functions is provided by the Network Flight Recorder, a network monitoring system that serves as the basis for some commercial network-based intrusion detection products. The N programming language is an interpreted language operating on a byte-code instruction and implementing a simple stack machine.

Figure 4.6   STALKER Misuse Detection Approach

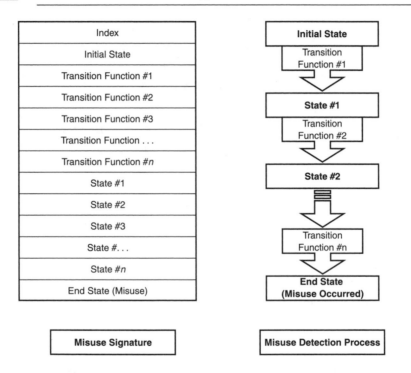

The language includes flow control, procedures, and 64-bit integer counter data types. It is customized to support network packet filter construction. Although these packet filters can be programmed to recognize network attacks, they can also be programmed to recognize other network activity.

Filters are written in N-code, which is input to the network monitoring engine, compiled, and stored as byte-code instructions to optimize filtering performance. Network packet traffic is reassembled using a table structure, which preserves the state of each current network session. This state preservation permits matching signatures against the entire lifetime of a connection or traffic stream.

The underlying engine also keeps statistics about the network performance, including timing statistics regarding packet arrival rate and network errors (as evidenced by broken packets or duplicate packet traffic). The engine also uses a statistical calculation to determine how long to retain state information about a connection before discarding it. In hybrid intrusion detection systems, this statistical information can be passed to an anomaly detection component.

Under the N-code packet filtering mechanism, the language binds a filter to the reception of a network packet. It can also support other specified events. The filter collects information from the packet, exporting it through either an alert or record mechanism. Alert mechanisms send alert messages to an alert management system, whereas record mechanisms send a data structure to a recorder function for various types of additional back-end processing.

The N language is included in the Network Flight Recorder product, which is available in source code form from the developers.[10]

4.3.1.3   *Information Retrieval for Batch Mode Analysis*

Although most current intrusion detection is based on real-time collection and analysis of event data, some approaches involve working with audit data archives, searching for evidence of interesting patterns of activity, or providing the ability to isolate the activities affecting a particular object or involving a particular user. This is of special interest to investigators and incident handlers.

One such approach comes from Ross Anderson and Abida Khattak of the University of Cambridge. They propose a functional separation between intrusion detection systems that discover new attacks and systems that allow security administrators to find instances of the attacks after they are identified. To handle the latter problem, Anderson and Khattak propose the use of information retrieval (IR) techniques. These techniques are currently widely utilized in the form of search engines (such as AltaVista) for the World Wide Web.

IR systems utilize inverted files as indexes that allow efficient searching for keywords and combinations of keywords. These systems also utilize algorithms that learn a user's preferences and use Bayesian inference to help refine searches. These differ from data mining in that they rely on indexing, not machine learning, to discover patterns of data.

This approach is limited to reviewing audit information after the fact (in batch mode). The researchers constructed a prototype utilizing the UNIX `lastcomm` system log and GLIMPSE, a search engine developed by the University of Arizona. They used a Perl script to sort the file into a selection of smaller files, one for each user. A GLIMPSE search was entered, searching for command-line sequences that matched the sequences associated with a particular attack. This process quickly and reliably located the attacks.

This approach is simple, yet powerful, and significant efficiencies are associated with the use of the IR techniques to perform the detection activity. The index utilized by GLIMPSE is compact (about 2%–4% of the indexed material) and can serve as an effective data reduction mechanism for audit trails. The presence of the index can also serve as a fail-safe mechanism, revealing situations in which hackers alter audit information to cover their tracks. Because GLIMPSE and proposed audit data sources are either free or included with standard operating system packages, this approach is also inexpensive, an advantage for many organizations that cannot afford other solutions.[11]

4.3.2   Anomaly Detection

Anomaly detection involves a process of establishing profiles of normal user behaviors, comparing actual user behavior to those profiles, and flagging deviations from the normal. The basis of anomaly detection is the assertion that abnormal behavior patterns indicate misuse of systems. *Profiles* are defined as sets of metrics. *Metrics* are measures of particular aspects of user behavior. Each metric is associated with a threshold or range of values.

Anomaly detection depends on an assumption that users exhibit predictable, consistent patterns of system usage. The approach also accommodates adaptations to changes in user behavior over time. The completeness of anomaly detection has yet to be verified (no one knows whether any given set of metrics is rich enough to express all anomalous behavior). Thus, additional research is required to know whether anomaly detection will ever be able to detect all scenarios of interest, representing a strong protection mechanism for systems.

4.3.2.1   Denning's Original Model

Dorothy Denning, in her landmark 1986 paper outlining the IDES model for intrusion detectors, asserts that four statistical models may be included in the system. Each model is deemed suitable for a particular type of system metric.

Operational Model

First is the *operational model*. This model applies to metrics such as event counters for the number of password failures in a particular time interval. The model compares the metric to a set threshold, triggering an anomaly when the metric exceeds the threshold value. This model, which applies to misuse detection as well as anomaly detection, corresponds to threshold detection, covered later in this section.

Mean and Standard Deviation Model

Denning's second detection model proposes a classic mean and standard deviation characterization of data. The assumption is that all the analyzer knows about system behavior metrics are the mean and standard deviations as determined from the first two moments. A new behavior observation is defined to be abnormal if it falls outside a confidence interval. This confidence interval is defined as d standard deviations from the mean for some parameter d. Denning hypothesizes that this characterization is applicable to event counters, interval timers, and resource measures. She also alludes to the ability to assign weights to these computations, such that more recent data is assigned a greater weight.

Multivariate Model

The multivariate model, the third of Denning's detection models, is an extension to the mean and standard deviation model. It is based on performing correlations among two or more metrics. Therefore, instead of basing the detection of an anomaly strictly on one measure, you might base it on the correlation of that measure with another measure. So instead of detecting an anomaly based solely on the observed length of a session, you might base it on the correlation of the length of the session with the number of CPU cycles utilized.

Markov Process Model

The final, most complex part of Denning's model is limited to event counters. Under this model, the detector considers each different type of audit event as a state variable and uses a state transition matrix to characterize the transition frequencies between states (not the frequencies of the individual states/audit records). A new observation is defined as anomalous if its probability, as determined by the previous state and value in the state transition matrix, is too low. This allows the detector to spot unusual command or event sequences, not just single events. This introduces the notion of performing stateful analysis of event streams.[12]

4.3.2.2   Quantitative Analysis

The most commonly used anomaly detection approach is quantitative analysis in which detection rules and attributes are expressed in numeric form. Denning includes this category of measures in her operational model. This set of techniques often presumes some computation, which can range from simple addition to more complex cryptographic calculations. The results of these techniques can be the basis for misuse detection signatures and anomaly detection statistical models alike. This section describes several common quantitative analyses and provides an example of an operational system that utilizes these techniques to accomplish data reduction and intrusion detection goals.

Threshold Detection

Probably the most common form of quantitative analysis is *threshold detection* (also known in some circles as *thresholds and triggers*). In threshold detection, certain attributes of user and system behaviors are characterized in terms of counts, with some level established as permissible. The classic example of a threshold is the number of permissible unsuccessful logins to a system. Virtually every early intrusion detection system contained a detection rule defining an intrusion in terms of this measure.

Other thresholds include the number of network connections of a particular type, the number of attempted file accesses, the number of files or directories accessed, and the number of network systems accessed. An inherent assumption in threshold detection is that the measurement is made over a particular time interval. This interval can be fixed in time (for instance, the threshold can be reset to zero at a particular time of day) or function over a sliding window (for example, the measurement is made over the last eight hours).

Heuristic Threshold Detection

Heuristic threshold checks take simple threshold detection a step further by adapting it to observed levels. This process increases the accuracy of the detection, especially when performing detection over a wide range of users or target environments. So, for instance, instead of having a threshold detection rule triggering an alert when the number of failed logins exceeds three in an eight-hour period, you can have a threshold detection rule that triggers an alert when an abnormal number of failed logins occur. "Abnormal" can be defined by various formulas. One that comes immediately to mind is a Gaussian function (such as chi-square) in which the mean number of failed logins is calculated and subsequent numbers of failed logins are compared to the mean plus some standard deviation.

Target-Based Integrity Checks

Another valuable quantitative analysis measure is a target-based integrity check. This is a check for a change in a system object that should not be subject to unpredictable change. The most common example of such an integrity check utilizes a message digest function to calculate a cryptographic checksum of the system object in question. After the checksum is calculated and stored in a safe place (for instance, read-only media) the system periodically recalculates the checksum, comparing it to the stored reference value. If a differential is found, an alarm is raised. The Tripwire™ product, found in both public domain and commercially supported versions, provides this capability.

Quantitative Analysis and Data Reduction

One of the more interesting uses of quantitative analysis in early intrusion detection systems used quantitative measures to perform data reduction. *Data reduction* is the process of eliminating superfluous or redundant information from often-voluminous event information. This reduces system storage loads and optimizes detection processes based on the event information.

An example demonstrating the use of quantitative methods to support effective data reduction comes from the NADIR system, developed by the Computing and Communications Division of Los Alamos National Laboratory. The NADIR developers utilized *data profiling*, which transforms user activity from audit logs into vectors of quantitative measures (most of them linear categorical or a combination of linear categorical and ordinal data). The profiles are aggregated over time (with weekly summaries) as well as over systems (with aggregate views of user activity per system). The reduced data is subjected to both statistical and expert system examination, with alarms and alerts handled by a staff investigator.[13]

4.3.2.3 Statistical Measures

The first worked examples of anomaly detection systems were based on statistical measures. These included approaches such as those utilized in IDES, mentioned earlier, and the follow-on NIDES project, as well as the Haystack system.

IDES/NIDES

IDES and NIDES, developed by researchers at SRI International, were two of the most prominent early intrusion detection research systems. They were both hybrid systems, including misuse and anomaly detection features; however, I focus on the statistical analysis here.

The statistical analysis techniques employed for IDES and NIDES support historical statistical profiles established and maintained for each user and system subject. These profiles are updated periodically, with older data aged so that the profiles adapt to reflect changes in user behavior over time.

The systems maintain a statistical knowledge base consisting of profiles. Each profile expresses normal behaviors for a particular user in terms of a set of measures or metrics. Once a day, new audit data is incorporated into the knowledge base (after the old vectors are aged by an exponential decay factor), based on the activity of the user during that day.

Let's take a look at how these statistics were calculated for IDES. Each time an audit record is generated, a summary test statistic is generated. This statistic, called the IDES score (IS), is calculated by the following formula:

$$IS = (S_1, S^2, S_3 \ldots S_n)C^{-1} (S_1, S_2, S_3 \ldots S_n)t;$$

where $(S..)$ $C-1$ is the inverse of a correlation matrix or vector and $(S...)$ t is the transpose of the vector. Each S_n measures some aspect of behavior, such as file access, terminals used, and CPU time used. Different S_n values can also represent different views of the same aspect of behavior.[14]

Haystack

Haystack, an anomaly detection system developed by Tracor Applied Sciences and Haystack Laboratories for the U.S. Air Force, employs a two-part statistical anomaly detection approach. The first measure determines to what degree a user session resembles an established intrusion type. This measure is calculated as follows:

1. The system maintains a vector of user behavior measures.

2. For each type of intrusion, the system associates a weight with each behavior measure, reflecting the relevance of the measure to the given intrusion type.

3. For each session, the vector of user behavior measures is calculated and compared to the threshold vector.

4. Those behavior measures for which threshold settings are exceeded are noted.

5. The weights associated with the measures exceeding threshold are summed.

6. The sum is used to assign a suspicion quotient to the session, based on the distribution of the weighted intrusion scores for all previous sessions.

The second, complementary statistical method detects deviations in a user's session activities from the normal user session profile. This method looks for session statistics that significantly deviate from the normal historical statistical profile for that user.[15, 16]

Strengths of Statistical Analysis

Statistical anomaly detection analysis originally targeted intruders masquerading as legitimate users. Although the assertion has been made that statistical analysis may also detect intruders who exploit previously unknown vulnerabilities who could not be detected by any other means, this assertion has yet to be proven in production use of a system. Early researchers also hypothesized that statistical anomaly detection could reveal interesting, sometimes suspicious, activities that could lead to discoveries of security breaches. This assertion was confirmed on at least one system, NADIR (in operation at Los Alamos National Laboratory), where developers reported that some of the information gained by using NADIR led to the discovery of system and security process errors, as well as discoveries that allowed them to improve the general management of Los Alamos's system complex.[17]

Another advantage often claimed for statistical analysis is that statistical systems do not require the constant updates and maintenance that misuse detection systems do. This claim may be true, but it depends on several factors. Metrics must be well chosen, adequate for good discrimination, and well-adapted to changes in behavior (that is, changes in user behavior must produce a consistent, noticeable change in the corresponding metrics). If these conditions are met, chances are excellent that the statistical analyzer will reliably detect behaviors of interest without requiring on-the-fly modifications to the system.

Drawbacks of Statistical Analysis

On the other hand, statistical analysis systems have significant drawbacks. First, most were designed to perform batch mode processing of audit records, which eliminated the capability to perform automated responses to block damage. This omission was not a problem at the time the systems were proposed because early systems were designed to monitor audit trails from centralized, mainframe target platforms. Although later systems attempted to perform real-time analysis of audit data, the memory and processing loads involved in using and maintaining the user profile knowledge base usually caused the system to lag behind audit record generation.

A second drawback affects the range of events that statistical analysis can characterize. The nature of statistical analysis precludes the capability to take into account the sequential relationships between events. The exact order of the occurrence of events is not provided as an attribute in most of these systems. In other words, the event horizon for these systems is limited to one event. Because many anomalies indicating attack depend on such sequential event relationships, this situation represents a serious limitation to the approach.

In cases when quantitative methods (Denning's operational model) are utilized, it is also difficult to select appropriate values for thresholds and ranges.

The false alarm rates associated with statistical analysis systems are high, which leads to users ignoring or disabling the systems. These false alarms include both type 1 (false negative) and type 2 (false positive) errors.

4.3.2.4   Nonparametric Statistical Measures

Early statistical approaches were similar in that they utilized *parametric* approaches to characterizing the behavioral patterns of users and other system entities. *Parametric approaches* refer to analytical approaches in which assumptions are made about the underlying distribution of the data being analyzed. For instance, in early versions of IDES and MIDAS the distributions of user usage patterns were assumed to be Gaussian or normal.

The problem with these assumptions is that error rates are high when the assumptions are incorrect. When researchers began collecting information about system usage patterns that included attributes such as system resource usage, the distributions were discovered not to be normal, and including these measures led to high error rates.

Linda Lankewicz and Mark Benard of Tulane University proposed that a way of overcoming these problems was to utilize nonparametric techniques for performing anomaly detection. This approach provides the capability to accommodate users with less predictable usage patterns and allows the analyzer to take into account system measures that are not easily accommodated by parametric schemes.

The approach Lankewicz and Benard utilized involved nonparametric data classification techniques, specifically *clustering analysis.* In clustering analysis, large quantities of historical data are collected (a *sample set*) and organized into *clusters* according to some evaluation criteria (also known as *features*). Preprocessing is performed in which features associated with a particular event stream (often mapped to a specific user) are converted into a vector representation (for example, $Xi = [f_1, f_2, ...f_n]$ in an n-dimensional state). A clustering algorithm is used to group vectors into classes of behaviors, attempting to group them so that members of each class are as close as possible to each other while different classes are as far apart as they can be.

In nonparametric statistical anomaly detection, the premise is that a user's activity data, as expressed in terms of the features, falls into two distinct clusters: one indicating anomalous activity and the other indicating normal activity.

Various clustering algorithms are available. These range from algorithms that use simple distance measures to determine whether an object falls into a cluster, to more complex concept-based measures (in which an object is "scored" according to a set of conditions and that score is used to determine membership in a particular cluster). Different clustering algorithms usually best serve different data sets and analysis goals.

Researchers at Tulane found that the clustering algorithm that best accomplished this goal using resource usage figures as evaluation criteria was the *k-nearest-neighbor* algorithm. This groups each vector with *k* of its nearest neighbors. *k* is a function of the number of vectors in the sample set, not a fixed value.

Experimental results using this analysis technique showed that clusters formed that reliably grouped similar system operations (such as compiling or editing files) and also grouped activity patterns according to user.

The advantages of nonparametric approaches include the capability to perform reliable reduction of event data (in the transformation of raw event data to vectors). This reduction effect was documented as more than two orders of magnitude. Other benefits are improvement in the speed of detection and improvement in accuracy over parametric statistical analysis. Disadvantages involve concerns that expanding features beyond resource usage would lessen the efficiency and accuracy of the analysis.[18]

4.3.2.5 Rule-Based Approaches

Another variation of anomaly detection is rule-based anomaly detection. The assumptions underlying this approach are the same as those associated with statistical anomaly detection. The main difference is that rule-based intrusion detection systems use sets of rules to represent and store usage patterns. Two such approaches are covered in this section: the Wisdom and Sense approach and the Time-Based Inductive Machine (TIM).

Wisdom and Sense

The first rule-based anomaly detection system was the Wisdom and Sense (W&S) system, developed by researchers at Los Alamos National Laboratory and Oak Ridge National Laboratory. W&S can operate on a variety of system platforms and can characterize activity at both operating system and application levels. It provides two schemes for populating rule bases: entering them manually (to reflect a policy statement) and generating them from historical audit data. The rules are derived from historical audit data by performing a categorical examination, expressing the patterns found in terms of rules. The rules reflect the past behavior of system subjects and objects and are stored in a tree structure, called a *forest*. Specific data values within the audit records are grouped into *thread classes* with which collections of operations or rules are associated.

An example of a thread class is "all the records containing the same user-file field values." Rules are applied to the data in a thread each time an activity associated with that thread occurs. Anomalies are detected this way: When transactions are processed, they are compared to the events of the matching thread to determine whether the events match the historical patterns of activity or represent an anomaly.[19]

TIM

The TIM system, proposed by Teng, Chen, and Lu, while they were associated with the Digital Equipment Corporation, utilizes an inductive approach to dynamically generate rules defining intrusion. The difference between TIM and other anomaly detection systems is that TIM looks for patterns in *sequences* of events, not in individual events. It effectively implements a Markov transition probability model, as proposed by Denning in her seminal intrusion detection work.

TIM observes historical event record sequence, characterizing the probability of particular sequences of events occurring. Other anomaly detector systems measure whether or not the occurrence of a single event represents a deviation from normal patterns of activity. TIM focuses on sequences of events, checking to see whether a chain of events corresponds to what would be expected based on its observation of historical event sequences.

For example, suppose events E_1, E_2, and E_3 are listed sequentially in an audit trail. TIM characterizes the probability of the occurrence of E_1 followed by E_2 followed by E_3, based on the history of sequences it has observed in the past. TIM automatically generates rules about the event sequences as it analyzes historical event data, and then stores the rules in a rule base. Because TIM groups event sequences, the amount of space required for the rule base is significantly smaller than that required for a single-event-oriented rule based system (such as Wisdom and Sense).

If a sequence of events matches the head of a rule, then the next event is considered anomalous if it's not in the set of predicted events in the body of the rule. The system also refines its analysis by deleting less predictive rules from the rule base. (Rule 1 is *more predictive* than rule 2 if rule 1 successfully predicts more events than rule 2 predicts.)

The advantages for TIM, especially when compared to statistical measures, are significant. This approach is well suited to environments where user patterns differ significantly from user to user, but where each user exhibits consistent behavior over time. Such an environment might be represented by a large corporation in which different users are responsible for accounting, administrative, programming, and personnel functions with very little crossover of user duties. This approach is also well suited for environments in which threat is associated with a few event types rather than the full complement of system events. Finally, this approach is not subject to problems associated with *session creep*, a defeat strategy associated with anomaly detection, in which an attacker gradually alters his/her behavior pattern over time to train the system to accept intrusive behavior as normal. This resistance to session creep attacks is due to the fact that the semantics are built into the detection rules.

However, as with other systems, weaknesses are associated with the TIM approach. It suffers the problem associated with all learning-based approaches in that the effectiveness of the approach depends on the quality of the training data. In learning-based systems the training data must reflect normal activity for the users of the system. Furthermore, the rules generated by this approach may not be comprehensive enough to reflect all possible normal user behavior patterns. This weakness produces a large false positive (type 2) error rate, especially at the beginning of the operation of the system. The error rate is high because if an event does not match the head of any rule (that is, if the system did not encounter the event type in the training data set), that event always triggers an anomaly.

This approach served as the basis for the Digital Equipment Corporation Polycenter intrusion detection product and forms the foundation for much subsequent anomaly detection research.[20]

4.3.2.6 Neural Networks

Neural networks use adaptive learning techniques to characterize anomalous behavior. This nonparametric analysis technique operates on historical sets of training data, which are presumably cleansed of any data indicating intrusions or other undesirable user behavior.

Neural networks consist of numerous simple processing elements called *units* that interact by using weighted *connections.* The knowledge of a neural network is encoded in the structure of the net in terms of connections between units and their weights. The actual learning process takes place by changing weights and adding or removing connections.

Neural network processing involves two stages. In the first stage (corresponding to the "building the detector" stage of the intrusion analysis model outlined earlier in this chapter), the network is populated by a training set of historical or other sample data that is representative of user behavior. In the second stage (corresponding to the second stage of the intrusion analysis model), the network accepts event data and compares it to historical behavior references, determining similarities and differences.

The network indicates that an event is abnormal by changing the state of the units, changing the weights of connections, adding connections, or removing them. The network also modifies its definition of what constitutes a normal event by performing stepwise corrections.

Neural network approaches hold a great deal of promise for anomaly detection. Because they don't use a fixed set of features to define user behaviors, feature selection is irrelevant. Neural networks don't make prior assumptions on expected statistical distribution of metrics, so this method retains some of the advantages over classic statistical analysis associated with other nonparametric techniques.

Among the problems associated with utilizing neural networks for intrusion detection is a tendency to form mysterious unstable configurations in which the network fails to learn certain things for no apparent reason. However, the major drawback to utilizing neural networks for intrusion detection is that neural networks don't provide any explanation for the anomalies they find. This practice impedes the ability of users to establish accountability or otherwise address the roots of the security problems that allowed the detected intrusion. This made it poorly suited to the needs of security managers. Although some researchers have proposed hybrid approaches as a means of overcoming these disadvantages, no published figures yet indicate the feasibility of neural network approaches.[21]

4.3.3 Alternative Detection Schemes

Some recent intrusion detection approaches fit neither misuse detection nor anomaly detection categories. These schemes may be applicable to either problem, perform precursor activity that can drive or refine either form of detection, or depart from the traditional monolithic view of intrusion detection in ways that affect detection strategies.

4.3.3.1 Immune System Approaches

In an innovative and promising research project, researchers at the University of New Mexico (Forrest, Hofmeyr, and Somayagi, among others) took a fresh look at the entire question of computer security. The question posed by the researchers was, "How does one equip computer systems with the means to protect themselves?" In answering this question, they noted marked similarities between biological immune systems and system protection mechanisms.

The key to both systems' functioning well is the capability to perform "self/nonself" determination—that is, the capability of an organism's immune system to determine which materials are harmless entities (such as the organism's own) and which are pathogens and other dangerous factors. As the immune system performs this determination by using peptides, short protein fragments, the researchers decided to focus on some computer attribute that could be considered analogous to peptides. The team hypothesized that sequences of UNIX system calls could satisfy those requirements.

In deciding to consider system calls as a primary source of information, the researchers considered a variety of goals for the data, including data volume, capability to reliably detect misuse, and suitability for encoding in a fashion appropriate for advanced pattern-matching techniques. They chose to focus on short sequences of the system calls, furthermore ignoring the parameters passed to the calls, looking only at their temporal orders.

The system as first proposed performs anomaly detection. (It can also perform misuse detection.) The system complies with the two-phase intrusion detection analysis process, with the first phase building a knowledge base that profiles normal behavior. This profile is a bit different from others discussed in this chapter in that here the behavior characterized is not user-centric, but system-process centric. Deviations from this profile are defined as anomalous. In the second phase of the detection system, the profiles are used to monitor subsequent system behavior for anomalies.

Sequences of system calls that result from running privileged processes were collected over time. The profiles for the system consisted of unique sequences of length 10. Three measures were utilized to characterize deviations from normal process behaviors: successful exploits, unsuccessful exploits, and error conditions.

The results were extremely promising because the three measures allowed the detection of several sorts of anomalous behavior spanning several historically problematic UNIX programs. The research also showed that the sets of execution sequences were remarkably compact.[22]

Subsequent research compared different approaches for characterizing normal behavior. It explored whether more powerful data modeling methods significantly improved the performance of this approach when monitoring more complex systems. Somewhat surprisingly, even powerful data modeling techniques (for example, hidden Markov models, which are extremely reliable, though computationally greedy) did not give significantly better results than the simpler time-sequence-based models.

Although the self/nonself techniques appear to constitute an extremely powerful and promising approach, it is not a complete solution to the intrusion detection problem. Some attacks, including race conditions, masquerading, and policy violations, do not involve the use of privileged processes. Therefore, these attacks are not subject to detection using this approach.[23]

4.3.3.2 Genetic Algorithms

Another more sophisticated approach to performing anomaly detection utilizes *genetic algorithms* to perform analysis of event data.

A genetic algorithm is an instance of a class of algorithms called *evolutionary algorithms*. Evolutionary algorithms incorporate concepts of Darwinian natural selection (survival of the fittest) to optimize solutions to problems. Genetic algorithms utilize encoded forms (known as *chromosomes*) with methods that allow combination or mutation of the chromosomes to form new individuals. These algorithms are recognized for their capability to deal with multidimensional optimization problems in which the chromosome is composed of encoded values for the variables being optimized.[24]

In the eyes of the researchers investigating genetic algorithm approaches to intrusion detection, the intrusion detection process involves defining hypothesis vectors for event data, where the vector either indicates an intrusion or does not. The hypothesis is then tested to determine whether it is valid, and an improved hypothesis is devised and tried based on the results of the test. This process repeats until a solution is found.

The role of genetic algorithms in this process is to devise the improved hypothesis. Genetic algorithm analysis involves two steps. The first step involves coding a solution to the problem with a string of bits. The second step is finding a fitness function to test each individual of the population (for instance, all the possible solutions to the problem) against some evaluation criteria.

In the system GASSATA, developed by Ludovic Mé of Supeleć, the French engineering university, genetic algorithms are applied to the problem of classifying system events by using a set of hypothesis vectors, H (one vector per event stream of interest) of n dimensions (where n is the number of potential known attacks). H_i is defined to be 1 if it represents an attack and 0 if it doesn't.

The fitness function has two parts. First, the risk that a particular attack represents to the system is multiplied by the value of the hypothesis vector. The product is then adjusted by a quadratic penalty function to eliminate unrealistic hypotheses. This step improves the discrimination among the possible attacks. The goal of the process is to optimize the results of this analysis so that the probability of a detected attack being real approaches 1 and the probability of a detected attack being false approaches 0.

Experimental results for the genetic algorithm approach to anomaly detection are encouraging. In experimental runs, the mean probability of true positives (accurate detection of real attacks) was 0.996, and the mean probability of false positives (detection of nonattacks) was 0.0044. The time required to construct the filters is also encouraging. For a sample set of 200 attacks, it took the system 10 minutes and 25 seconds to evaluate audit records generated by an average user over 30 minutes of intensive system use.

The following drawbacks are noted in this approach to misuse detection:

- The system can't take into account attacks characterized by event absence (for instance, rules in the form of "programmer does NOT use cc as compiler").

- Because of the binary expressional form for individual event streams, the system can't detect multiple simultaneous attacks. The possibility exists that nonbinary genetic algorithm approaches could solve this problem.

- If the same event or group of events is common to several attacks and an attacker uses this commonality to execute multiple simultaneous attacks, the system can't find an optimal hypothesis vector.

- Perhaps the largest drawback is that the system doesn't precisely locate attacks in the audit trail. Therefore, no sense of temporality occurs in the results of the detector.

(Note that this drawback is similar to problems noted in neural network approaches.) Therefore, genetic algorithm approaches must be backed up with post hoc search or other investigative aids if such support is required.[25]

4.3.3.3   Agent-Based Detection

Agent-based approaches to intrusion detection are based on software entities that perform certain security monitoring functions at a host. They function autonomously—that is, they are controlled only by the operating system, not by other processes. Agent-based approaches also run continuously with the understanding that this type of operation allows them to learn from experiences, as well as to communicate and cooperate with other agents of similar construction.

Agent-based detection approaches can be very powerful due to the range of capabilities with which one can imbue an agent. An agent can be extremely simple (for example counting the number of times a particular command is invoked in a time interval) or complex (looking for evidence of a set of attacks for a particular environment), depending on the whim of the developer.

The range of agent capabilities can allow an agent-based intrusion detection system to provide a mixture of anomaly detection and misuse detection capabilities. For instance, an agent can be programmed to adapt its detection capabilities to changes in the local environment. It can also monitor for very subtle patterns over a long time interval, thereby detecting slow attacks. Finally, an agent can enact extremely fine-grained responses to a detected problem (for instance, changing the priority level of a process, effectively slowing it down).

Autonomous Agents for Intrusion Detection

A prototype of an agent-based intrusion detection system, Autonomous Agents for Intrusion Detection (AAFID), was developed by researchers at Purdue University. It serves as the basis for this discussion of agent-based solutions.

This architecture for agent-based intrusion detection systems calls for a hierarchically ordered control and reporting structure for agents, as pictured in Figure 4.7. Any number of agents can reside on a host. All agents on a particular host report their findings to a single transceiver. Transceivers monitor the operation of all the agents running in the host, with capabilities to issue start, stop, and reconfiguration commands to agents. Transceivers also perform data reduction on information reported by the agents and report results to one or more monitors, the next level of the hierarchy.

Figure 4.7   AAFID Architecture

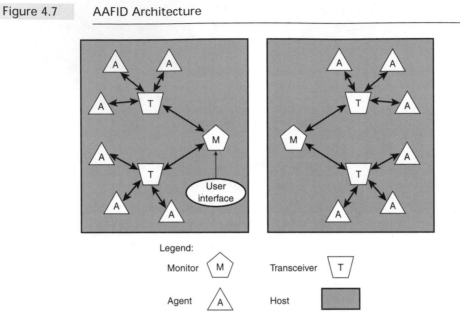

Monitors, which can be hierarchically structured in multiple layers, control and consolidate information from several transceivers. The architecture of AAFID allows redundancy in reporting from transceivers to monitors so that the failure of a monitor doesn't jeopardize the operation of the intrusion detection system. Monitors have the capability to access data from the entire network and therefore perform higher-level aggregation of results from transceivers. This feature enables the system to detect multihost attacks. Through a user interface, the user of the system enters commands to control the monitors. They, in turn, control the transceivers based on these user commands.

APIs exported by each component accomplish communications between agents, transceivers, monitors, and users.

The advantages of AAFID and other such agent-based approaches include the following:

- They appear to be more resistant to insertion and evasion attacks than other intrusion detection systems.

- The architecture is more easily scaled, with provisions for adding new components or replacing old ones as needed.

- Agents can be tested independent of the full system before they are deployed.

- Because they can intercommunicate, agents can be deployed in groups in which each performs a different, simple function but contributes to a complex result.

The following deficiencies are also associated with the AAFID architecture:

- Monitors are single points of failure. If a monitor ceases to work, all the transceivers under its control stop producing useful information. Possible solution strategies exist, but they are as yet untested.

- If duplicated monitors are used to address the first problem, it is difficult to deal with the consistency and duplication of information. This situation requires additional mechanisms.

- Access control mechanisms to allow different users to have different modes of access to the intrusion detection system are missing. This significant deficit must be addressed at each level of the architecture.

- Problems occur because of the propagation time for evidence of attackers to reach the monitor level. This problem is common to all distributed intrusion detection systems.

- As in the rest of intrusion detection, a significant need remains for more insight regarding designing user interfaces for intrusion detection systems. This need extends from presentation schemes to policy structures and specification schemes.[26]

EMERALD

A second architecture that utilizes distributed agent approaches to performing intrusion detection is the EMERALD system, researched and prototyped by Phillip Porras (whose previous intrusion detection work includes the STAT state transition analysis system) of SRI International. EMERALD includes numerous local monitors in a framework that supports distributing local results to a global array of detectors that, in turn, consolidate alarms and alerts.

EMERALD, like IDES and NIDES, SRI's previous intrusion detection systems, is a hybrid intrusion detector, utilizing both signature analysis and statistical profiling to detect security problems.

EMERALD is notable in that it separates the analysis semantics from the analysis and response logic, thereby enabling much easier integration throughout the network. EMERALD also supports analysis at different layers of abstraction, an important capability. Futhermore the design supports interoperability, another important issue in modern intrusion detection systems.

The central component of EMERALD is the EMERALD Service Monitor, which is similar in form and function to the AAFID autonomous agent. Service monitors are programmable to perform any function and are deployed to hosts. They can be layered, to support hierarchical data reduction, with service monitors performing some local analysis and reporting results and additional information to higher-level monitors. This approach yields some scalability not commonly found in network intrusion detection products. The system also supports a wide range of automated response, which is of great interest to customers responsible for critical large-scale networks.

EMERALD, as it builds on considerable corporate insight gathered in the IDES and NIDES efforts, holds great promise for protecting large distributed networks.[27, 28]

4.3.3.2 Data Mining

An approach that is similar to some of the rule-based anomaly detection efforts involves utilizing data mining techniques to build intrusion detection models. The objective of this approach is to discover consistent useful patterns of system features that can be used to describe program and user behaviors. These sets of system features, in turn, can then be processed by inductive methods to form classifiers (detection engines) that can recognize anomalies and misuse scenarios.

Data mining refers to the process of extracting models from large bodies of data. These models often discover facts in the data that are not apparent through other means of inspection. Although many algorithms are available for data mining purposes, the three that are most useful for mining audit data are *classification*, *link analysis*, and *sequence analysis*.

- *Classification* assigns a data item to one of several predefined categories. (This step is akin to sorting data into "bins," depending on some criteria.) Classification algorithms output *classifiers*, such as decision trees or rules. In intrusion detection, an optimal classifier can reliably identify audit data as falling into a normal or abnormal category.

- *Link analysis* identifies relationships and correlations between fields in the body of data. In intrusion detection, an optimal link analysis algorithm identifies the set of system features best able to reliably reveal intrusions.

- *Sequence analysis* models sequential patterns. These algorithms can reveal which audit events typically occur together and hold the key to expanding intrusion detection models to include temporal statistical measures. These measures can provide the capability to recognize denial-of-service attacks.

Researchers have developed extensions to standard data mining algorithms to accommodate some of the special needs of audit and other system event logs. Initial results of experiments using live data are interesting, but the work is not yet ready for transfer into commercial products. Additional research is planned to refine the approach.[29]

4.4   Conclusion

In this chapter, you've seen the different approaches to the core function of intrusion detection: analysis. In analysis, which involves isolating patterns of behavior known to represent problems (misuse detection) and using mathematical approaches to characterize user behaviors that are abnormal (anomaly detection), intrusion detection systems address several system protection challenges.

Although many approaches have been explored for doing both misuse and anomaly detection, most commercial products confine themselves to performing pattern matching and elementary statistical characterization of user activity and usage patterns. Refining advanced analysis techniques and transferring them to commercial products represent significant challenges for the intrusion detection research and development community. However, this step is necessary if intrusion detection products are to be effective in protecting real systems, both now and in the future.

Endnotes

1. Lunt, T., A. Tamaru, and F. Gilham. "IDES: A Progress Report." Proceedings of the Sixth Annual Computer Security Applications Conference, Tucson, AZ, December 1990.

2. Ranum, M. personal communication, June 1999.

3. Kumar, S. "Classification and Detection of Computer Intrusions." Ph.D. thesis, Department of Computer Sciences, Purdue University, 1995.

4. Ilgun, K. "USTAT: A Real-Time Intrusion Detection System for UNIX." Master thesis, Computer Science Department, University of California, Santa Barbara, CA, November 1992.

5. Porras, P. "STAT, A State Transition Analysis Tool for Intrusion Detection." Master thesis, Computer Science Department, University of California, Santa Barbara, CA, July 1992.

6. Kumar, S. and E. H. Spafford, "A Pattern Matching Model for Misuse Intrusion Detection." Proceedings of the Seventeenth National Computer Security Conference, October 1994: 11–21.

7. Mounji, A. "Languages and Tools for Rule-Based Distributed Intrusion Detection." Thesis, Faculte's Universitaires Notre-Dame de la Paix Namur, Belgium, September 1997.

8. Smaha, S. and S. Snapp. "Method and System for Detecting Intrusion into and Misuse of a Data Processing System." US555742, U.S. Patent Office, September 17, 1996.

9. `http://www.nai.com/asp_set/products/tns/ccmonitor_intro.asp`.

10. `http://www.nfr.net`.

11. Anderson, R. and A. Khattak. "The Use of Information Retrieval Techniques for Intrusion Detection." Presentation at the First International Workshop on the Recent Advances in Intrusion Detection, Louvain-la-Neuve, Belgium, September 1998.

12. Denning, D. "An Intrusion Detection Model." Proceedings of the Seventh IEEE Symposium on Security and Privacy, May 1986: 119–131.

13. Hochberg, J., K. Jackson, C. Stallings, J. McClary, D. DuBois, and J. Ford. "NADIR: An Automated System for Detecting Network Intrusion and Misuse." *Computers and Security*, vol. 12, Elsevier Science Publishers, Ltd., 1993: 235–248.

14. Javitz, H. S. and A. Valdes. "The SRI IDES Statistical Anomaly Detector." Proceedings IEEE Symposium on Security and Privacy, Oakland, CA, May 1991.

15. Smaha, S. E. "Haystack: An Intrusion Detection System." Proceedings of the Fourth IEEE Aerospace Computer Security Applications Conference, Orlando, FL, December 1988.

16. Mukherjee, B., L. T. Heberlein, and K. N. Levitt. "Network Intrusion Detection." *IEEE Network*, vol. 8, no. 3, May/June 1994: 26–41.

17. Hochberg, J. et al., op cit.

18. Lankewicz, L. and M. Benard. "Real Time Anomaly Detection Using a Nonparametric Pattern Recognition Approach." Proceedings of the Seventh Annual Computer Security Applications Conference, San Antonio, TX, December 1991.

19. Liepins, G. E. and H. S. Vaccaro. "Intrusion Detection: Its Role and Validation." *Computers and Security*, vol. 11, Elsevier Science Publishers, Ltd., 1992: 347–355.

20. Teng, H. S., K. Chen, and S. Lu. "Adaptive Real-Time Anomaly Detection Using Inductively Generated Sequential Patterns." Proceedings of the IEEE Symposium on Security and Privacy, May 1990.

21. Debar, H., M. Becker, and D. Siboni. "A Neural Network Component for an Intrusion Detection System." Proceedings of the 1992 IEEE Symposium on Security and Privacy: 240–250.

22. Hofmeyr, S. A, S. Forrest, and A. Somayaji. "Intrusion Detection Using Sequences of System Calls." *Journal of Computer Security*, vol. 6, no. 3, 1996.

23. Warrender, C., S. Forrest, and B. Pearlmutter. "Detecting Intrusions Using System Calls: Alternative Data Models." Proceedings of the Twenty-Fifth IEEE Symposium on Security and Privacy, Oakland, CA, May 1999.

24. Howe, D. Free On-line Dictionary of Computing (FOLDOC), available at `http://foldoc.doc.ic.ac.uk`.

25. Mé, L. "GASSATA, A Genetic Algorithm as an Alternative Tool for Security Audit Trails Analysis." First International Workshop on the Recent Advances in Intrusion Detection, Louvain-la-Neuve, Belgium, September 1998.

26. Balasubramaniyan, J. S., J. O. Garcia-Fernandez, D. Isacoff, E. H. Spafford, and D. Zamboni. "An Architecture for Intrusion Detection Using Autonomous Agents." COAST Technical Report 98/05, Purdue University, June 1998.

27. Porras, P. A. and P. G. Neumann. "Emerald: Event Monitoring Enabling Responses to Anomalous Live Disturbances." Proceedings of the Twentieth National Information System Security Conference, Baltimore, MD, 1997.

28. Neumann, P. G. and P. A. Porras. "Experience with EMERALD to Date." First USENIX Workshop on Intrusion Detection and Network Monitoring, Santa Clara, CA, April 1999.

29. Lee, W., S. J. Stolfo, and K. W. Mok. "A Data Mining Framework for Building Intrusion Detection Models." Proceedings of the Twentieth IEEE Symposium on Security and Privacy, Oakland, CA, 1999.

CHAPTER 5

Responses

After the analysis is done, and the system has identified problems, it's time to let someone know about them (and in some cases, to take additional action). In the intrusion detection process model, this is handled by the *response* section. Ideally, this portion of the system is feature-rich and serves all the members of the security management team by tailoring responses to each of them.

This chapter covers numerous ways in which intrusion detection systems can handle the results of analysis and outlines some options for responses to detected problems. These options include passive responses, in which the system simply notes and reports the problem; and active responses, in which the system (automatically or in concert with the user) takes action in order to block or otherwise affect the progress of the attack). Finally, we discuss ways of tying the results back into the site security management process.

5.1 Requirements for Responses

Many considerations come into play when designing response features for an intrusion detection system. Some responses can be designed to reflect current standards for security management or incident handling; others can reflect local management concerns and policies. When designing response features for commercial products, vendors should provide end users with the capability to tailor response mechanisms to fit their particular environment.

In the early days of intrusion detection system research and design, most designers focused on the monitoring and analysis sections of the system, leaving the crafting of the response component to the user. Although there was a great deal of discussion of what users really wanted in a response component, no one had a clear idea of the operational environment in which intrusion detection systems were likely to be fielded. In one of the first intrusion detection research conferences, an intrusion detection system researcher presented his tongue-in-cheek design for "the perfect intrusion detection system" (pictured in Figure 5.1). It remains one of my favorite designs, because it so accurately captures my experience with early users of the technology!

Note

A question that arises from time to time has to do with the generic term *user*. Who is the "standard user" of an intrusion detection system?

I've found three general categories of users for these systems in my experience so far. First are network security specialists or managers. Specialists are sometimes brought in as consultants to the systems management staff. Because these security specialists interact with various commercial intrusion detection systems, these people are often very knowledgeable about the various tools. However, the specialists are not always as knowledgeable about the underlying systems that they are monitoring or testing.

Second are the system administrators who are using the intrusion detection products to monitor and protect the systems they manage. In some cases, these are the power users of the intrusion detectors, with a good technical understanding of both the tools and the system environments they protect. System administrators can be the most demanding users of intrusion detection systems, sometimes requiring features seldom used by the other user constituencies of the products.

Finally, we have security investigators, members of a system audit staff or a law enforcement agency, who use the intrusion detection product to monitor compliance with legal regulations or to support an investigation. These users may not possess the technical acumen to understand either the tools or the underlying systems. However, they do understand the process of investigating problems and can be the source of important insight for intrusion detection system designers.

In this chapter, we will refer to these three groups of users as *security managers*, *systems administrators*, and *investigators*, respectively. The term "user" will refer to all three groups.

Figure 5.1   The Perfect Intrusion Detection System[1]

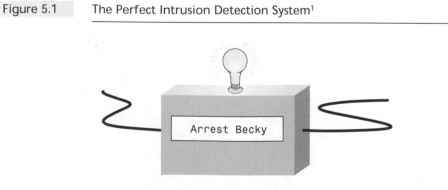

Users rely on intrusion detection systems to perform complex and exacting analysis on huge volumes of system event data. Ultimately, they want the system to be reliable and accurate and to convey the results of the analysis to the right people at the right time in straightforward, easy to understand terms. Many considerations color these requirements, but the goal remains the same.

5.1.1 Operational Environment

When designing a response mechanismm, an obvious consideration is the nature of the operational environment in which the intrusion detection system is operating. The alarm and notification requirements of an intrusion detection system that has a number of attended control consoles lining the wall of a network operations center are likely to be quite different from the requirements of an intrusion detection system installed on a desktop system in a home-based business.

The information provided by the intrusion detection system as part of the notification also depends on the environment. Network operations center staffers might prefer to use products that provide details about low-level network traffic (contents of fragmented packets, for instance). A graveyard-shift security manager might consider anything beyond a simple alarm with a message to contact the proper person to be worthless.

Audible alarms are perfectly suitable for installations in which one person is responsible for monitoring the results of multiple intrusion detection systems. Such alarms can be a massive annoyance for those managing multiple operations on a complex network from a single console.

Visual alarms and activity graphs may be of value to installations that have a full-time operator who sits in front of the system console. They are especially helpful when monitoring other components of the security infrastructure (such as encryptors or firewalls) that might not be visible from the management area.

Visual alarms are likely to be irrelevant to operators who are not present to view them. Color-coded alarm status displays are of little value to operators who are color-blind (as are a significant percentage of military system operators) or to those who are visually challenged.

5.1.2 System Purpose and Priorities

Another factor driving response requirements is the monitored system's function. The need to provide active responses (for instance, terminating the network connections of a user recognized as the source of an attack) is driven in part by systems that provide critical data and services to users. An example of this type of system is a medical record server for an emergency room. Another is a Web server for a high-traffic, high-revenue electronic commerce site.

In these cases, the impact of a successful denial-of-service attack (or a series of such attacks) can be devastating. In both cases, the value of preserving the availability of the systems far outweighs any additional overhead associated with providing active responses to detected intrusions.

5.1.3   Regulatory or Statutory Requirements

Other factors driving specific response capabilities include regulatory or statutory requirements for intrusion detection. In certain military computing environments, intrusion detection capabilities are required for certain types of processing to take place. For instance, a system might be accredited to handle classified information of a certain level of sensitivity only if an intrusion detection system is present. In these environments, regulations govern the operation of the intrusion detection systems, and reporting requirements govern the format and delivery schedule for the results of the intrusion detection system's operation. If the intrusion detection system is not running, the regulations dictate that the classified information cannot be processed on the system.

In online stock-trading environments, the Securities and Exchange Commission requires trading systems to be accessible to customers during trading hours. Any denial of access can result in fines and other penalties levied on the site. This situation requires both automated responses that can block attacks and well-targeted, concise explanations of detected problems—so that damage recovery can be completed as quickly as possible.

5.1.4   Conveying Expertise to Users

One need that intrusion detection products often neglect is providing guidance to users along with or as part of the detection responses. In other words, whenever possible, the system should accompany the detection results with explanations and advice to the user that allow him to take appropriate action. This area is one in which an immense disparity exists among products. A well-designed set of response mechanisms can structure information and explanations so that users are guided through a series of decisions, in the proper order, that ultimately lead them to the appropriate resolution of the problem.

Such a response mechanism also allows the tailoring of the presentation of results to users possessing different levels of expertise. As noted in the description of user constituencies in the author's note, different users of intrusion detection systems have different information needs. System administrators are probably able to make sense of sequences of network service requests or raw packet traces. Security specialists might be able to understand the difference between a "port scanner" and a "sendmail buffer overflow." Investigators might require the capability to track the sequence of commands a particular user makes, along with the system objects that user affects.

Intrusion detection system developers should accommodate a wide range of user capabilities and expertise levels. In this fast-growing market (that did not exist 10 years ago) the expert user is likely to be rare for a few more years!

5.2 Types of Responses

Intrusion detection system responses can be classified as *active* or *passive*. In active responses, the system (automatically or in concert with the user) blocks or otherwise affects the progress of the attack. In passive responses, the system simply reports and records the problem.

Active and passive responses are not mutually exclusive. Intrusion detection systems should, as a matter of course, always log detection results, regardless of whether other responses are enabled.

An essential part of including intrusion detection in a site security process is determining which intrusion detection responses to enable and deciding which actions should occur as a result of those responses.

5.2.1 Active Responses

As stated above, responses can be classified as active or passive. Active responses involve taking action based on the detection of an intrusion. Several options are available for active responses; most of these options fall into one of the following categories:

- Take action against the intruder

- Amend the environment

- Collect more information

Although the first option, taking action against the intruder, is extremely popular in some circles, it is not the only active response. Furthermore, because it has serious legal and practical implications, this response should not be the most common active response you use!

There are two forms of active response: those that are user driven and those that are performed automatically by the system.

5.2.1.1 Take Action Against the Intruder

The first option in active response is to take action against intruders. The most aggressive form of this option, tracing back the intruder to the source of the attack and then taking action to disable the intruder's machine or network connection, has captured the imagination of many an information warfare groupie. This approach is also of considerable appeal to the long-suffering security manager who has been the target of one too many hacker denial-of service-attacks!

Unfortunately, this option can also represent one of the biggest briar patches of security. The hazards represented by striking back include the following:

- Given the general *modus operandi* of network hackers, the system identified as the source of the attack on your system probably belongs to another victim of the hacker. Network hopping, in which a hacker successively hacks a system and then uses it as a platform for attacking another system, is a common practice. If you target the system from which the attack was launched, you are probably targeting an innocent party.

- Even if the attacker is coming from a system over which she or he has legitimate control, spoofing the IP address of the source of attacks is common practice. Therefore, the IP address that appears to be the source of the attack on your system may actually be "borrowed" from another (innocent) victim.

- You may find that striking back simply provokes an escalation of the attack. What might have begun as a routine surveillance or scan of your system could develop into a full-scaled hostile attack, placing the availability of your system resources in jeopardy.

- In many situations, by striking back you expose yourself to a significant risk of criminal charges or civil legal action. If your actions attack an innocent party, that party may sue you for damages. Furthermore, your reaction in itself may violate computer crime statutes, and you may be subject to charges. Finally, if you work for a government or military organization, you may be violating policy and may be subject to disciplinary action or dismissal. Law enforcement officials advise contacting authorities for assistance in dealing with attackers.[2]

Taking action against intruders can also occur in more benign forms. For instance, the intrusion detection system might simply terminate the network session by resetting TCP connections. The system might also direct a firewall or router to block packets coming from the IP address that appears to be the source of the intrusion.

Another response is to automatically spawn email to the administrator of the system from which the intruder appears to be coming and request assistance in identifying and dealing with the problem. This can be productive when the hacker is connected to that system by a dial-up connection. As traceback capabilities improve for the communication infrastructure as a whole, it may become possible to utilize features in the telephone system (such as caller ID or trap and trace) to assist in establishing accountability for intrusions.

User-Driven Responses

Many active response capabilities originated in the days when "super security geeks" performed them manually. Although many of the responses can be automated to deal with attacks in real time, this doesn't mean you should.

For instance, suppose an attacker discovers that your system's automated response to a denial-of-service attack is to "shun" (that is, terminate the current connection and refuse subsequent TCP connections with the source IP address) the ostensible source of the attack. The attacker may use IP-spoofing tools to generate denial-of-service attacks that appear to come from a list of your most important customers, resulting in those customers being denied access to your critical resources. What is even worse is that in strictest terms, this denial of service is being enabled by your own intrusion detection system!

Automatic Responses

On the other hand, automating at least some of the active responses is necessary because of the sheer speed with which attacks take place. Most of the attacks that come from the Internet utilize attack software and scripts. These attacks progress at a pace that prohibits manual intervention. Intrusion detection designers should consider whether a particular active response can be handled manually (with the intrusion detection system providing guidance and information to the user). If the intervention must be automated, measures should be taken to minimize the risk of the automated response being used as a vehicle for attack. We will return to this topic in Chapter 12, "For Designers," when we cover design issues for intrusion detection.

5.2.1.2 Amend the Environment

The next option for active response is to amend the system environment. Although this type of response to intrusions is quieter and less glamorous than other approaches, it is often the optimal response scheme, especially in combination with responses that provide investigative support. The concept of amending the system environment to "heal" flaws that allow intrusions to occur is consistent with the vision for critical systems articulated by many researchers. "Self-healing" systems are equipped with defenses analogous to the body's immune system in which problems can be recognized, the causative factors isolated, and a suitable response generated to address the problem.

In some intrusion detection systems, this category of response could alter the operational characteristics of the analysis engine, perhaps increasing sensitivity levels. It could also alter expert systems by inserting rules that increase the suspicion level for certain attacks or increase the scope of the monitoring to collect information at a finer granularity than usual. This strategy is analogous to those used in real-time process control systems in which the outcome of the current system process is used to tune and refine subsequent processes.

5.2.1.3   Collect Additional Information

The third option in active response is to collect additional information. This option is of special interest when the system being protected is critical and a system owner might want to pursue legal remedies. At times, this logging response is coupled with the use of a specialized server, established to serve as an environment into which intruders can be diverted. This server is known by a variety of names. Most common are "honey pots," "decoys," or "fishbowls." Such servers are equipped with file systems and other spoofed system attributes that are designed to mimic the appearance and content of critical systems.

Note

The design of decoy servers was first explored in 1992, in Bill Cheswick's classic paper, "An Evening with Berferd in Which a Cracker Is Lured, Endured, and Studied."[3] This paper outlines the steps that Cheswick took to design, build, and field a decoy server into which he redirected a Dutch hacker who attacked Cheswick's systems. The use of a decoy server was reported by Cliff Stoll in his classic book *The Cuckoo's Egg*.[4]

Decoy servers are of value to security managers who are collecting threat information on intruders or who are collecting evidence to support taking legal action against them. Using a decoy server allows the victim of an intrusion to determine the intent of the intruder, logging extensive information about the activities of the intruder without placing the actual system contents at risk of damage or divulgence. This information can also be used to construct custom detection signatures.

Information collected in this way is also of value to those performing trend analysis of network security threats. This information is of particular interest in systems that must operate in hostile threat environments or that are subject to large numbers of attacks (such as government Web servers or high-profile electronic commerce sites).

5.2.2   Passive Responses

Passive responses are those that provide information to the user, relying on the user to take subsequent action. In early intrusion detection systems, all responses were passive. Passive responses are important, however, and in many cases represent the sole response form for the system. In this section passive responses are presented in order of criticality to the user. (This criticality is the primary difference between alarm mechanisms and problem reports.)

5.2.2.1 Alarms and Notification

Most intrusion detection systems provide options for generating alarms in a variety of forms. This flexibility allows a user to tailor the alarms to fit the organization's system operating procedures.

Alarm Display Screens

The most common alarm and notification feature provided by intrusion detection systems is an onscreen alert or window. This alarm and message appear on the intrusion detection system console or on other systems as specified by the user in the intrusion detection system setup. Different systems provide different levels of detail in the alarm message, ranging from a simple "an intrusion has occurred" to extensive records outlining the ostensible source of the problem, the target of the attack, the apparent nature of the intrusion, and whether it was successful. In some systems the contents of the alarm message can also be customized.

Remote Notification of Alarms and Alerts

Organizations that run attended systems around the clock use another alarm/alert option. In these situations, intrusion detection systems can issue alarms and alert messages by dialing pagers or cellular telephones issued to system administrators and security personnel. Email messages are another means of notification, although this approach is not recommended in cases of on-going or persistent attacks (the attacker is likely to read or, worse, block the email message). In some cases, the notification option allows users to configure additional information or alarm codes sent to these units.

5.2.2.2 SNMP Traps and Plug-Ins

Some intrusion detection systems are designed to function in concert with network management tools. These systems can utilize the network management infrastructure to send and display alarms and alerts on the network management console. Some products spawn Simple Network Management Protocol (SNMP) messages or traps as an alarm option.

This option is currently provided in some commercial products, but many believe that intrusion detection and network management systems can be much more thoroughly integrated. Several benefits are associated with this integration, including the ability to utilize common communications channels and the ability to provide active responses to security problems that take into consideration the network environment at that time. Furthermore, SNMP traps allow users to move the processing load associated with responding to a detected problem to the system receiving (and acting upon) the trap.

5.3 Covering Tracks During Investigation

Part of the effectiveness of an intrusion detection system relies on its capability to provide silent, reliable monitoring of attackers. When a system is under attack, it is wise to handle alarms and notification in a fashion that is invisible to the intruder. This approach allows investigative activity to take place while the intruder's session is still underway, allowing accountability to be established. In these cases, alarms and notification may be performed over encrypted channels. Other needs for encrypted channels are discussed in the following section on fail-safe considerations.

5.3.1 Fail-Safe Considerations for Response Components

Several fail-safe measures should be taken in this component of intrusion detection systems.

First, as in the rest of the system, the design of the response system and all of its components should assume that an adversary will target them as part of the attack. The attack strategy is likely to involve either monitoring the response channels, searching for signs of detection, or else disrupting or intercepting the alarm and alert channels so that operators are not notified of the attack.

Utilizing encrypted tunnels and other cryptographic means of hiding and authenticating intrusion detection communications is required for the reliable operation of the system. This measure precludes a variety of attacks targeting both the response components and the rest of the intrusion detection system.

Alarms generated by intrusion detection systems should be redundant, utilizing multiple channels. For example, users might want to configure an intrusion detection system to trigger three alarms for a certain severity of attack on a critical system, sending one alarm to the notification unit via normal network communications, a second via encrypted channels, and a third via a dial-up channel.

The logs generated by the response component that document all detection results should be protected from alteration or destruction. Because they are likely to be used in any investigation and to support any legal action, this protection is especially important. One way to protect these logs is to use write-once media (such as CD-ROMs) with an optional hard copy backup to line printers. For especially critical systems, redundant logging mechanisms are recommended.

5.3.2 Handling False Alarms

One problem that exists in intrusion detection systems and that requires some embedded intelligence in the response component of the system involves false alarms. These alarms can be false positives, in which the system identifies attacks when there are none, and false negatives, in which the system fails to identify attacks when they occur. False negatives are a problem of analysis and are best handled in that component. However, false positives can in themselves present problems to the response component.

When a faulty network component corrupts packets, triggering a false indication of network attack, the analysis system sends an alarm to the response component, which will in turn generate alarm messages. If the corrupted packets trigger false alarms at even two per second, the response component may be flooded with service requests and ultimately crash. Therefore, response components should give users the capability to limit the number of alarms triggered by the same source and signature during a time interval. This technique not only serves to protect the integrity of the response component but also reduces the possibility that the user will ignore the alarms generated by the detector.

5.3.3 Archive and Report

The longer-range portion of passive response involves archiving detection results for later use. Some intrusion detection systems store the results in databases. This approach allows the user to generate a wide range of reports, targeting each to a particular audience. This feature of intrusion detection products is very popular because it allows security managers to regularly inform executive management about the state of system security, targeting details of problems to those best equipped to deal with them.

Another task that is important to the security process is to maintain an intrusion detection result log, structured in much the same way as system logs and audit trails. This log should be written to write-once media to protect it from alteration or deletion. This log is important because it provides a long-term sequential record of intrusions against the target system. This material can be important as documentation of the progress of a long-term problem and can, even more importantly, serve as evidence should the organization decide to seek legal remedies for the problem. Such evidence is critical regardless of whether the remedies pursued are in criminal or civil venues.

5.4 Mapping Responses to Policy

A successful security management program effectively blends policy and supporting technology. To optimize the utility of intrusion detection systems, it should be included in organizational security policy and procedures. One way to do this is to include provisions to specify which activities should correspond to detected intrusions or security violations. These activities are divided into the following four categories, ordered by the time and criticality of the activities: immediate or critical, timely, local long-term, and global long-term.

5.4.1 *Immediate*

Immediate or critical actions are those required of system management immediately following an intrusion or attack. These include the following:

- Initiating incident-handling procedures

- Performing damage control and containment

- Notifying law enforcement or other organizations

- Restoring victim systems to service

The time span associated with immediate or critical action can be determined by local policy and can be further refined to accommodate the severity of the attack.

5.4.2 *Timely*

Timely actions are those required of system security management following detected attacks or security violations. The elapsed time can range from hours to days, and these actions usually follow those in the immediate/critical category. Activities that should take place in a timely fashion include the following:

- Manually investigating unusual patterns of system use

- Investigating and isolating the root causes of the detected problems

- Correcting these problems when possible (by applying vendor bug patches or reconfiguring systems)

- Reporting the details of the incident to proper authorities (if they were not involved in the incident-handling process)

- Altering or amending detection signatures in the intrusion detection system

- Instigating or pursuing legal action against the perpetrator

- Dealing with publicity associated with the attack and notifying shareholders, regulators, and others for whom there may be statutory reporting requirements

5.4.3 *Long-Term—Local*

Local long-term actions refer to system management activities that are less critical than actions that fall in the immediate or timely categories but are still important to the security management process. The impact of these activities is local to the organization. These activities might be scheduled as part of a regular review.

Activities that fall into this category include the following:

- Compiling statistics and performing trend analysis

- Tracking patterns of intrusion over time

These patterns of intrusion and security violation should be evaluated to isolate areas requiring amendment or improvement. For instance, a large number of attacks targeting a vulnerability that has been corrected by a vendor might lead to a security policy requirement that systems software be patched on a regular schedule. A large number of false alarms might indicate a need to review the detection signatures or configuration of the intrusion detection system or else to look at an alternative intrusion detection product. Finally, large numbers of problems that are due to user error might indicate a need for additional training of personnel.

5.4.4 Long-Term—Global

Global long-term actions refer to system management activities that are noncritical but nonetheless important to the state of security on a societal level. The impact of these activities is not confined to the organization. These activities are likely to be conducted in the context of an industry organization or consortium.

Activities in this category include the following:

- Notifying vendors of the problems the organization has suffered due to security problems in their products

- Lobbying lawmakers and the government for additional legal remedies to system security threats

- Reporting statistics regarding security incidents to law enforcement or other organizations that maintain statistics

Many critical issues in system security simply can't be addressed at a local level. Thus community-level activity allows you and your organization to be part of the larger remedy.

5.5 Conclusion

In this chapter we covered the third and final component of the intrusion detection process model: response. This component handles the output of the analysis component, generating both active and passive responses to intrusions that are detected.

We explored requirement definitions for this functional component and defined a classification scheme for binding the results of the intrusion detection process to the organizational security management process.

Endnotes

1. Smaha, Steve. Presentation, First Experts Conference on Future Directions in Computer Misuse and Anomaly Detection, Davis, CA, April 1992.

2. Yasin, R. "Think Twice Before Becoming a Hacker Attacker." *Internet Week*, December 14, 1998.

3. Cheswick, W. "An Evening with Berferd in Which a Cracker Is Lured, Endured, and Studied." Proceedings of the USENIX Security Conference, San Francisco, CA, Winter 1992: 163–174.

4. Stoll, Clifford. *The Cuckoo's Egg: Tracking A Spy Through the Maze of Computer Espionage.* New York, NY: Doubleday, 1989.

6

Vulnerability Analysis: A Special Case

One of the earliest product strategies proposed for security management was that of *vulnerability analysis*. I consider vulnerability analysis a special case of intrusion detection. The discussion of concepts and definitions of intrusion detection in Chapter 2, "Concepts and Definitions," explains the difference between *static* and *dynamic* analysis schemes. Vulnerability analysis is a static analysis scheme.

Static analysis is also called *interval-based analysis*, referring to the fact that the information source is sampled and analyzed at intervals, not continuously. This difference is analogous to the difference between snapshots and movies—the information source may well be the same, but it is sampled at different frequencies.

The deficiency of this approach to system monitoring is obvious—a knowledgeable adversary can simply note the times at which information is sampled, and then time an intrusion to fit between the collection times. Given the numerous hacker tools for erasing evidence of someone's presence on the system, an adversary can come and go without being detected. This problem is of particular concern when the goal of the intrusion is to violate confidentiality (for example, to copy intellectual property or access classified documents). When intruders violate system integrity (by placing back doors in the system), they leave artifacts that will be detected at the next sampling interval.

Although vulnerability analysis does not represent a complete solution to intrusion problems, it is a valuable security management tool for a variety of reasons. This chapter explores those reasons and delves into the techniques used in this special case of intrusion detection.

Note

Because vulnerability analysis is the predominant working example of a static analysis approach to monitoring the system security state, I use the terms *vulnerability analysis* and *static analysis* interchangeably in this chapter, favoring the former because of its common usage in the industry.

6.1   Vulnerability Analysis

Vulnerability analysis is the analysis of the security state of a system or its components, on the basis of information collected at intervals. This process is different from dynamic analysis, which is the analysis mode most commonly associated with intrusion detection systems. The general strategy for static analysis is as follows:

- A predetermined set of system attributes is sampled.

- The results of the sample are archived in some data store.

- That store is organized and compared to at least one reference set (in some cases, a manually generated template of an "ideal configuration").

- The differences between the two are noted.

6.1.1   Rationale for Vulnerability Analysis

Vulnerability analysis is an excellent way to monitor the security-relevant configuration of systems. It can deliver a measurable improvement in the security state of a system for a modest investment in time and expense.

Three benefits are traditionally associated with vulnerability analysis. First, vulnerability analyzers can be educational, structuring otherwise arcane security details of systems in a fashion that allows system administrators and other security management personnel to learn how to secure systems. Second, vulnerability analyzers are time-saving devices, allowing an administrator to automatically check systems against a list of hundreds of settings, any one of which might portend a security problem. Third, vulnerability analyzers are consistent, offering a means of sanity-checking the security of systems after the systems are altered, as they might be when new software is installed or organizational structures change. This feature provides a safeguard against simple human error on the part of users or system administrators.

6.1.2   COPS—An Example of Vulnerability Analysis

Perhaps the best-known early example of a vulnerability analysis program is the Computer Oracle and Password Security System (COPS) written by Dan Farmer and Gene Spafford in 1989. Spafford, a professor at Purdue University and Farmer, then an undergraduate at Purdue, continue to work in computer security and intrusion detection. (Spafford is the director of the CERIAS Security Research Center at Purdue University and Farmer is a commercial security expert.)

COPS is structured as a set of small programs, each of which performs a particular security check on the target system. It checks for thirteen different types of security problems. COPS was written to evaluate a variety of UNIX platforms and continues to be a standard part of many security administrators' operational toolkits. Table 6.1 outlines the components of COPS, the system objects that each component checks, and the objectives of each check.[1]

Table 6.1   COPS Checks and Configurations

Name of Routine and Target:	Configuration File:	Default Configuration:	Check for:
Dir.chk -checks vital directories	Dir.chklst	/, /etc, /usr, /bin, /Mail, /usr/spool, /usr/adm, /usr/etc, /usr/lib, /usr/bin, /usr/spool/mail, /usr/spool/uucp, /usr/spool/at	Word writable
File.chk-checks vital files	File.chklst	/.* /etc/* /bin/* /usr/etc/yp* /usr/lib/crontab /usr/lib/aliases /usr/lib/sendmail	Word writable
Dev.chk-checks critical files NFS file system	Files- variable NFS=/ect/fstab	/dev/kmem, /dev/mem, /etc/fstab/*, /netrc, /usr/adm/sulog, /etc/btmp	Word readable (files) or unrestricted NFS file system
Suid.chk-checks all for SUID status	N/A uses "find" from root directory to create file listing	All files	Did files gain SUID privilege or lost SUID priv
Passwd.chk-check password files and yellow pages (NIS) password files for user ID problems?	/etc/usr/passwd, other passwd files as needed, compare to reference normal; flag exceptions	/etc/usr/passwd	Null passwords? improper number of fields? Non- unique userIDs? Blank lines? Nonnumeric group IDs? Non alphameric Userids?

continues

Table 6.1   Continued

Name of Routine and Target:	Configuration File:	Default Configuration:	Check for:
Group.chk-checks password files and yellow pages (NIS) password files for group ID problems	Reads through password files, comparing to reference normal; flags exceptions	/etc/usr/passwd	Groups with passwords? Improper number of fields? Nonunique group IDs? Blank lines? Duplicate users in groups?
Pass.chk-checks user passwords	Uses stock "crypt" command to compare encrypted password stored in passwd file to encrypted guesses		Does password match: Login ID? Information in gecos field? Single letter?
Root.chk-checks root path and critical files	Checks rootpath, umask, /etc/ftpuser, /.profile, /.cshrc		Are any directories word writable? Is "." anywhere in the path? Is umask set to create word-writable files?
Rc.chk-checks commands in /etc/rc*	Examines all commands in /etc/rc	All entries starting with "/"	Are any strings starting with "/" world-writable?
Cron.chk-checks /usr/lib/crontab	Examines all strings in /usr/lib/ crontab, occurring after line 5	All entries starting with "/"	Are any entries word-writable?
Home.chk-checks all user home directories	Uses system call getpwent() to get all user home directories; checks write directories against bit mask		Are any user home directories writable?
Usr.chk-checks important user files	Uses system call getpwent() to get all home	All files with "." prefix Rhost, profile, logging,	Are any of these files world-writable?

Name of Routine and Target:	Configuration File:	Default Configuration:	Check for:
	directories,then checks against bit mask	cshrc, kshrc, tcshr, crhost, netrc, forward, dbxini, distfile, exrc, emacsrc	
Kuang.chk- performs intelligent probe of system permissions	Run kuang.chk shell-adapted from U-Kuang (Baldwin, MIT)	Any user-group pair in system	Can I get to the root from an unprivileged account?

The vision of COPS was, at the time of its inception, extremely powerful, and the program was widely celebrated and adopted worldwide. At that time, almost all networks were based on UNIX, which is a somewhat complex and nonintuitive operating system—especially for nontechnical users. Acquiring the requisite skills to manage security for UNIX systems can take years. In the late 1980s, "security through obscurity" was the coping strategy of choice for many who were charged with system security. In other words, information about hacking techniques and attacks was closely held, and rarely discussed or published in the general technical community.

COPS enabled security novices to check their systems for known configuration problems and other common security flaws. Furthermore, it offered these capabilities in a fashion that did not yield roadmaps for hackers. Therefore, COPS was considered to be of acceptable risk for sensitive environments. A COPS output example follows:

```
ATTENTION:
Security report for Wed Jun 23 12:14:56 PDT 1999

from host baruntse, 1999_Jun_23

Bad config variable at line 12 of ./cops.cf:
              $SECURE_USERS   = "foo@bar.edu";
              In string, @bar now must be written as \@bar at (eval 3) line 1,
near "foo@bar"

Warning!  NFS file system /usr/home exported with no restrictions.
Warning!  /etc/security is _World_ readable!
Warning!  Passwd file, line 1, does not have 7 fields:
              root:*:0:0:Charlie &:/root:/usr/local/bin/tcsh
Warning!  Passwd file, line 2, does not have 7 fields:
              toor:*:0:0:Bourne-again Superuser:/root:
Warning!  Passwd file, line 2, user toor has uid == 0 and is not root
              toor:*:0:0:Bourne-again Superuser:/root:
```

```
Warning!  Passwd file, line 3, does not have 7 fields:
                    daemon:*:1:1:Owner of many system processes:/root:/sbin/nologin
Warning!  Passwd file, line 4, does not have 7 fields:
                    operator:*:2:5:System &:/usr/guest/operator:/bin/csh
Warning!  Passwd file, line 5, does not have 7 fields:
                    bin:*:3:7:Binaries Commands and Source,,,:/:/sbin/nologin
Warning!  Passwd file, line 6, does not have 7 fields:
                    games:*:7:13:Games pseudo-user:/usr/games:/sbin/nologin
Warning!  Passwd file, line 7, does not have 7 fields:
                    news:*:8:8:News Subsystem:/:/sbin/nologin
Warning!  Passwd file, line 8, does not have 7 fields:
                    man:*:9:9:Mister Man Pages:/usr/share/man:/sbin/nologin
Warning!  Passwd file, line 9, does not have 7 fields:
                    uucp:*:66:66:UUCP pseudo-
```

6.1.3 Issues and Considerations

Although static analysis is a logical portion of any security management strategy, it is not without problems, including the following:

- As with many other security products, intrusion detection among them, people want to treat static analysis tools as security panaceas. Therefore, the user regards the product as a one-shot miracle cure for all the security problems that exist in the system. Unfortunately, security products do not provide miracle cures.

- Many static analysis tools only diagnose problems, stopping short of prescribing or suggesting cures. Although the best of the commercial products are improving in this regard, it is still important to emphasize the importance of acting on the results of the analysis and eventually correcting the problems that are revealed.

- Attackers can use these tools to profile your systems to identify holes that might be exploited. This risk is inherent in any knowledge-driven diagnostic tool. The fact that many vulnerability analysis tools indicate only that a particular problem exists (not how that problem is exploited, suggesting an attack script or tool) helps to defuse this issue.

6.2 Credentialed Approaches

The monitoring approaches that vulnerability analysis products use can be divided into two categories: *credentialed* (also known as *passive*) and *noncredentialed* (also known as *active*). I found the credentialed/noncredentialed labels suggested by Shostack and Blake[2] to be much clearer than the traditional passive/active labels.

The basis for this differentiation is whether the information analyzed is gained with or without credentials. *Credentials* are passwords or other access tokens that allow someone to legitimately use system services. Therefore, credentialed checks are typically done by accessing a system data object, whereas noncredentialed checks are done by re-enacting exploits to provoke a run-time reaction from the system. Because credentialed approaches were the first to be proposed and used in vulnerability assessment tools, we will address them first.

6.2.1   Definition of Credentialed Approaches

Credentialed monitoring approaches for vulnerability assessments assume some legitimate system access. Checks run in credentialed mode use system data sources such as file contents, configuration information, and status information. This information is gained from nonintrusive sources; that is, it is gained by performing standard system status queries and inspection of system attributes. In UNIX systems, this information is gathered at the host or device level; therefore, credentialed approaches are also *host-based* approaches. Windows NT handles the gathering of this status information differently. Windows NT systems allow many native calls to be used on either local or remote systems, depending on the credentials used; therefore, the correlation between credentialed and host-based approaches does not always apply.

6.2.2   Determining Subjects for Credentialed Approaches

The effectiveness of credentialed approaches to vulnerability analysis depends on the subjects being analyzed. The security policy for the system in large part determines suitable targets for credentialed approaches; so does threat information provided by expert sources. Most vulnerabilities revealed by credentialed checks involve *privilege escalation* (that is, users gaining superuser privilege).

Much of the value added by commercial vulnerability-analysis products is in the form of expert collection and evaluation of current threat information, translated into guidance for vulnerability-analysis systems. Part of this guidance is determining whether credentialed or noncredentialed checks are more effective for detecting a particular problem. Given the extensive and dynamic nature of the threat environment, this is a powerful contribution.

The network security community is quite knowledgeable about the security vulnerabilities that affect UNIX systems (compared to other operating systems). The COPS system (illustrated in the output example in Table 6.1) constructed one of the first definitive sets of configuration checks for common UNIX problems. Some checks are for blatant mistakes in configuration that should simply never occur. For instance, only systems administrators should be able to alter critical system files and directories. And only trusted systems administrators should be able to read certain critical configuration files. The default assumption in most environments is that users should have some expectation of privacy and control over their own file spaces; therefore, COPS checks assure that only users have default write privileges for their own directories.

A special case of credentialed analysis is that of target-based monitoring—specifically, file integrity assurance mechanisms. These protective mechanisms use cryptographic message digest algorithms to protect files and objects from unauthorized alteration. A credentialed vulnerability analyzer might include tables of critical files and objects, along with corresponding reference checksums. In this case, one is interested in detecting any change since the last analysis. In commercial products, some vendors also use these checksums to perform another check of immense value to users: to determine whether vendor-supplied bug patches have been applied to system binaries.

6.2.3   Strategy and Optimization of Credentialed Approaches

One strategy for structuring credentialed vulnerability analyses uses separate assessment routines to conduct each type of check. This approach allows the system administrator to run checks in parallel; it also allows the division of effort across multiple platforms where desired. Another strategy for optimizing credentialed analysis across multiple networked hosts employs software agents that conduct most of the assessment local to the monitored node, forwarding the results of the assessment to a centralized management console for reporting.

Other schemes call for performing simple analyses and checks locally, and forwarding more complex (and, therefore, more computationally greedy) portions of the analysis to a more powerful system.

Credentialed approaches are by nature much more tightly targeted to the operating system platform. This feature represents both a blessing and a curse. The capability to optimize the scans results in improved accuracy. On the other hand, part of the assessment engine running on the local host inflicts a performance hit on the system being monitored. The required tailoring to operating system platform also means that one has to maintain a variety of these operating system-specific tools when running on heterogeneous networks. This can be costly in both support dollars and time. Finally, the credentials (as well as much of the information that the assessment engine can access using the credentials) must be protected. Otherwise, the system itself represents a security vulnerability.

Note

An atypical but significant early security approach is the Kuang system, which was developed by Robert Baldwin when he was a student at MIT. Kuang, which inspired a great deal of the subsequent work in vulnerability assessment and intrusion detection (including COPS and the Network Security Monitor), is an expert system that allows a system administrator to perform "what-if" analyses outlining the security impact of a particular configuration change. Figure 6.1 shows a typical Kuang decision tree and interpretation that is produced by the tool. Kuang allows the user to provide a particular hacker goal, a set of conditions (usually in the form of user group and permissions). It then automatically answers the following question: Given access to a particular set of privileges, can an attacker achieve superuser privileges? Baldwin's insight with regard to the UNIX protection model is considerable, and KUANG represents one of the most elegant approaches to conceptualizing security impacts of system configurations. A Kuang tree is an IF rule tree, so any one of the leaf conditions is sufficient to satisfy the root.[3]

Figure 6.1   A Kuang Rule Tree

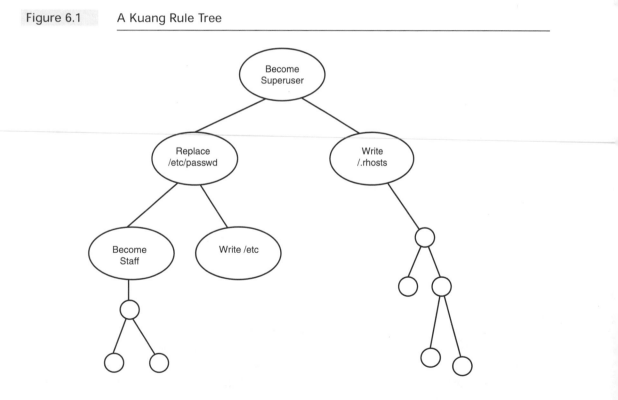

6.3   Noncredentialed Approaches

In recent years, *noncredentialed* approaches have become popular in vulnerability analysis. Many members of the Internet community believe that noncredentialed vulnerability analysis *is* intrusion detection. Some products billed as intrusion detection products are, upon closer inspection, actually vulnerability analyzers that use noncredentialed monitoring approaches. The correlation between credentialed and host-based approaches also applies to noncredentialed and network-based approaches.

6.3.1   Definition of Noncredentialed Approaches

Noncredentialed approaches for vulnerability analysis actually reenact system attacks, noting and recording system responses to these attacks. Therefore, noncredentialed approaches are more intrusive than credentialed monitoring approaches. The former have additional monitoring and detection capabilities that complement those of credentialed approaches, allowing users to assess vulnerabilities associated with network services.

6.3.2   Methods for Noncredentialed Vulnerability Analysis

Various techniques are used for noncredentialed vulnerability assessment. Before we discuss them, here are the attributes that can be used to gauge their effectiveness:

- **Accuracy** Whether the analysis technique correctly diagnoses the presence of a vulnerability.

- **Reliability** Whether the analysis technique consistently diagnoses the presence of a vulnerability.

- **Intrusiveness** The degree to which the analysis technique affects the normal operation of the targeted system.

- **Resource usage** The amount of computing and network bandwidth consumed by the analysis technique—this information is of great interest because it affects the speed with which networked systems can be assessed.

6.3.3   Testing by Exploit

Testing by exploit is the analysis technique whereby the system reenacts an actual attack. The test scripts are usually fashioned so that the exploits return a status flag, not the root shell that the actual attack would return. Although the accuracy and reliability of exploit techniques are greater than those of inference techniques, a number of issues in strategizing and executing affect this form of assessment.

To reliably diagnose the presence of a vulnerability, you must isolate signs of that vulnerability from the information returned from the target host, or else use additional steps to obtain the data. This process can be difficult, given the uneven performance that vendors have demonstrated in software quality and compliance with standards.

Testing by exploit can be very intrusive, which is obviously an issue when performing checks for denial-of-service vulnerabilities. However, there are numerous examples of situations in which a test for a vulnerability that is not a denial-of-service attack provokes a system crash.

Other strategies offer some of the advantages of testing by exploit while reducing the level of intrusiveness. These strategies include a strategy of "escalation," in which users perform less-intrusive checks, proceeding to actual attack reenactment only after less-intrusive checks do not yield the necessary information. For instance, you might check for the existence of a Web server before running an exploit script for a denial-of-service vulnerability in an application that requires a Web server to run.[4]

6.3.4   Inference Methods

Inference methods encompass the analysis techniques that do not actually exploit vulnerabilities, but look for evidence that the vulnerabilities have been exploited. Early vulnerability assessment tools, including Security Administrator's Tool for Analyzing Networks (SATAN), used inference techniques.

Specific inference techniques include the following:

- **Version checks** Rely on a version number or other identifier provided by a server (sometimes in response to a query) to infer whether a vulnerability exists.

- **Port status checks** Query ports to determine which ports are open. The fact that certain ports are open serves as reliable evidence that some vulnerabilities exist.

- **Protocol compliance checks** Done in conjunction with port status checks, protocol compliance checks exercise network services with simple requests for status or information.

Inference methods have the advantage of being less intrusive than testing by exploit. Therefore, inference methods can safely perform denial-of-service checks. The resource usage for these techniques is also low. However, they are not usually as accurate or reliable as testing by exploit.[2]

6.3.5   A Historical Note

Another feature of noncredentialed approaches is a colorful history! The entire computer community was introduced to noncredentialed vulnerability assessment in 1995 when SATAN was released. Developed by Dan Farmer and Wietse Venema, the tool was surrounded by a great deal of controversy, complete with doomsday predictions. Farmer and Venema are both respected security experts. (As noted earlier in this chapter, Farmer's COPS product was one of the first widely used UNIX vulnerability analyzers. Venema is the author of many security tools, including the widely used TCPwrapper, a utility that allows users to log network accesses and restrict access to servers according to source IP addresses and other attributes). Prior to releasing SATAN, Farmer and Venema published a paper outlining the design and justification for the tool that openly discussed the network security problems prevalent at the time, complete with attack information.[4]

This paper challenged the prevalent attitudes of the time by openly discussing the details of attacks. Perhaps more significantly, the authors also challenged the security community to take a more aggressive, noncredentialed approach to protecting systems. Before this time, most computer security focused on preventing problems by emphasizing procedural control of both systems and threat information. This credentialed approach, although suitable for an era in which computers were few, expensive, and centralized, was ineffective given the explosive growth in the number and power of networked personal computers and work-stations (and the corresponding growth in threat to those systems). The challenge mounted by Farmer and Venema was for security professionals to "hack your own systems and fix the problems before someone else hacks you." The SATAN software then provided the means for users to perform the hacks easily.

The reaction of many in the security community and press was drastic and unfavorable. Several prominent members of the computer security community asked Venema and Farmer not to release SATAN. Some accused the authors of threatening the very existence of the Internet as a functional communication medium; others accused them of writing the tool for purposes of self-aggrandizement. One of the authors even lost his job. The SATAN software received front-page coverage in most major newspapers in the United States, and almost every computer trade publication carried articles on the tool and interviews with Farmer and Venema. Two tools designed specifically to detect SATAN were developed and released at the same time that SATAN was posted to the Internet. And the Internet (and for that matter, the world) survived the release of SATAN, and life went on.

Ironically, SATAN was not the first, nor was it the most aggressive network vulnerability assessment tool available at the time. Christopher Klaus' ISS (freeware version) was released in 1993 and is acknowledged as a smaller, much more aggressive scanner. According to data from the Computer Emergency Response Team (CERT) at Carnegie Mellon University, of 111 security incidents in which scanning toolkits were detected, 93 involved ISS and 21 involved SATAN.[5]

SATAN offers a nice combination of features and design elegance, especially for a public domain software package. It also reflects the authors' considerable expertise in network security. Therefore, it is used here as a case study of a noncredentialed vulnerability analysis system.

6.3.6 Architecture of SATAN

The architecture of SATAN is pictured in Figure 6.2. It consists of four major functional elements:

- Target acquisition engine

- Data collection and analysis engine

- Policy engine

- Trust analysis engine

These elements are controlled by an inference engine, and driven by a set of configuration and rule files. The data collection and analysis engine generate additional information that is stored in canonical form in a main database. The results of the analysis are communicated to the user via a Web browser interface. Let's take a look at the system in more detail (see Figure 6.2).

Figure 6.2   SATAN System Architecture

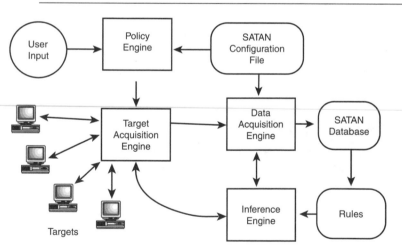

6.3.6.1   Target Identification

The *target acquisition engine* generates the list of systems that SATAN is to test. As targets can refer to single hosts or whole subnetworks of hosts, the first step in target acquisition is expanding targets into lists of IP addresses, each corresponding to a single host. After this expansion is done, the target acquisition engine uses the internal SATAN tool `fping` to determine which hosts in the list are alive. `fping` takes the expanded target list of IP hosts, then invokes the network utility `ping` for each host, recording each response. `ping` issues Internet Control Message Protocol (ICMP) echo packets to IP hosts in order to determine that they are present and communicating. Because some network security devices interfere with this test (for instance, networks using filtering routers or firewalls may block the ICMP protocol on which `ping` relies), SATAN enables users to specify that certain IP addresses are to be tested regardless of whether they respond to `fping` checks.

6.3.6.2   Policy Definition

The *policy engine* handles two types of controls: the *coverage* of the testing (that is, the specific hosts that are targets of the testing) and the *attributes* of the test (that is, the number of attacks or attributes that is checked on each host). The testing attributes are specified in terms of *severity settings*. In SATAN, severity can be set to low, medium, or high; low is the default setting. The policy engine is driven by the SATAN configuration file (`satan.cf`), which includes the severity settings as well as a list of target hosts that are not to be scanned.

6.3.6.3   Assessment and Analysis

The *data acquisition engine* actually drives the testing by launching small scanning processes, each of which targets a specific security hole for a specific host address. The input to the processes is a host name (derived from the configuration file), and they generate output in the form of a database record.

The *inference engine* analyzes the information written to the SATAN database by the processes of the data acquisition engine. To perform this analysis, the inference engine uses a set of six automata that act as rule engines. A list of these automata and their functions follow.

- **Drop**   Specifies which information should be ignored. This engine is loaded with statements of known exceptions to general security problem-detection rules. In other words, the experts writing SATAN know that, in general, some system settings are terrible except for one particular scenario. Drop allows the experts to tell the system not to take detections that occur in this scenario seriously, thereby eliminating a false alarm.

- **Facts**   Extracts security-relevant data from text messages that are returned from tools and service banners.

- **Host type**   Determines the operating system of a host being scanned. This information is extracted from banners.

- **Services**   Converts reports of detected network services to human-readable form.

- **Todo**   Handles the case in which a scan result suggests that another scan should be done. For instance, if a well-known vulnerability is associated with a particular service (say, Telnet), Todo instructs the data acquisition engine to run a scan for that vulnerability only if the first scan for the presence of that service indicates that it is running.

- **Trust**   Recognizes trust relationships between scanned network hosts based on a set of cases (for example, if NFS exports are recognized from scan results), and then translates these relationships to human-readable form. This automaton identifies chains of trust, using a Kuang-style engine. Thus, even if the target host is not vulnerable, if any of the upstream hosts (that is, hosts with which the target host has a trust relationship) are vulnerable, the attack can exploit that host and follow the chain of trust down to the target. These trust relationships were seldom justified, nor were they documented.

6.3.6.4   User Interfaces
SATAN uses a Web browser interface, which makes the tools easy to operate. This approach was quite novel at the time. Many other vulnerability-assessment tools now use Web browsers or other graphical user interfaces to configure systems and report results.

6.3.7   Fail-Safe Features
Several features in SATAN allow users to control the scope of the tool's operation. One such feature is the specification of targets in terms of distance (in network hops) from the system on which SATAN is running. Another is the capability to specify both hosts that should be tested and those that should never be tested. Several advisory notes in the system documentation recommend against allowing IP forwarding on any firewalls serving as a testing perimeter for SATAN. Finally, SATAN was designed to have a large characteristic footprint, which makes it easier for a system defender to spot and recognize an unauthorized SATAN test.

6.3.8   Issues Associated with SATAN
Although SATAN is a good example of a network-based, vulnerability-analysis system, it has some areas in which improvement is possible. The developers acknowledge that their intent in writing SATAN was as much to develop a vehicle for conducting further security

research on the Internet as to produce a public domain tool. They also allude to areas in which improvement is possible. One is the choice of a development environment. SATAN is coded primarily in Perl, which is interpreted and therefore slower than a compiled system (such as C or C++). Perl relies on an HTML user interface, which extracts a performance hit from the system on which SATAN runs. In this application, graphic mapping of the networks being assessed would be extremely helpful. Despite these issues, the system is still a fine working example of a well-designed security assessment tool.[6]

Note

One amusing reaction to the furor surrounding the naming of SATAN was the SANTA conversion tool. If you didn't like the name SATAN, the SANTA script replaced all references to the angel of darkness with a reference to a break-in artist rumored to strike during winter!

6.4   Password-Cracking

A necessary portion of vulnerability analysis that does not neatly fit into either noncredentialed or credentialed approaches is password assessment. Because it is included in most vulnerability-analysis tools, it is included here. The test of the strength of system passwords addresses one of the most common system vulnerabilities, that of password-cracking. Password-cracking enacts a common attack (called the *dictionary attack*) against the contents of a UNIX system password file.

6.4.1   Concepts of Operation

In UNIX, user passwords are not stored in plain text in the password file. Instead, the operating system generates a value by encrypting a block of zeros, using a one-way function [`crypt()`] with the password as key and storing that value in the password file. When a user logs in, the system takes the password entered and repeats the zero-block encryption operation, comparing the encrypted value with that stored in the file. If they match, then the user is allowed access to the system; if not, access is denied.

The `crypt()` function is cryptographically strong. Thus, given the encrypted string in the password file, an attacker cannot directly derive the password. However, if the user picks an easily guessed password, the attacker can simply guess passwords, replicate the zero-block encryption operation performed by the operating system, and check for matches with the encrypted value within the password file. *Password crackers* are designed to do this job, encrypting likely passwords (from extensive hacker "dictionaries") and comparing them with the encrypted values stored in the password file.[7] Most vulnerability analysis tools include password-cracker functions. The size of dictionaries varies from tool to tool, with some commercial products including extremely comprehensive password checkers.

6.4.2 Password Crackers as Vulnerability Analysis Tools

The size and quality of dictionaries used in the password crackers included with vulnerability analysis packages vary widely. Some look for only 20 or 30 of the most blatantly weak userID-password pairs (for instance, the userID "field" and password "service" that were shipped as a system default on older operating system versions and often never changed). If a user wants to include the output of a strong password cracker in his or her system vulnerability analysis, Alec Muffet's Crack software package is generally acknowledged as excellent, with well-optimized code and one of the most comprehensive dictionaries. The hacker group L0pht's L0phtcrack software package performs the same for Windows NT function environments.

As with other security tools, certain fail-safe considerations are associated with password crackers. Because password crackers are often successful in capturing weak or otherwise badly chosen passwords, the results of password cracker runs should be either encrypted or otherwise stored in a protected location.

6.5 Strengths and Weaknesses of Vulnerability Analysis

When all the definitions are voiced and discussed, one question remains. What are the most effective approaches for performing vulnerability analysis? As in other areas, each approach has its benefits and drawbacks.

In general, vulnerability analysis is of significant value as a part of security monitoring. This tool allows security managers to detect problems on systems that simply cannot support a more dynamic monitoring technology. Vulnerability analysis also fills a need for a security-oriented configuration tester for use in baselining systems at the start of a security program, or when a baseline needs to be re-established. (One example is when software changes are made and installed into an operational system.) Finally, when configured to operate on a regular schedule, vulnerability analysis can reliably spot changes, alerting security managers to many problems before they can negatively affect a site.

6.5.1 Strengths of Credentialed Analysis Techniques

Because credentialed analysis techniques allow the sampling and testing of system objects at host level, they are well suited to detect fine-grained artifacts of attacks. Thus, in cases in which hackers have attacked a system and left a trail of back doors, strange data files, or other artifacts of their activity, credentialed analyzers can usually find these more rapidly than noncredentialed analyzers can. In such cases, noncredentialed analyzers can detect the outcome of a security problem, but may miss some details or other forensics associated with the incident. This consideration is important when attacks inflict more damage, and organizations want to pursue attackers more aggressively.

Because credentialed approaches are tightly matched to specific hosts and operating system platforms, these approaches are usually more accurate and reliable than noncredentialed approaches are. Finally, credentialed analyzers that are run on regular schedules can time-bracket some problems. (That is, they can reveal, within a rough order of approximation, when a problem occurred by noting when a transition from "secure" to "insecure" occurred for a variety of system objects.) However, because time-bracketing may not be a reliable form of detection, especially given an expert intruder, other techniques should serve as the primary detection mechanism.

6.5.2 Strengths of Noncredentialed Analysis Techniques

Noncredentialed approaches are valuable, as well. They are largely platform-independent. Thus, a single, noncredentialed analyzer can support a number of operating system platforms, scaling to cover a heterogeneous network environment. Noncredentialed analyzers can also detect a susceptibility to network-based attacks (for example, attacks against the TCP/IP suite of services, attacks based on malformed packets, and denial-of-service attacks).

6.5.3 Disadvantages

There are disadvantages, as well, associated with vulnerability analysis approaches. The tight fit between credentialed analyzers and operating system platforms means that these analyzers cannot scale easily across heterogeneous networks; and they are likely to be more expensive to build, maintain, and manage. The platform independence possessed by non-credentialed analyzers makes them less accurate and more subject to false alarms. The capability to test systems for susceptibility to denial-of-service attacks can backfire on non-credentialed analyzers because a denial-of-service test can easily become indistinguishable from a denial-of-service attack! Unfortunately, some tests for vulnerabilities that are not in themselves denial-of-service attacks can have the same effect.

Issues also exist in coordinating vulnerability assessment products with intrusion-detection systems. Noncredentialed checks, especially denial-of-service attacks, can trigger intrusion detection system responses, ultimately blocking subsequent scans. Similar problems are associated with repetitive checks (such as those associated with scanning large networks of target hosts). Vulnerability assessment checks can trigger false alarms and throw off the accuracy of intrusion detection systems. Furthermore, frequent checks can retrain some intrusion detection systems so that they ignore real attacks when they occur.

Finally, many political issues are associated with running both types of analyzers, ranging from concerns about privacy issues to controversy regarding enacting hacking attacks against systems that may be in other political control domains. Because vulnerability assessment systems carry an embedded knowledge of system vulnerabilities to attack, the analysis tools themselves are of great appeal to system attackers and intruders. Furthermore, the figures from the CERT cited earlier in the chapter indicate that attackers have used these systems to identify targets for attack. This factor should not discourage you from using vulnerability assessment systems; in fact, it should serve as the most powerful of incentives to use them!

Privacy issues abound with regard to monitoring systems, and vulnerability assessment systems are no exception. In 1994, Technet, at that time the only commercial ISP in Singapore, used active scanning against its subscribers. The scanning resulted in a subscriber being arrested for downloading sex films from the Internet, the first enforcement of a national Internet regulation.[8]

6.6   Conclusion

Given their widespread distribution and adoption within the operational information technology community, vulnerability analysis products are here to stay. They are a valuable entry in the security management arsenal, allowing system managers to spot correctable problems in system configurations. Vulnerability analysis products also allow managers to check their networks for signs of prior intrusion and to baseline a system as a way of bringing it under management control. This chapter covered the different approaches used in vulnerability analysis, cited cases and working examples of the packages, and outlined the strengths and weaknesses associated with the different approaches as well as vulnerability analysis itself.

Endnotes

1. Farmer, D. and E. H. Spafford. "The COPS Security Checker System." Proceedings of the Summer USENIX Conference, Anaheim, CA, June 1990: 165–170.

2. Shostack, A. and S. Blake. "Toward a Taxonomy of Network Security Assessment Techniques." Proceedings of the 1999 Black Hat Briefings, Las Vegas, NV, July 1999.

3. Baldwin, R. W. "Rule-Based Analysis of Computer Security." Massachusetts Institute of Technology, Cambridge, MA, June 1987.

4. Farmer, D. and W. Venema. "Improving the Security of Your Site by Breaking into It." Internet white paper, 1993: http://www.fish.com.

5. Howard, J. D. "Analysis of Security Incidents on the Internet." 1989–1995. Doctoral thesis, Carnegie Mellon University, April 7, 1997.

6. Farmer, D. and W. Venema. "Security Administrator's Tool for Analyzing Networks." `http://www.fish.com/zen/satan/satan.html`.

7. Garfinkel, Simson and E. H. Spafford. *Practical UNIX and Internet Security.* O'Reilly and Associates, Sebastopol, CA, 1996.

8. Global Internet Liberty Campaign. "Privacy and Human Rights: An International Survey of Privacy Laws and Practice." `http://www.gilc.org/privacy/survey/`.

CHAPTER

7

Technical Issues

Although intrusion detection is rapidly becoming a standard component in security management infrastructures, it is still a young technology. Many issues stand in the way of optimizing the performance of intrusion detection, especially as it evolves with the network landscape it's charged with monitoring and protecting. In this chapter, we will discuss some of these issues, along with strategies that might rectify them.

7.1   Scalability

As the reach of computer networking increases, monitoring large mission-critical networks (such as those belonging to major Internet service providers [ISPs] or backbone providers) becomes a gargantuan feat. As the threat environment becomes more hostile and customers demand more secure network connectivity, monitoring also becomes more vital to these organizations.

Scalability refers to how well a particular solution to a problem works when the size of the problem grows. Several challenges are associated with scaling intrusion detection approaches to large complex networks. Given the traditional approaches to performing network audit and intrusion detection, the issues in scalability extend across different dimensions. We consider the two most common issues, scaling over time and scaling over space.

7.1.1   Scaling over Time

Consider the issues associated with scaling intrusion detection over time. Intrusions, you may recall from Chapter 4, "Analysis Schemes," appear to the analysis engine as partially ordered sequences of events or state transitions. Therefore, to recognize suspicious activity, the intrusion detection system must consider the event stream as a function of time. This requirement is usually not an issue when monitoring for events driven by an attack script or intrusion tool because the progression of events is rapid.

However, what if an attacker, in a deliberate attempt to defeat the intrusion detection system, does a "slow attack" in which the steps of the attack are stretched over minutes, hours, days, or longer? This situation is worrisome, both because the scarcity of attack data allows the attacker to bury the attack in the background noise of event traffic and because most systems don't keep enough event data to track across an extended time interval.

Although some slow host-level attacks might be blocked by session timeout rules, (especially when augmented by integrity checkers to detect alterations in system executables), other scenarios can show up as slow attacks. An example of such a scenario is an insider attack (that is, an authorized user overstepping his or her privileges on a particular system) in which existing protections rely on anomaly-detection-based characterization of user behavior. In this scenario, the user gradually changes his or her pattern of behavior until the system allows misuse.

In current intrusion detection systems, efficient memory utilization is critical, lest data structures grow to the extent that they overflow available memory, ultimately crashing the intrusion detection engine. Therefore, many operational intrusion detection systems limit the amount of event data they retain over time. These memory limitations constrain the time window over which the system can "see" the progress of an extended attack, enabling attacks to mount slow attacks. In fact, "slow scan" tools, which have been posted to many hacker sites, are already in common use.

7.1.2   Scaling over Space

The other aspect of intrusion detection scalability is how well it works when the network monitored increases from hundreds of hosts to thousands or even millions of hosts. As networked systems become ubiquitous, this scenario is common in large organizations. The issues associated with this scalability translate into a plethora of other issues covered elsewhere in this chapter.

For instance, how can an intrusion detection system track attacks that are traversing a large global network, utilizing a variety of communications media, so that link speeds vary, thereby distorting the time sequence of monitored information? Certain large networks must contend with significant *clock skew* (that is, the differential between individual system clocks) when no central time server is available.

Another such situation exists in designs that utilize hierarchical intrusion detection architectures to organize monitoring systems into reporting or control tree structures. These require a means of aggregating the monitoring results at various points in the tree, allowing some regional reduction of data.

Finally, issues are associated with displaying the results of large, network-wide intrusion detection systems so network managers can interpret them. There may be a need to overlay these results on information from a network management system.

7.1.3   Case Study—GrIDS

One approach to dealing with scaling intrusion detection to large networks comes from a research project sponsored by the Defense Advanced Research Projects Agency (DARPA). The Graph-Based Intrusion Detection System (GrIDS) project at University of California, Davis, uses a hierarchical aggregation scheme to scale to larger networks. By allowing a significant reduction of activity information at each level of the hierarchy, the approach addresses one of the management obstacles to scalability: the reluctance of domain administrators to exchange activity information collected within their domains.

GrIDS constructs activity graphs of network hosts and activities, which allow it to recognize attacks whose hallmarks involve movement across networks. Two examples are a "sweep" attack, or vulnerability scan, and a "worm" attack. An example of a sweep is the freeware ISS tool or SATAN; an example of a worm is the Internet worm of 1988, which spread to thousands of systems on the Internet, resulting in massive denial of service.[1]

GrIDS is designed to accept input from a variety of intrusion detection systems, constructing graphs, which are passed up the hierarchy, with a function that collapses the graphs into coarser resolution at each level. The graph engine is driven by a rulebase, which allows security administrators to specify how graphs can combine, which graphs represent "bad" activity, and which action to take when bad activity is recognized. A policy language is included to specify the conditions under which intrusion triggers should be reported. The system is dynamically reconfigurable, so it accommodates changes in network structure and configuration.

Although GrIDS does not deal with scalability over time, it represents a promising strategy for scaling intrusion detection systems across huge networks of interest.[2]

7.2   Management

Another pressing issue is dealing with the management of intrusion detection systems. This issue directly follows from the scalability problems noted in Section 7.1. As the size and complexity of networks under the control of a single organization grow, so do security issues and the need for intrusion detection. Clearly, many of the workable solutions for intrusion detection call for numerous, highly distributed sensors and detection agents. However, unless these components are well managed, they will contribute nothing to, or worse, jeopardize the function of the intrusion detection system, compromising the security of the target system.

7.2.1 Network Management

Network management is defined as "controlling a network to maximize its efficiency and productivity." The International Standards Organization (ISO) network management model divides it into five categories: security management, fault management, accounting management, configuration management, and performance management.

Fault management is identifying and locating faults in the network. This activity includes finding the problem, isolating the source of the problem, and repairing (or isolating the rest of the network from) the problem. Configuration management involves identifying, tracking, and modifying the setup of network devices, such as routers and file servers. Performance Management involves measuring the performance of various components of the network. This activity includes using the results of those measurements to optimize the network performance.

Although ISO defines security management as controlling (granting, limiting, restricting, or denying) access to the network and resources, security management also includes functions that are associated with intrusion detection systems, such as finding intrusions, identifying entry points for intruders, and repairing or otherwise closing those avenues.[3]

Many commercial intrusion detection systems acknowledge the overlap between the information consumed by network management and intrusion detection systems. Despite this awareness, few intrusion detection systems actually utilize this commonality in purpose beyond providing the response option of generating Simple Network Management Protocol (SNMP) traps.

Intrusion detection systems can benefit network management by enabling the network management system to understand, at a finer level of detail, the events occurring on the network. Network management systems can benefit intrusion detection systems by providing information that can improve the accuracy of decisions made about intrusion or other activity of interest. The newest versions of SNMP (v.3) offer secure messaging and management features, which may be suitable for use in intrusion detection. However, the integration of network management and intrusion detection requires some preparatory modifications.

First, network management engines need to provide a rich enough set of alerting and response functions to support the security goals of intrusion detection systems. Many current problems associated with generating SNMP traps in response to detected attacks reflect the inability of listeners to react appropriately to the traps.

Furthermore, the complexity of the major network management systems interferes with their accommodating existing intrusion detection systems without significant modification.

This situation is especially troublesome because such modification involves customizing the intrusion detection system to each network management platform as well as to each network installation in which the system is to run.

Despite these issues, the fact remains that as network traffic and complexity levels grow, so will the need to more tightly integrate intrusion detection functions with network management systems.

7.2.2 Sensor Control

Another ongoing debate within intrusion detection research circles concerns the centralization of management control of intrusion detection sensors, agents, and analysis engines. As with other issues, costs and benefits are associated with centralized and decentralized control strategies.

Most of the arguments in favor of distributed controls are similar to those associated with the Transmission Control Protocol/Internet Protocol (TCP/IP) suite itself. Distributed control strategies provide systems that are more robust, fault tolerant, resilient in the face of attack, and capable of surviving catastrophic failures of the part of the system infrastructure. Depending on the level of intelligence embedded in the sensor or distributed analysis engine, the amount of information that is conveyed to the central management system is less than if raw data is collected and forwarded without any preprocessing.

On the other hand, distributed controls have significant deficiencies. It is hard to maintain control in a consistent fashion and, furthermore, very difficult to protect distributed sensors from subversion. Another deficiency affecting low-bandwidth network environments is that distributed control inflicts an overhead load on network bandwidth because the control system and the distributed agent must exchange control information.

The increasing number of high-speed networks used in ISP, backbone provider, and major corporate installations is driving requirements for hardware sensors. The obstacles already noted for software sensors still apply (although some of the problems associated with integrity breaches are mitigated), however, the capability to adapt sensor features to address new attack scenarios may be lost. It is unclear what support will be available for managing embedded sensor hardware. It is even more unclear is which architecture is optimal for utilizing these devices in an intrusion detection context.

7.2.3 Investigative Support

Current intrusion detection systems do not adequately serve the needs of those who investigate and resolve security incidents. This lack of support can be devastating to system owners, as it effectively prohibits them from controlling costs associated with incident handling without sacrificing the quality of the investigation.

At a minimum, intrusion detection systems should allow investigators to tell that incidents occurred, isolate the entry points of the intruder, determine the means utilized to accomplish the intrusion, and determine the effects of the intrusion on the system itself as well as the data stored on the system. This information allows the system owners and administrators to repair any damage done by the intruder, to take steps to prevent additional intrusions, and to consider additional responses to the incident.

To allow system owners to pursue legal remedies for intrusions, intrusion detection systems must include support for legal processes. The first wave of computer crime prosecutions, as outlined in Chapter 9, "Legal Issues," taught the security community some lessons regarding the special needs of these processes.

Many of the functions required to support the investigation and prosecution of intrusions present a special challenge to intrusion detection system designers. They often represent a significant resource commitment and require additional protections (for instance, cryptographic protection of event logs with access logging mechanisms to indicate who collected and otherwise handled the data). Shoehorning these additional features into a system that is already resource-constrained is difficult.

To better support investigators working within classic investigative protocols, mechanisms that allow seamless connection across different communications networks are needed. This feature would allow an investigator to trace a session from the Internet through the telephone network and back again, possibly traversing cellular or satellite networks.

7.2.4 Performance Loads

Intrusion Detection in network environments can generate a significant system load, at both host and network levels. For intrusion detection systems not to represent a denial-of-service attack themselves, these system loads must be manageable in the context of the operational environments in which they are running. This calls for functions that allow system administrators to perform activities such as load balancing and run-time tuning of intrusion detection systems.

7.3 Reliability

Even when the obstacles to optimizing the core functions of intrusion detection are overcome, other issues remain. To be of any value, intrusion detection systems must be reliable, both at component and at system level. This means that the system must be resilient to incidental failures as well as the attacks an adversary might launch against it as part of an intrusion. These requirements apply to each functional component of intrusion detection, as each represents a potential point of failure. They also apply to the system as a whole.

7.3.1 Reliability of Information Sources

Information sources encompass a multitude of system mechanisms. These include sensors, agents, audit mechanisms, and other components that feed analysis engines and, in some cases, preprocess and otherwise reduce event data.

Encryption mechanisms represent special challenges for intrusion detection systems because traditional approaches involve reading information from clear-text channels at various points in the system. With encryption (provided by such mechanisms as virtual private networks or link encryptors) these channels are scrambled and therefore lost as information sources.

Two common scenarios illustrate this problem. Almost all electronic commerce is performed with Web browsers that provide Secure Socket Layer (SSL) encrypted links. When a customer proceeds to the payment portion of an e-commerce transaction, the browser's SSL features establish an encrypted channel between the buyer and seller sites. This practice obscures the view of the network traffic that passes between the buyer and seller sites (which is indeed the goal of using SSL in these situations). However, this step can also disable the detection capability of a network-based intrusion detection system.

Another scenario is a virtual private network (VPN), often built in compliance with the IPSEC standard for VPNs. In this situation, as in the e-commerce situation, the traffic between the sender and receiver sites is obscured from outside view, including the view of a network-based intrusion detection system.

Similar issues arise in connection with switched networks, which operate by instantiating connections between pairs of communicating systems. This behavior prevents most network monitors, which rely on tapping into traffic for entire network segments, from seeing more than one connection at a time unless a workaround is devised. The most common workaround is to utilize a special port (a spanning port) on network switches. This port allows you to see all of the traffic flowing through the switch.

This workaround is ultimately doomed, given trends in modern network switch design. In these, no one port can have enough bandwidth to equal the sums of the other ports. Therefore, the ability to see more than a single connection is endangered, and the ability to utilize common promiscuous-mode network monitors disappears. This situation drives requirements to use host-level monitors as an alternative scheme for capturing the network traffic.

At applications level, problems are associated with audit trails generated at the object level. Given object reuse and naming conventions for objects, making sense of information gathered at object levels is difficult.

7.3.2 Reliability of Analysis Engines

Many issues are associated with the reliability and robustness of analysis components of intrusion detection systems. First, profile-based systems face issues associated with maintaining profiles for all subjects and objects in a large system without having problems associated with memory management. The profile data can grow to the point of exhausting memory, thereby risking a system failure. Structuring the profile data is one strategy for dealing with this situation, but that approach can cause other problems, such as performance degradation.

Signature-based systems have similar problems, also associated with dealing with steadily growing numbers of subjects and objects in target systems, as well as attacks that target them. As the number of attacks increases, so does the number of attack signatures the system must recognize. After a point, the ability of the system to accommodate this growth in the signature database without performance reduction suffers.

Network-based systems must deal with problems associated with monitoring high-speed networks. Current network-based monitoring systems tend to underestimate the speed and memory needed in the monitoring platform. One network monitoring product vendor reports that to correctly monitor a saturated Fiber Distributed Data Interface (FDDI) network (averaging 17,000 packets per second), a monitoring system needs about 128MB of RAM. The memory is utilized to buffer packets that are collected out of order. This buffering is needed to do consistent reassembly of TCP sessions, necessary to detect many modern attacks.[4]

Without adequate provisions for such buffering and optimization, the monitoring system will miss a great deal of traffic, thereby reducing the reliability of the intrusion detection system.

Another issue in network-based intrusion detection systems is that of hackers bypassing or nullifying the analysis capabilities of the systems. For instance, hackers can use nonstandard ports for services (thereby defeating intrusion detection analyzers that pattern match against particular ports and services). Other recorded incidents involve hackers using trivial encryption (in this case, a substitution cipher) to evade regular expression-based intrusion detection analysis.[5] Both of these attack forms can involve some degree of collusion (in which an insider assists the attacker by providing tunnels or port services for an outsider). These attacks also reflect problems that might be mitigated by exercising other protective mechanisms, both intrusion detection as well as firewalls.

As network bandwidth increases, researchers have explored schemes for increasing the performance of network-based systems. One approach is to place multiple intrusion detection engines in parallel, dividing the monitoring and analysis load among them. This scheme presents significant challenges to intrusion detection designers because it introduces issues of correctly dividing the analysis load and maintaining temporal ordering of the traffic.

7.3.3 Reliability of Response Mechanisms

The reliability of response components is critical for several reasons. The first is obvious: An intrusion detection system, robbed of the capability to notify users that it has detected a problem, is of little, if any, value.

A second issue is a bit more disconcerting. When automated responses are enabled, a suborned response component can allow an adversary to utilize the intrusion detection system as a vehicle for attack against the system it is supposed to protect, as well as other innocents. Even when responses are limited to "shunning" connections or other relatively benign reactions, the capability of adversaries to corrupt and redirect response components can result in selective denial-of-service attacks against trusted allies.

Let's take a look at how such an attack might work. Corporation A and Corporation B, who are strategic partners, both run intrusion detection systems with automated responses set to block sources of certain attacks. The attacker, knowing this (by having probed both sites and ascertaining that each intrusion detection system indeed responds to common attacks by blocking subsequent traffic) launches an attack against Corporation A, using source IP addresses for Corporation B. Corporation A's intrusion detection system recognizes the attack and responds by blocking all subsequent traffic from Corporation B. If the attacker wants to go a step further, she might launch the same attack against Corporation B, spoofing Corporation A's IP address as the source of the attack. The result is that the corporations are blocked from communicating with each other, with a possible loss of revenue from the interruption of communications between the two organizations.

Another issue that comes up in connection with response components is recording information that is destined for use as legal evidence of attack. If response components are not reliable and robust in the face of attack, the information that they log about detected problems is subject to corruption. This nullifies its value as evidence in a legal action.

Although managing response components of intrusion detection to assure their reliability and robustness is difficult, mechanisms that allow the management portion of the intrusion detection system to track the health of response components at least allow the system to determine when response components are attacked and corrupted. These mechanisms can comprise cryptologic "heartbeat" (poll-response) functions. These heartbeat functions can be either push or push/pull in form. A push heartbeat function simply provides that the agent send an encrypted message (perhaps some combination of the system clock and an identifier) to the intrusion detection management engine at a particular interval. A push/pull involves the intrusion detection management engine initiating a communication with the agent, sending a challenge string to the agent, which then applies an encryption algorithm to the challenge string to generate a response. In either case, the management engine decrypts the message, recording either a success (heartbeat) or failure (death/corrupted sensor).

7.3.4 Reliability of Communications Links

Yet another set of reliability concerns involves the communications links utilized by intrusion detection systems. These concerns run the gamut from the stability of those communications in the face of hostile attack, to dealing with adversaries who hack the communications infrastructure itself as a means of covering their tracks.

In situations where customers are concerned about controlling access to critical information, the ability of attackers to use steganography to successfully smuggle out that information represents a major issue. (*Steganography* is hiding information by encrypting it and then using a specialized algorithm to embed it in other information.) The use of host-based intrusion detection that is capable of characterizing and analyzing information flows could be helpful in these scenarios.

In the fail-safe arena, the ability of attackers to defeat intrusion detection systems by using a "man in the middle" attack, in which the attacker inserts himself in the communications link between two parts of the intrusion detection system, intercepts traffic, and then replaces it with his own, represents a serious issue.

One approach to dealing with this set of issues is to use encryption to hide legitimate traffic between intrusion detection system components. The rationale for this strategy is that attackers cannot target what they cannot see.

Utilizing redundant communications channels, switching from one to another at randomized intervals, is another scheme for hardening these channels and making them more resilient. This approach has worked for TCP/IP itself, as well as for other information survivability technologies. The final option is to use totally out-of-band communications links when the system is under attack. Such links might include using private wireless communications systems or even, in extreme cases, actually running cable between systems.

7.4 Analysis Issues

Many issues are yet to be resolved in intrusion detection analysis. These range from difficulties characterizing goals to difficulties refining results.

7.4.1 Training Sets for AI-Based Detectors

Many see great promise in utilizing nonparametric or other artificial intelligence (AI) approaches for performing intrusion detection analysis. These techniques are dependent on large training sets of data from which to draw detection rules. However, significant problems are still associated with the existence of appropriate training sets and the generation of new ones that are feasible for training analysis engines.

Unlike other problems to which AI approaches have been applied, the capability to manually differentiate between "correct" and "incorrect" data is not yet present in intrusion detection. Given a set of event data large enough to utilize as a training set, balancing the following three constraints on the data is currently impossible:

- It must be complex enough to be authentic.

- It must be clean of attacks you don't want to consider as part of normal activity.

- It must be free of local bias if you want to be able to generalize results across large networks. (That is, if Acme Corporation, our organization, uses a learning set, management will likely want that training set to serve all hosts across the Acme network environment.)

7.4.2 False Positives/Negatives in Anomaly Detection

Tuning statistical anomaly detection engines continues to be a significant challenge. This process is considered to be a major impediment to wider adoption of anomaly detection in commercial products. If the anomaly detection engine is tuned so that the sensitivity of the detection mechanism is high, the false alarm (false positive or Type I error) is high. In this case, users of the intrusion detection system lose faith in the reliability of the system because it isn't reliably telling the difference between normal activity and intrusions.

If the false negative (or Type II error) rate is high, users lose faith because the system isn't reliably detecting when intrusions are taking place. In either case, users react by turning the intrusion detection system off or else ignoring its results.

7.4.3 Trends Analysis

There is a recognized need to enable intrusion detection systems to recognize entire categories of attacks, not just a particular attack within that category. This capability would allow the system to generalize the signature of a newly reported attack in order to recognize other attacks that take on the same attributes.

7.4.4 Composition of Policies

Building security policies, especially those suitable for specifying signatures and rule-bases, remains a major issue in intrusion detection. A great deal of effort is needed to translate administrative policies into monitoring and detection policies and rules. This situation is due, in part, to the fact that the perspective from which administrative policy is formulated and written is quite different from that required for writing monitoring and detection policies.

The U.S. Department of Defense attempted to tackle this sort of inconsistency when it initiated the Trusted Systems Initiative that produced the set of security references known as the Rainbow series. These references set forth the conditions that operating systems should meet to be considered secure enough to protect classified information.

The Orange Book (Trusted Computer System Evaluation Criteria, or TCSEC) outlines these conditions for single computer systems, ranking the strength of systems according to a rating scale. Elaborate measures are specified for the highest levels of trusted systems, complete with requirements for rigorous mathematical proofs of the security properties (which form the enforced security policies) of the systems.

However, when the Red Book (Trusted Network Interpretation), which is the interpretation of the Orange Book as applied to computer networks, was written, an effect was noted. For even when you connect two secure systems with a secure communications channel, in most cases you form a network that is much less secure than its parts! This effect is called the *cascade vulnerability problem*, and a great deal of research in computer security has been devoted to this topic. The cascade problem is but one of many reminders that even rigorously constructed and verified policies are not foolproof when devised for a complex or distributed system.[6]

Administrative policies, as they are to apply to human users, are written to describe behaviors, both desired and undesired. As such policies are usually written to target organizations, not specific hardware or software platforms, these behaviors are described in terms of goals, intentions, directions, and outcomes of human users, not the machines they use.

Intrusion detection system users must, on the other hand, specify monitoring and detection policies in terms of events that occur on a particular computer system. Even current means of classifying and organizing repositories of computer vulnerability and threat information do not serve these needs well. The information required for detection purposes must be expressed in terms of the results yielded by the exploitation of vulnerabilities, not the vulnerabilities themselves. Vulnerabilities can sometimes be used to drive static analysis (as in vulnerability scanners). However, their utility in constructing monitoring schemes and policy is often limited to using them to construct exploitation scripts. This script would be used in laboratory reenactments to isolate patterns of event activity associated with attackers targeting the vulnerability in question.

Some measures that appear to be helpful to users devising security policies are serviceable for both administrative and intrusion detection purposes. One such measure is providing automated policy-building tools that enable users to build policies using templates proven to be secure. Users can interface with these tools by way of structured questionnaires or other interview schemes.

The advantages represented by this sort of policy-building assistance are immense. The policy builders improve the quality of administrative as well as intrusion detection and monitoring policies by eliminating major omissions and errors commonly found in ad hoc policies. Such a structured policy can be used to configure full suites of security tools (including firewalls, encryption tools, and I&A) and, in some cases, can be pushed out into other system components. In fact, this policy-based practice is the goal of many who advocate the integration of security tools with network and system management platforms.

Other needed features are extensions to policy-builder interfaces that allow users to specify policies in terms that are relevant to their operational environment. This could include specifying policies at the application level (because many administrative policies specify behaviors only in terms of allowed and disallowed activities associated with a particular application package) or simply translating nomenclature to that employed in the user's environment. Such extensions could also facilitate building monitoring and detection policy at the application level.

7.5 Interoperability

As network environments become more complex, monitoring and detection needs also increase. Experience has taught the intrusion detection community that the most powerful monitoring solution is one that allows the collection of information from multiple levels of abstraction in the system, from multiple hardware and software platforms, and in different data formats. How does an intrusion detection system gather and combine all that information in a way that allows the system to make sense of it?

Another lesson learned is that the best point solutions across a complex problem space are almost never delivered by any single vendor or developer. This rule is even stronger when the solution depends on the developer's mastery of a proprietary operating system or hardware environment. How does a security manager who wants an intrusion detection system that combines solutions from six different vendors get her wish?

Finally, perhaps the most important lesson of the past is that if users are provided with a security mechanism that is not manageable, reliable, or relevant to the environment, they will simply not use it. How do you blend solutions and features in a way that allow users to operate them in a manner appropriate to their operational environments?

The feature addressing all of these needs is interoperability. *Interoperability* is the capability of a system or product to work with other systems or products without special effort on the part of the customer. Interoperability is the key to the proliferation of a particular technology.

Interoperability is part of modern life. For instance, you can plug a variety of devices into electric outlets without having to alter the devices or the electric outlet. You can purchase auto tires from different manufacturers without having to alter the tire rims or the location of the bolts that hold them on to your car. You can fill your car with gasoline at any fuel station and be assured that the car's engine can run on the fuel and, furthermore, that the gas pump nozzle will fit the neck of the gas tank on your vehicle.

In the area of information technology, interoperability relies on two general approaches. The first is published interface standards. These standards specify the format and content of interfaces between different system components. Examples of such standards include TCP/IP, HTTP, and IPSEC.

The second approach to achieving interoperability is specifying a specialized suite of software that serves as a "broker" to convert one product's interfaces to another. These operate in real time. An example of such a broker is the Common Object Request Broker Architecture (CORBA), which converts interfaces between distributed program objects in a network. This approach allows client programs to use objects without having to understand the network location or interface details of the objects.

In intrusion detection, the need for interoperability became apparent in the development of early commercial products. Although a few nascent standards have emerged, there are pressing needs for more.

7.5.1 CIDF/CRISIS Effort

At this time, the most ambitious effort addressing interoperability is the Common Intrusion Detection Framework (CIDF) project. CIDF is a DARPA-funded project to establish a common architecture under which different intrusion detection and response tools can be interconnected. This effort allows the systems to pool discoveries and share information and processing resources.

CIDF lays the groundwork for this architecture by outlining the ways in which intrusion detection components could interact and then by specifying a language that would enable those interactions. Another project, Critical Resource Allocation and Intrusion Response for Survivable Information Systems (CRISIS), extends the CIDF work, adding the capability to allocate critical resources in the face of an attack, allowing the system to balance the need for intrusion detection and response with the need to support ongoing computational needs of the target system (that is, the real work of the system).[7]

7.5.2 Audit Trail Standards

The common audit trail standard has been a topic of debate in intrusion detection circles for a long time. Operating system audit trails, the first common information source for intrusion detection systems, have always varied wildly from platform to platform. Many audit trail standards have been proposed over the years, with none reaching broad acceptance. The lack of these standards is recognized as a major obstacle to interoperability.

7.5.2.1 Orange Book

The Defense Department's TCSEC (the Orange Book mentioned earlier in this chapter), as well as its audit-specific subtext (the Tan Book) provide a great deal of information about the desired properties of auditing mechanisms. However, they specify these properties in terms of the content of the audit log. They never specify the format in which that content should be reported.

The criteria also specify which operating system events should be auditable, but never those that should, as a matter of course, be audited. The result has been a crazy quilt of operating system audit trail formats, leading to great frustration on the part of both intrusion detection developers and security managers.

7.5.2.2   Denning's IDES Audit Format

Dorothy Denning, in her seminal paper on intrusion detection, proposes a simple, six-element, platform-independent audit format.[8] Unfortunately, the proposed audit trail does not provide adequate information to describe operating system activity in sufficient detail to support misuse detection.

7.5.2.3   Smaha's SVR 4++ Audit Data Interchange Format

Steve Smaha, at the time with Haystack Laboratories, proposed a UNIX audit data interchange format, called SVR4++, which Haystack used as the basis for its line of commercial audit analysis and intrusion detection tools (Stalker). The format was proposed to POSIX and X/OPEN as a standard. Although never formally adopted, the format was used by several other organizations that developed intrusion detection products based on audit data.[9]

7.5.2.4   Bishop's Audit Format

Matt Bishop, of the University of California, Davis, proposed a standard audit trail format, which specifies field separators, character formats, delimiters, and operations. The format deliberately does not specify standard attributes and is intended to apply to all system platforms, regardless of operating system or application platform.[10]

7.5.2.5   Standards Bodies

Many audit-related standards have been proposed in software-standards groups. POSIX, ISO, and X/OPEN have all proposed audit standards. However, the standards proposed specify Application Programming Interfaces (APIs) or attributes of audit mechanisms, not audit trail formats.

7.5.2.6   IETF/IDWG

The Internet Engineering Task Force (IETF) has also chartered a working group on issues of interoperability. The Intrusion Detection Exchange Format Working Group is specifying a set of data exchange formats and transport mechanisms for use in an intrusion-detection-system-specific messaging system. This messaging system will consolidate information from intrusion detection systems, allowing systems to share information about detected intrusions, the status of monitored hosts, and other system events.

The working group will write two additional specifications as part of this standards effort: a data format specification, which will outline the format for the messages about suspicious events to be exchanged by systems; and a communication specification, which will identify protocols that are best suited to conveying this alarm data.[11]

7.6 Integration

Along with interoperability issues come those of integration. Integration involves combining parts into a coherent entity, resolving problems in interaction between the components. Such problems that exist in current intrusion detection systems include problems integrating intrusion detection systems with heterogeneous systems, especially when they include legacy systems running old or custom-built software. As the underlying semantics may differ wildly from system to system, resolving interaction conflicts in this scenario can be challenging, if not impossible.

Another significant integration challenge is that of integrating an intrusion detection system with an environment that uses multiple network protocols. Although the host systems attached to these networks may share common operating systems, the underlying communications protocol still differs. The difficulty increases when parts of the network are encrypted, switched, or otherwise obscured from view.

7.7 User Interfaces

Finally, the area of user interfaces remains an open issue in intrusion detection, as in other areas of security. The usability of security mechanisms to a large degree determines whether they are effective. If the user interface is badly designed, so that users find it difficult to interact with the system, they will in many cases choose not to use the system. In extreme cases, users will circumvent or sabotage the system.

User interfaces for intrusion detection systems represent a special challenge. The amount of information gathered in the course of monitoring system events is huge. Displaying this information in a fashion that allows users to identify activity that represents violations of policy or other scenarios requiring further investigation is a formidable task. User's needs and preferences in such interfaces vary widely; furthermore, each user's needs vary with the monitoring environment and the user's level of expertise.

Given the diverse information sources and analysis schemes provided by intrusion detection systems, user interfaces must support various schemes for displaying the output of a system. For instance, in anomaly-detection systems using statistical profiles and other quantitative means of analyzing data for intrusions, graphic display options such as bar charts and graphs can be helpful. In systems where network traffic is captured and characterized, numeric tables may represent the clearest way to express the results of analysis. In other systems, simple tabular text displays are appropriate, perhaps augmented with color or graphic tags for exceptional event records. In the GrIDS system discussed earlier in this chapter, network attacks over large networks were discernable when the attacker's connections were converted to a graph representation.

To meet the needs for appropriate user interfaces for intrusion detection systems, flexibility and clarity are essential. The user interfaces must be easily customized to a system environment. Furthermore, user interfaces should be adaptable to accommodate a variety of user expertise levels, from novice to guru. Finally, the user interface should present information in a way that allows the user to easily identify the patterns activity that require further action.

7.8 Conclusion

In this chapter, I've discussed technical issues in intrusion detection systems. Some of these may be corrected to some extent by standards activities and advances in the state of the art. Others, such as scalability and usability, are likely to continue to plague the community for the foreseeable future. Almost all will continue to represent research challenges for some time to come.

Endnotes

1. Spafford, E. H. "The Internet Worm: Crisis and Aftermath." Communications of the ACM, 32(6):678–687, June 1989.

2. Staniford-Chen, Cheung, Crawford, Dilger, Frank, Hoagland, Levitt, Wee, Yip, and Zerkle. "GrIDS—A Graph-Based Intrusion Detection System for Large Networks." Proceedings of the Nineteenth National Information Security Conference, Baltimore, MD, October 1996.

3. Leinwand, A. and K. Fang-Conroy. *Network Management: A Practical Perspective.* Addison-Wesley, 1995.

4. Ranum, M. personal communication, August 1999.

5. Neuman, M. personal communication, August 1999.

6. National Computer Security Center. "Trusted Network Interpretation." v1, NCSC-TG-005, Rainbow Series, July 1987.

7. Kahn, C., P. Porras, S. Staniford-Chen, and B. Tung. "A Common Intrusion Detection Framework." submitted to *Journal of Computer Security,* July 1998.

8. Denning, D. "An Intrusion Detection Model." Proceedings of the Seventh IEEE Symposium on Security and Privacy, p. 223, May 1986.

9. Smaha, Stephen E. "A Common Audit Trail Interchange Format for UNIX." Technical report, Haystack Laboratories, Inc., Austin, TX, October 1994.

10. Bishop, Matt. "A Standard Audit Log Format." Proceedings of the Eighteenth National Information Systems Security Conference, Baltimore, MD, October 1995.

11. Wood, M. "Intrusion Detection Exchange Format Requirements." Internet draft, Internet Engineering Task Force, June 1999.

8

Understanding the Real-World Challenge

Now that you understand the principles of intrusion detection, it's time to take it for a test drive in the real world. This chapter introduces the root causes of security vulnerabilities and takes you step by step through a typical hacker attack. The discussion then turns to exploring the differences between security engineering and more traditional engineering disciplines. Finally, I talk about specific challenges associated with securing intrusion detection systems.

8.1 The Roots of Security Problems

Intrusion detection systems exist to help computer system managers deal with security problems. To understand where intrusion detection fits in the security world, you should understand the cause of system security problems. Several models address the etiology of security problems in computer systems. I find it helpful to group system security problems into three categories. Most security scenarios result from problems that fall into one or more of these areas.

- **Problems in system design and development**   Problems resulting from errors and omissions occurring in the system design and development process.

- **Problems in system management**   Problems resulting from mismanagement of systems after they are placed in operational use. This area includes making mistakes in system configuration; disabling security mechanisms on systems (or never enabling them!); or failing to establish security management policies, procedures, and practices.

- **Problems in allocating trust appropriately**   Problems resulting from a failure to accurately assess trust. This area encompasses situations in which there is an assumption of trustworthiness when no compelling evidence supports that assumption. This area includes problems in network protocols (Transmission Control Protocol/Internet Protocol, or TCP/IP, features many notorious examples), cryptographic protocols, and policy.

Researchers have proposed numerous taxonomies to describe and categorize system security vulnerabilities. I use this three-part classification scheme because it lends itself to exploring the nature of security problems from the perspective of preventing them. However, the classification also helps a security manager understand how to prevent, detect, and/or block subsequent occurrences of each exploitation of a vulnerability. This approach is especially useful when multiple vulnerabilities are exploited in the course of a single attack.

For example, consider a typical attack in which an adversary, pretending to be a security administrator, deceives a user into revealing his or her password. The adversary uses the password to gain access to the system and then executes a buffer overflow attack to gain superuser privilege. As a superuser, the adversary substitutes trojan horse executables for several system utilities, adds user accounts to the system password file, and takes steps to cover his or her tracks before leaving. The adversary is likely to utilize the system alterations in future attacks.

Using the vulnerability categories outlined above, let's consider the components of this attack and how a security manager might address the causative factors. The first *social engineering* hack might be mitigated by increasing user awareness training and amending security policy. The buffer overflow may be addressable by either notifying the software vendor and requesting a bug patch or else noting the pattern of system events corresponding to the exploitation of the flaw and using that pattern to build a detection signature for an intrusion detection system. The alteration of system executables, as well as the covering of tracks, can be detected by integrity checkers and/or nonalterable logging mechanisms. Both scenarios lend themselves to detection signatures.

The key to managing system security is to optimize those protections over which you have control while leveraging attempts to correct other problems in the longer term. Therefore, the long-term solution for problems in the first vulnerability category is obvious—better software quality from software vendors. However, the track record of most commercial software vendors providers is not encouraging. Furthermore, some flaws in design and development are difficult to recognize with standard quality assurance practices. Given the growth in size and complexity of operating system software, the probability of eliminating all software design and implementation flaws is miniscule. Therefore, savvy security managers will compensate by devising other coping strategies.

8.1.1 *Problems in Design and Development*

As mentioned already, the first source of security woes are errors and omissions occurring in the system design and development process. These occur in both software and hardware. The description covers design and implementation faults and flaws that occur as software developers design and build systems. Examples of these problems can be easily found in current operating systems.

Many security vulnerability taxonomy efforts have explored this category of problem, classifying problems in terms of the path of introduction of the problems, the point in the software development process when the problems are introduced into the software, when the problems are most apt to surface, and the input and output associated with the exploitation of the problem. In this section, I'll examine one of the first of these efforts, the RISOS project, consider some problems in detail, and then talk about the ongoing research in this area.

8.1.1.1 RISOS

The RISOS project, of the mid-1970s, was a study of operating system software in an attempt to understand the origin of security problems. The goal of the study was to articulate the root causes of security breaches, with the hope of developing software engineering techniques to prevent these problems in subsequent systems. The problems identified by the RISOS team follow:

- **Incomplete parameter validation** This problem is a failure to check the parameters corresponding to the procedure calls used to effect interprocess communication. The validation checks should include data types, number and order, value and range, access rights to storage location, and consistency. This error is particularly devastating when the call is made by a process operating at one level of privilege to a process operating at a higher level of privilege. Invalid parameters in this case can cause the privilege level of the process to increase, resulting in a security breach.

- **Inconsistent parameter validation** Although this problem appears to be the same as incomplete parameter validation, the two are different. Inconsistent parameter validation is considered a design error, not a validation error. If the validation criteria in a system are inconsistent (for instance, when a series of isolated spot checks is performed and the process takes action based on a single check), a problem occurs when the process takes action based on a condition it considers to be valid.

- **Implicit sharing of privileged/confidential data** This term refers to information leakage from a process or user possessing a high level of privilege to a process or user possessing a lower level of privilege.

- **Asynchronous validation/inadequate serialization** This term refers to a violation of an assumption that the steps of process execution occur in a particular order. An example of this problem is the time-of-check-to-time-of-use errors, also known as a *race condition exploit*. These errors usually allow system penetration during a particular interval, called a *timing window*.

- **Inadequate identification/authentication/authorization** Authorization grants access rights and permissions based on identification and authentication of individuals and resources. It allocates these rights and permissions in a controlled fashion. The problems in this category occur when the operating system omits authorization requirements entirely or fails to uniquely identify the resources involved in the authorization.

- **Violable prohibition/limit** These problems involve data overflow conditions in fixed-size data structures such as tables or stacks.

- **Exploitable logic errors** These problems include improbable timing conditions, incorrect error handling, or instruction side effects. This area covers a wide range of questionable programming practices, most of which can be isolated by quality assurance methods during the development process.[1]

8.1.1.2 Examples

Ironically, when a group of intrusion detection researchers gathered in 1993 to review the state of operating system vulnerabilities, we found that the list of security vulnerabilities in UNIX operating systems was virtually identical to those listed in RISOS! Despite 20 years of advances in operating systems, the problems remained the same.[2]

Stack Smashing

Let's take a closer look at how one of these vulnerabilities is exercised. One of the most common problems exploited by system attackers is that of buffer overflow (or "violable prohibition/limit," the sixth problem category in the RISOS report). In C programming slang, exploiting this vulnerability by overwriting the end of a dynamic auto array is called "smashing the stack."

This attack works thanks to several structural attributes of computer processes. These attributes include the stack, which is a block of contiguous memory used to implement procedure calls and returns, a critical concept of structured programming in high-level languages. The stack—a last in, first out (LIFO) data structure as shown in Figure 8.1— keeps track of the location of the instruction following the procedure call so that control of the program can pass back to that instruction. The stack is also used to dynamically allocate local variables and to handle parameters passed to and values returned from the procedures.

Because the stack serves to manage the orderly return of program control from procedure calls, corrupting the stack can cause the system to return to a random address. Attackers use this feature to induce the system to execute arbitrary code. In a stack-smashing attack, the attacker crafts a character string that overwrites the buffer so that the contents of the frame pointer and return pointer fields are overwritten with alternate values. These alternate values, in turn, cause the system to execute a command. (For instance, the shell command is a common entry in attacks.)

Figure 8.1   System Stack Format

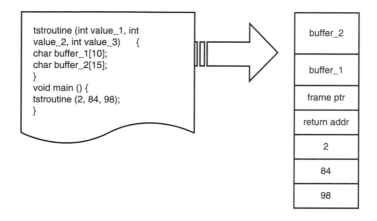

This ability to execute commands at will is especially significant if we consider it in the context of privilege management in UNIX and other systems that allow running processes to take on superuser privilege to perform critical tasks. For instance, sendmail must have write access to private mail directories and files for all users on a system; hence it requires root privilege to do its job. If an attacker targets sendmail with a buffer overflow attack in which a shell is spawned, the shell will take on the privilege level of sendmail, root. The attacker therefore takes control of the system with root privilege and is at liberty to access everything on the system.[3]

Race Conditions

Another common vulnerability is the *race* condition, a problem that falls within RISOS category 4. One instance of race condition occurs when a timing window exists between the time an attribute is checked and the time it is actually used. A trivial (but consistent) example of this error occurs when a program contains a call to the function access() followed by an open() operation.

A recent example of this problem occurred in the print daemon (printd) for Sun's Solaris operating system (version 2.6). When printd is used to print a large file, it creates a lock file in the directory /tmp. To exploit the race condition, an adversary creates a symbolic link to the printd /tmp lock file, pointing toward a system file or other file that the adversary wants to create or modify. The adversary then invokes printd to print a large file.

When printd is finished, the file to which the symbolic link is pointing contains the print daemon's process ID and has permissions of 640 (owner readable and writable, group readable, no read or write access to the world).

A second exploitation of this vulnerability allows an adversary to print a file for which he or she has no read access. In this exploit, the adversary creates a symbolic link to the file printed before the print queue is flushed. After printing commences, the print daemon queuing mechanism does not check the access permissions associated with the file being printed, thereby allowing the adversary to feed the print daemon additional files.[4]

8.1.1.3 Research

A great deal of security research has explored schemes for classifying and organizing system vulnerability information so that the security community could better understand the nature of security vulnerabilities. In addition, an active research community is exploring ways to spot problems in design and development, in hopes that future operating systems and applications software will contain fewer vulnerabilities. You can find more information about past research efforts in Appendix B, "Bibliography," and about ongoing efforts in Appendix C, "Resources."

8.1.2 Problems in Management

Even in a world where vendors produced stable, reliable software, information security would still be an active area. For even the best of machines are fielded in system environments with huge ranges of physical, personnel, and organizational goals and behaviors. Vendors can provide very little in the way of protection that cannot be undone by user error or willful noncompliance with policy.

Some of these problems arise when organizational needs collide at security control points. A classic example occurs at system firewalls, where best current security practices clearly dictate a policy of disabling all connections, enabling each one only as needs require. Best network administration practices, however, indicate that network hardware should be configured to optimize network bandwidth, blocking traffic only when absolutely necessary. Which is correct? One can't make any hard and fast determination because both the security management and the network management personnel are correct. In such situations, only local business management can make the final decision, which might call for a more formal decision process—risk analysis.

This scenario of conflicting but legitimate needs is not typical of problems in this section. I focus here on systematic errors that are a result of oversights and omissions in managing security in systems.

8.1.2.1. Absence of Security Management Infrastructure

The most extreme case of problems arising from mismanagement of systems is the total omission of security: no security policy, no procedures or guidelines, no requirement for security at any level of the organization. This situation is still quite common, especially in small organizations. In larger organizations, it is pointless to proceed with installation of intrusion detection systems in this situation. Even if a company realizes some improvement in security related to the intrusion detection systems, it's of questionable duration and significance without a security policy and other protections. Also, as noted in Chapter 11, "For Strategists," there is a Zen to building a security infrastructure for an organization, and installation of intrusion detection is not the first step of the construction process!

8.1.2.2 Failure to Ship/Correct Default System Configurations

Probably the most common class of security problems occurs when vendors ship operating systems and software to customers with configurations that disable access restrictions. This situation occurs when default permissions on critical system files are set to allow any user to access or worse yet, modify them. Another common scenario occurs when password files or other files containing identification and authentication information are configured to allow anyone to access, download, or modify them. The history of computer security is peppered with examples of systems shipped with security mechanisms (such as password challenges) disabled or default accounts and passwords included in the system password files. The severity of this problem has led to the formation of organizations dedicated to lobbying software vendors for more conservative, security-sparing default configurations in shipped systems.

8.1.2.3 Failure to Coordinate Components of Protection Scheme

A common problem associated with system management is that of administrators installing protective mechanisms but configuring them in ways that nullify their protective effect. Another instance of this problem is the failure to coordinate protection features when multiple mechanisms protect a network of interest. Examples include the following situations:

- Password files for firewalls or intrusion detection systems are stored so that they are remotely accessible and therefore subject to password cracking attacks.

- Encryption software is installed, but secret keys are kept in world-readable files or directories.

- Intrusion detection system or firewalls are installed on operating systems that have not been scanned for vulnerabilities.

- Protection mechanisms are configured for remote access and control by clients that have weak or no authentication.

- Encryption software encrypts information sources critical to an intrusion detection system, and the intrusion detection system is unable to decrypt the information.

Designers of a security protection infrastructure must consider the interactions and dependencies on a system-wide basis. Furthermore, any security infrastructure should be subjected to thorough testing and periodic security audits.

8.1.2.4　*Failure to Adequately Train Personnel*

An often neglected part of security practice is the training of personnel. Training of technical personnel in security is especially critical, given the fact that few computer scientists and engineers receive any exposure whatsoever to computer security in their formal education. Furthermore, many of those who do receive college-level training in computer security receive exposure to a small subset of the requisite topics—usually cryptography and the Trusted System Criteria (Rainbow) series from the National Computer Security Center. Every new wave of technological advances requires additional training to enable technical personnel to keep up with associated security challenges.

Users also require training, both awareness training (to sensitize them to the need for security and to gain their support) as well as policy training in which they learn the security-related procedures and practices required by organizations. Problems have resulted from the failure to train users to properly protect authentication tokens (such as smart cards) and information (such as passwords). Social engineering attacks (adversaries deceiving users into giving them critical information or access) are still common, and awareness training plus strong policy are the only ways of dealing with this category of problem. Training also serves to inform users that protections are in place on your network. This knowledge can discourage insider abuse if the potential abuser perceives a high risk of detection and subsequent punishment for such activity.

8.1.2.5　*Human Error in Managing Systems*

Another problem area in security management is that of human error. In this case, the user or administrator is well trained, is working from a current security policy, is knowledgeable about the system and organization, and simply makes a mistake. For instance, in setting up permissions for a new user directory, the administrator may inadvertently type the wrong group number or name for the user, granting that user greater privilege than is suitable. A user may forget to encrypt a critical file before sending it to others. A user, called away from his or her desk during an emergency, may neglect to log out of a corporate network or database. These errors are a normal part of life, and although they create very real security problems, they will likely continue.

8.1.2.6   Intrusion Detection and Management Problems

There is some good news regarding the problems in this category. Intrusion detection and vulnerability assessment tools represent a reliable means of diagnosing and correcting problems associated with system misconfiguration and human error. These tools allow a system manager to deal with this common category of problems, taking corrective action before an adversary exploits these weaknesses to launch an attack.

8.1.3   Problems in Trust

A third category of root causes for security problems addresses the very essence of security. These vulnerabilities result from trust assumptions that are not intrinsically incorrect, just inappropriate for the environment at hand. Consider a physical analogy.

When you visit a foreign city for the first time, you may be very suspicious of your environment. Depending on the number of people around, the way in which those people act, and the news reports about crime in the area, you might not be willing to take a midnight stroll in the neighborhood. If you stay in a hotel room in that city, you may demand a strong door lock or window bars to protect you from intruders. You may decide not to wear flashy jewelry in public. In extreme cases, you may carry a weapon or hire a body-guard. When you do venture out, you may monitor your environment constantly, looking for signs of impending trouble.

Now how would this decision process be affected if you could neither see nor hear? What if you were unable to gain any information about the trustworthiness of the environment? Would you be more conservative, maybe even to the extent of refusing to visit a new city? Would you take more precautions?

Many users of the Internet face this situation. They are in a setting where a great deal of activity takes place, much of it transparent to them. (Although they realize that they are connected to the Internet, they fail to realize that the Internet is connected to them!) Furthermore, there is often no basis for judging the appropriate level of trust one should invest in the environment. Many generalize their physical environment to the network: If I access the network from the comfort of my home or office in small town America, why would I consider the network to be more dangerous than my immediate surroundings? This belief is a common misperception and a disastrous one at that.

The third category of security problem, problems of trust, does not result from flaws in the systems or management of the systems per se; rather this problem is a result of a difference between the trust assumptions held by many network users and the trustworthiness of the network environment. This problem spans the entire system from initial requirements to common use.

8.1.3.1 Roots of Trust Issues

Much of the Internet was designed with trust assumptions that were perfectly appropriate for a research network with limited physical access. The early Internet had a limited number of users, many with common interests and goals. Early users of the Internet and Usenet speak wistfully of a close-knit community where newsgroups on Usenet gathered for parties, and close personal and professional alliances were forged within this environment of trust.

This trust environment, when added to the original goals of the Internet Protocol (which gave priority to robustness of the network, not security or control) yields some of the most profound network security problems of the current era. These problems arise when the protocol assumes trustworthiness of network hosts when no basis for that assumption exists. Similar issues arise when considering the trustworthiness of other system components, be they data objects or users.

8.1.3.2 Personnel Trust and Security Perimeters

One subset of this category is associated with the personnel dealing with your system. The notion of defining a security perimeter for your system is addressed in Chapter 2, "Concepts and Definitions," as part of the fundamental concepts of security. When considering the management of security in operational environments, this perimeter must be drawn to include the user as part of the system. Furthermore, the level of threat represented by those users must be controlled. Controlling the level of threat does not mean that security requirements should represent a computing handicap to the users. It does mean, however, that all users should be governed by appropriate use and security policies. Enforcement of these policies should be supported with mechanisms, such as strong identification and authentication, monitoring, intrusion detection, and access control.

8.1.3.3 Network Interhost Trust Issues

Many operating systems designed to support network operations have features that establish trust relationships between hosts on a network. These trust relationships, driven in many cases by host tables in the file systems, allow carte blanche access to one system from another, based on whether a user has accounts under the same username on both systems. This practice is particularly worrisome because this access is allowed without a password challenge!

This concept of interhost trust can also be extended to provide the same capabilities between a particular user and the operating system. If the user is listed as a trusted user, she or he can log into the system without a password. Furthermore, the trust extended to a user or host is transitive: If you trust host abc, and host abc trusts systems def, ghi, and jkl, then you also trust def, ghi, and jkl! The files associated with these trust mechanisms include the UNIX .hosts.equiv, .rhosts, and .shosts files.

The problems associated with this extension of trust and associated privilege are amplified by the fact that most implementations of this scheme make decisions regarding trust on the basis of a system's IP address or name. As discussed before, IP addresses and system names require additional strong authentication mechanisms to be trustworthy.

Another common attack enabled by interhost trust relationships is the IP spoofing attack. In this attack, an adversary sends packets from a host pretending to come from another IP address identified as a trusted host to the target system. The target system allows the adversary access without requiring a password or any other authentication. Firewalls are helpful for controlling this sort of risk because they can block connections coming from the Internet that spoof trusted internal IP addresses.

8.1.3.4 Protocols and Trust Issues

Network and cryptographic protocols have been the source of many vulnerabilities thanks to trust assumptions gone awry. Several examples of these problems exist in the Internet Protocols. For instance, the protocol assumes that legitimate users will not attack the fabric of the network infrastructure itself. This belief leads to a plethora of current network vulnerabilities and attacks. Some examples of these, with the corresponding problems in trust assumptions are as follows:

- IP is subject to eavesdropping (network sniffer) attacks in which the contents of network communications are readable by other than the sender and recipient. Trust assumption: No protection of packet contents is necessary because those other than the intended destination can be trusted not to read a message.

- Domain Name Service (DNS) is subject to many attacks ranging from DNS flooding (in which an adversary floods a client system with numerous invalid DNS responses, leading the client to accept a false name service response to the DNS lookup) to spoofed DNS servers (in which an adversary runs a DNS server that provides invalid information in response to client lookup requests). Trust assumption: DNS provides trustworthy mapping of IP addresses to names. Secondary trust assumption (bonus headache!): IP addresses or hostnames provided by DNS are suitable bases for authentication.

- Routing Internet Protocol (RIP) is used by Internet gateways to publish information about new gateways and networks. In many implementations, RIP trusts information that affects the routing of IP packets, regardless of the source or validity of that routing information. This condition can lead to the "black hole" network denial-of-service attack in which a rogue router broadcasts a false message asserting that it provides the shortest route to all destinations. The result is a scenario in which all packets for a portion of the network are sent to this router, which then drops all the packets. Another attack enabled by this vulnerability is a network eavesdropping attack in which packets are routed through a network segment on which a packet sniffer is running. Trust assumption: Any RIP packet is by default considered trustworthy.

8.1.3.5   *Using Intrusion Detection for Metering Trust*

You've probably noted by now that problems in this category are more subjective than those in the other two. Some instances here, especially those problems involving network trust models and protocols, can be handled by perimeter protections, such as firewalls. The rest require more finesse.

As in the physical world, operating in an environment sheltered enough to support liberal trust relationships between entities is often more efficient than operating in settings that require greater levels of suspicion. However, also as in the physical world, when the environment is hostile, utilizing sound practices and technologies to prevent attacks is much more efficient than razing and rebuilding structures every time attackers inflict damage. Furthermore, environmental threat and demand for availability is dynamic. This characteristic makes the task of balancing protection against availability a challenge to even the most expert security administrators.

The key to handling problems that fall in this category is policy. Predefining security goals enables security managers to define a security-sparing way of dealing with trust issues. Policy allows management to direct users to modify their usage patterns. Security tools and technologies such as firewalls and intrusion detection systems can put teeth into these directives by blocking violations and measuring compliance.

Intrusion detection systems can help. They give administrators capabilities to apply policies, test user compliance levels with these policies, and define specific scenarios that require intervention. In some cases, intrusion detection systems also allow administrators to automate that intervention. Managing these capabilities from a central location allows a security administrator to flex the security mechanisms according to organizational needs, responding to problem situations as they arise.

8.2   Through a Hacker's Eyes

If you ask system professionals why network security measures are necessary, most will answer, "To protect against hackers." Hackers spend a great deal of time and energy exploring systems and networks, searching for ways of penetrating system defenses, often utilizing the access they gain to disastrous effect. News accounts of hacker exploits are routine, with many government, corporate, and organizational systems on the list of sites taken out of commission for days, even weeks. Although one still sees hackers celebrated as evil geniuses, that perception is changing as the list of victims grows longer and the damage associated with the attacks becomes more indiscriminate.

Note

In this book, I use the term hacker to describe those who engage in system intrusion and other violations of security protections. I agree that the label has been unfairly corrupted from the original hacker community, whose members were notable for their bold innovation and exploration of emergent technology. However, the use of cracker as an alternative label has never been widely accepted.

If you are charged with protecting a system, understanding the approach intruders take as they carry out an attack can sometimes be helpful. This knowledge is valuable for a number of reasons.

- It enables you to spot certain activity patterns as they happen, recognizing the elements of an attack.

- It enables you to look at your systems proactively before the attacker gets to them, correcting vulnerabilities that would be found by any attacker searching your site.

- It gives you the insight necessary to make good decisions about protection strategies. Numerous products are marketed for the purpose of protecting systems. Some are a better fit for your environment than others.

- It enables you to make wiser decisions in managing your systems and your users. Security management is a constant balancing act between accommodating needs for access and honoring needs for protection. A knowledge of the threat from one attempting to attack your system gives you a better sense of the impact of tightening or loosening security stances.

8.2.1   Identifying a Victim

The first step in a system hack is to decide which system to attack. Two major attack motivations become apparent at this stage of the attack. In the first, the motivation is entertainment or challenge, and the victim selection is almost random. Here the attacker (or a group of cooperating attackers) might use vulnerability scanners to search part of the IP address space, recording hosts that have security vulnerabilities. A subset of this process involves the use of *war dialer* software to identify dial-up network connections. War dialers sequentially dial ranges or lists of telephone numbers, noting those that are connected to modems.

The second motivation for selecting a hacking target is self-aggrandizement or other tangible incentives (including intellectual property theft and discovery of sensitive information). Here the targeting of the victim is much more focused, with the attacker gaining knowledge of the victim system through research and information collection. This is usually followed by a more deliberate search and seizure of the desired information.

The motivation for targeting your site can include the following:

- You may be in business competition with the hacker or an entity that has employed that hacker.

- The hacker may have some personal interest in your site, for example, a relative who is an employee of your firm, or a fascination with a product your organization produces.

- Your site may have an odd or amusing domain name.

- Your site may have received press coverage.

- Your organization may be involved in a political or ideological matter of interest to the hacker.

8.2.2 Casing the Joint

Once the target of the hack is identified, the hacker determines the goal of the attack. In cases where a particular site has been identified as the target, this determination is likely to include collecting information about the system. The information can come from the InterNIC and other public sources and can include items such as the system platforms (both hardware and operating system), personnel involved in the management of the system, telephone numbers, MX records, registered servers, and other information. If the attacker hasn't done it already, he or she may run a vulnerability assessment tool against the site, recording the results.

8.2.3 Gaining Access

With the victim selected and sufficient information gathered to identify possible approaches to attacking the site, the attention of the attacker is likely to shift to gaining access to a site system. In many cases the vulnerability assessment tool run as part of casing the site has identified a vulnerability that allows the attacker to log on. In cases where no vulnerabilities were found, the hacker has several options.

The attacker could utilize social engineering techniques for gaining entry. This approach consists of steps such as making telephone calls to users, pretending to be system maintenance or network management personnel, asking for passwords or information. Another option is to introduce a trojan horse into the system, accomplished by duping an unwitting authorized user into installing the trojan horse by including it on a disk or network download containing data or software, or by sending it as an email attachment.

Should these measures fail, the next step depends on the determination and expertise levels of the attacker. If both are high, he or she is likely to undertake a more systematic, rigorous, analysis of the target system. For instance, the hacker might review all the system documentation, searching for known problems. If the operating system or applications source code is available, she or he might search it for vulnerabilities. If the attacker has a system on which to test possible attacks, he or she might construct several test attacks, checking to see whether any were indeed successful.

Once an avenue into the system is isolated, the final item in the strategy is to determine the timing of the attack. Many attackers time attacks for late night or early morning when they believe that no one is likely to be using the system. As globalization of organizations with time zone differences has increased the possibility that someone will be utilizing the system at almost any time, day or night, off-hours timing might not be as feasible as before. In any event, some attackers target attacks for peak hours so that their activity will blend into the "noise floor" of other system activity.

8.2.4 Executing the Attack

After the strategy is set, it's time to actually execute the attack. Some attackers, utilizing intrusion scripts and other process optimizations, are able to launch a targeted attack and then cover their tracks in a matter of minutes, even seconds. Others, who wish to take a more leisurely approach, might watch the system activities, waiting until the system has no other users logged on to proceed. On UNIX systems in which the finger daemon is enabled, executing a finger command with the name of the targeted system ("finger@targetedhost.com") returns a list of current users who are logged on the system.

When the attacker determines that the coast is clear, she or he will actually use an intrusion script or "borrowed" userIDs and passwords to log on to the machine. Depending on the privilege level of the account, the attacker might be in the system with user privilege. In this case, the attacker may utilize additional hacker tools to "break root," gaining superuser privilege, which will provide carte blanche access to the entire system.

8.2.4.1   Installing a Back Door

The first thing that some hackers do after they have entered the machine as superuser is install back doors, system utilities equipped with custom vulnerabilities that allow the hacker to access the machine at a later time. More expert hackers import precompiled system trojan horses with back doors, devised so that the file statistics do not differ from the original system binaries. Furthermore, the transfer of these trojan horses may be done with remote commands that are not logged by the system.

Part of this step can include installing "trojaned" versions of critical system binaries that log information about system processes and network connections. These binaries are altered to hide the presence of the attacker.

In systems where remote access is enabled (by placing entries in the .rhosts file), the attacker may alter the .rhosts file to allow access to the system, using remote shell commands.

Looking Around

When the ability to reenter is established, depending upon the motive of the intruder, the next step might be to explore the system. This phase can be leisurely or even clueless as in the case of the "script kiddie" (novice) hackers. Many early security-incident handlers have stories of monitoring sophisticated intrusions only to find the attacker attempting to execute inappropriate commands on the hacked system (such as entering dir, a DOS command on a UNIX system!).

The activities of the attacker at this point can range from relatively benign searches of the various systems on the network to devastating destruction or corruption of critical systems and data. Another common behavior is to use the current system as a platform for launching an attack on another organization. In one case in the mid-1990s (covered in more detail in Chapter 9 "Legal Issues"), a U.S. Air Force team watched in horror as a hacker used their system as a platform for attacking a system belonging to the South Korean Atomic Energy Research Institute. The political implications of such an attack being noted by the victim system's administrators are grave. Regardless of political sensitivities, the issue of downstream liability is of major concern to many in the network security field. I explore this topic in greater detail in Chapter 9, "Legal Issues."

One activity that has been noted while monitoring attacks is the cyber equivalent of looking over one's shoulder. This activity involves frequently invoking commands such as who and ps, searching for signs that the attacker has been noticed. Several early signature-based systems noted this activity pattern (nicknamed "paranoia") and included it as a signature of attack.

Collecting the Goods

A hacker can cash in on a successful intrusion in various ways. Here are typical payoffs:

- Password or other authentication files, especially those metering access to other systems

- Customer databases, especially those with credit card or other charge code information

- Email files

- Source code or other intellectual property

- Business records that might be of use to competitors

A common method intruders use to transport information out of systems is to establish a hidden file (beginning with a period so that a `list` command does not show the file) or directory, copy the information to that hidden repository, and then utilize one of the back doors to transfer the information out of the enclave at a later time. Incident handlers have also reported that intruders often use encryption to obscure the files.

8.2.4.2 Covering Tracks

Obscuring the evidence associated with the attack is a critical part of most attack strategies. Attackers have two separate sets of concerns:

- Covering those tracks that might lead a victim or investigator back to the attacker

- Eliminating evidence internal to the system indicating that the attack occurred

Path of Attack

Hackers usually use one or more of the following techniques to cover the trail establishing accountability for the attack. The "standard issue" hacker will use the following techniques to cover their real network addresses:

- Network hopping through compromised hosts using `telnet` or `rsh`. Some use the hacker tool `telnet gateway` that uses a single UNIX socket and a nonstandard port to provide `telnet` connections that are difficult to monitor. Many hackers deliberately include a host located in a foreign country as they network hop, in hopes of being perceived as having come from a country in which hacking is not considered criminal activity.

- Hopping through LAN hosts using WinGate (a popular software package that allows multiple systems to share a single dial-up network connection).

- Using IP-spoofing software to change the source IP address associated with the connection.

A second group of hackers, who are also proficient in phreaking (hacking telephone switches and exchanges), may also use these additional techniques:

- Using toll-free (1-800) lines to connect to ISPs by hacking private branch exchanges (PBXs) equipped with direct inward system access (DISA). DISA allows authorized personnel to call in on toll-free lines and then make outgoing toll calls that are billed to the PBX.

- Using modem dial-up connections to intersperse telephone system connections with Internet connections.

Because few law enforcement and incident investigators have successfully established a means of tracing connections that use both the Internet and the public switched telephone network, hackers who use these techniques are extremely difficult to trace back. Furthermore, because the toll-free numbers allow global connections, the hackers can access the ISP from anywhere in the world.

Evidence of Attack

Eliminating evidence that the hacker ever accessed the system is a common subject of discussion in the hacker community. Here are techniques hackers use to eliminate evidence:

- Wiping evidence of the hacker from the /etc/utmp file (which supports the who command). The two most commonly used hacker tools for removing evidence from this file are zap and z2.

- Wiping evidence of the hacker's connections from the /var/adm log files. Hacker sources recommend the simple editor pico or modifying the log files.

- Wiping evidence of the hacker's presence from the lastlog, /etc/utmp, and /etc/wtmp logs. This process uses lled (lastlog editor) and wted (wtmp/utmp editor).

- Wiping evidence of the hacker's presence or identity (userID) from the event logs of a Windows NT system.

- Wiping out the history file.

The hacker tools cloak and hide automate these processes for victim systems running UNIX.

8.2.4.3 Publicizing the Result

For some hackers, especially those operating as part of a group, the final step in an attack is publicizing the exploit to others. This step is more likely to occur if

- Your site has high name recognition (such as a popular e-commerce site, a major newspaper, or a government agency).

- The attacker is a juvenile, or otherwise not subject to criminal prosecution for the offense.

This publicity and resulting notoriety are often considered part of the motivation for the hack. If the hacker is a professional who was compensated for taking intellectual property or other sensitive information from your site, you will probably never see this stage of the attack.

8.2.4.4 Studying Predator and Prey

As you encounter and deal with intrusions in your environment, you may see many variations on the themes presented in this section. My point in presenting this information is that your ability to understand the goals of intrusion detection and the suitability of various monitoring and detection strategies depends on your understanding of the threats you hope to counter. Although I repeatedly make the point that the ability to hack a system doesn't necessarily indicate a similar ability to protect the system, those who can best protect the system do understand how an attacker approaches the system. Only by studying the tradecraft of your adversary can you shift the balance of power in your favor. Knowledge is the key to changing your role in this relationship from prey to predator.

8.3   Security versus Traditional Engineering

In some ways the design and development of security tools and techniques is an engineering specialty. However, significant differences exist between classic engineering practice and security engineering. In this section I outline some of those differences. *Engineering* is defined as "the application of science and mathematics by which the properties of matter and the sources of energy in nature are made useful to people."[5]

8.3.1   Traditional Engineering

Engineering principles allow us to design products and processes that do useful things. The value associated with those products and processes is measured by the things that they do and how well they do them. Typical engineering goals include reliability, resistance to failure, consistent quality, and optimal performance.

8.3.2   Security Engineering

Security engineering is different from traditional engineering. For instance, whereas traditional engineering values products according to what they do, security engineering values them for the things they prevent or block. Traditional engineering involves making things work. Security engineering attempts to itemize all the things that make things fail and then prevent those failures. Traditional engineering tries to assure that things continue to work in the face of random faults. Security engineering attempts to assure that things continue to work despite the best efforts of a dedicated, knowledgeable, and persistent adversary with the advantage of knowing exactly how to optimize the attack.

Ross Anderson and Roger Needham point out that the challenges of security engineering are those of "programming a computer which gives answers that are subtly and maliciously wrong at the most inconvenient possible moment."[6] In essence a designer must assume that the computer is under the control of an intelligent and malicious opponent.

8.3.3   Rules of Thumb

Does security engineering sound even more hopeless to you than managing the all too chaotic world of system security? Some of the work of exploring security engineering was done originally to explore problems in cryptographic protocols. Fortunately, some of the findings are also helpful to those dealing with network security products.

Two approaches are helpful in dealing with the black art of designing robust security systems. Formal methods can be helpful in identifying problems early on and can help structure sanity checks of systems in a fashion that allows you to spot trouble early and correct it. However, many systems and functions are simply too complex for current formal methods to characterize. In this case, rules of thumb that provide guidance toward good practice are helpful in that they help us tune our intuitions. The key concept is explicitness: As intrusion detection system designers, we should be explicit about our starting assumptions and goals, as well as those vulnerabilities that can be used in an attack on our systems. In records and profiles, we should be explicit about subjects and objects, shooting for unique identifiers for each. (For instance, information sources should include full pathnames for files and should use a user identification scheme that binds a userID to the system on which the userID resides.)

Another critical rule of thumb is redundancy. In other words, if information sources are key to monitoring a critical system, we should have multiple monitoring points with a good bit of overlap. This practice addresses the risk of an attacker disabling the information sources as a first step of an attack. Similarly, because temporal order and binding to audit records is important in the information source, measures should be taken to protect the clock from which the audit event time stamps are derived.

8.4   Rules for Intrusion Detection Systems

As in other dynamic protection schemes, intrusion detection involves a balancing act between security and availability. Because several special conditions apply to intrusion detection systems, both designers and users need to understand the issues that apply to this technology.

Carrying forward the ideas regarding security engineering, additional assumptions must be brought to bear when considering intrusion detection.

- The system will function in a hostile environment. Because evading detection and erasing evidence of activities is integral to hacker tradecraft, we must assume that any intrusion detection system will be subject to attack itself.

- The system must run on a platform that itself is trustworthy. Any system on which a security product is to run should be subjected to the maximum level of protection afforded in the organizational systems complex. Critical services (such as the system clock) should be hardened, too.

- The information sources on which the system relies must be reliable, redundant, and difficult to alter. As in other systems areas, "garbage in, garbage out" applies. Many successful detection cases have demonstrated the value of running extra, unpublished logging mechanisms. Running multiple logging mechanisms and then comparing the outputs is a reliable way of spotting problems. When the information sources are ubiquitous and distributed (as in agent-based approaches), crypto heartbeat functions should be utilized to note failed agents and to mitigate the possibility of an adversary attacking an agent and then spoofing its input to distort the results of the detector.

- The operation of the system, the management of its environment, and the veracity of its findings will be subject to legal challenge. To utilize the system for one of its most important functions, supporting legal remedies or else defending the organization from groundless accusations of wrongdoing, the system must be operated so that it can withstand a cross-examination in a court of law by a hostile adversary. This topic will be explored in more detail in Chapter 9.

- If the system is difficult to manage or run securely, users will allow it to be neither managed nor run securely. This fact should be considered in both system design and organizational policy. Administrators should have clear directions on how to set up and operate the intrusion detection capability for the organization.

- The intrusion detection system should itself be audited, with event records generated as a part of normal operations. In some environments where multiple intrusion detection systems exist, a single system should be assigned the task of monitoring the operation of the other systems, with organizational policy and practices dictating that failure of a system be treated as a critical systems attack.

- The system must be operated in compliance with the law. Given the amount and quality of information that intrusion detection systems collect and analyze, many laws regulate the handling of monitored information. Violation of these statutes can result in criminal or civil penalties for your organization or worse yet, you or other users of the system! Furthermore, as the results of intrusion detection often provide definitive records of security violations, the results should be generated and protected in a fashion that protects the legal admissibility of the evidence in a court of law. I discuss these legal requirements in Chapter 9.

- The system will fail—it should be designed and run in a configuration that allows it to fail gracefully with quick recovery. Computer systems, although they can be quite reliable, are not perfect. Security devices must be designed to fail in a security-sparing fashion (that is, no fail-open designs) with minimal impact on the rest of the security infrastructure. They should also have good diagnostics that can help isolate the cause of the failure; and quick, reliable recovery and restoration to service.

8.5 Conclusion

In this chapter, I've explored the roots of the challenges intrusion detection designers and users must meet. These challenges range from the root causes of security problems to the hacker threat. I also discussed the Zen of security engineering, which is different from traditional engineering practice. An understanding of these issues will allow you to better understand what features are needed as a part of intrusion detection and why.

Endnotes

1. Abbott, R. P., E. H. Spafford, D. Farmer, D. Bailey. "Security Analysis and Enhancements of Computer Operating Systems." Technical report NBSIR 76-1041, Institute for Computer Science and Technology, National Bureau of Standards, 1976.

2. Abbott, R. P., et al. "System Vulnerabilities." Panel Discussion, Second Experts' Workshop on Computer Misuse and Anomaly Detection, Davis, CA, September 1993.

3. Aleph One. "Smashing the Stack for Fun and Profit." Phrack, 7:49, 1997, available from `http://www.securityfocus.com`.

4. Silicosis. "Solaris printd Security Vulnerability." L0pht Security Advisory, L0pht Heavy Industries, February 1998, available from `http://www.l0pht.com/advisories/printd26.txt`.

5. *Merriam-Webster's Collegiate Dictionary, Tenth Edition*. Merriam-Webster, Incorporated, sv "engineering." 1998.

6. Anderson, R. and R. Needham. "Programming Satan's Computer." *Computer Science Today*, Springer LNCS v 1000: 426–441.

Legal Issues

In 1992, during my stint as a government research manager, I sponsored a workshop for intrusion detection researchers. The first of the workshops was held at the University of California, Davis, and featured a cast of experts drawn from areas that had direct bearing on intrusion detection systems. This included experts in system vulnerabilities (because during this time members of the computer security community refused to divulge actual vulnerabilities or attack information to each other). We also had experts in a variety of advanced analysis and computing topics, ranging from signals processing to machine learning.

On a whim, I proposed including a session dealing with legal issues associated with intrusion detection and monitoring. The program committee for the workshop debated whether to include a non-technical topic in the program, ultimately agreeing to add the topic in hopes that it might be a welcome break from the heavy technical content of the rest of the workshop.

We invited the head of the then recently formed Computer Crime Division of the U.S. Department of Justice, Scott Charney, to the workshop. Charney, a seasoned federal prosecutor with a good understanding of computing technologies, presented information on the current computer-related statutes and how they affected intrusion detection systems. That presentation, and the ensuing discussions, was rated by the workshop participants as the most valuable of the entire workshop.

A significant number of the workshop participants went home and changed the way they administered their systems, affixing legal login banners and warnings to their user interfaces. Perhaps more important, members of the community continued to work with the Justice Department and other law enforcement agencies to develop computer crime and fraud statutes that allowed systems administrators to monitor and use intrusion detection to protect their systems. The legal issues session was included in subsequent intrusion detection workshops and remained one of the most popular events of the series.

Intrusion detection systems represent an important part of the operational security management infrastructure because they often provide the first notification to users that their systems have been attacked. Because intrusion detection systems also handle and interpret many of the artifacts of the attack, they are also critical to the steps that customers take in the wake of the attack, namely, investigation and resolution. For attacks involving loss of information or significant financial damage, criminal and civil legal remedies may be appropriate reactions. In this chapter, I discuss a few of the legal issues that affect the design, development, and operation of intrusion detection systems.

Disclaimer

The author is not a lawyer, nor does she claim to be a legal expert. By raising certain legal issues for discussion involving legal considerations and potential legal consequences, the author is not in any way providing the reader or anyone else with legal advice. If this chapter succeeds in its limited purpose, that is, to identify certain legal standards, restraints, and some examples as applied, which can come into play when computer security is being considered, it will better enable the reader to formulate appropriate questions for his or her lawyer.

You should consult with a lawyer for legal advice concerning the issues introduced and discussed herein. Although in the past, computer security professionals have often been called upon to fend for their own legal rights, the author believes that this honeymoon is over! Computer security professionals should study the legal statutes referred to in this chapter and reach their own conclusions as to what they mean. In this undertaking, the best source of legal advice is a good lawyer. The interplay of law and technology is steadily accelerating, and that interplay involves complex technologies that are themselves changing rapidly. This situation requires continuous legal advice from competent counsel to avoid liability or costly litigation based on alleged negligence, invasion of privacy, or the violation of any rights or property interests of users or third parties.

Therefore the publisher and the author disclaim any liability for damages, direct or indirect, attributable to any discussions contained in this book.

9.1 Law for Geeks

Access logs and system files may constitute evidence in legal proceedings. Furthermore, the outputs (reports) of intrusion detection systems may also be required as evidence. Because an aggressive legal process allows victims of intrusions to halt further intrusions at the source, this goal of providing persuasive evidence to support legal action is an important one.

Certain legal statutes also limit the activities that system managers can use to protect their systems. These limitations should be reflected in the features and options provided by intrusion detection systems. This means that anyone working on or with intrusion detection systems should have a knowledge of the legal provisions that affect them.

In this section, I discuss some of the principles of legal systems, focusing on those factors that should be taken into consideration in designing and using intrusion detection systems. Because much of the referenced activity has taken place in the United States and Great Britain, the focus of these discussions is on legal process in these countries. However, where possible, I include information that applies to other legal systems also.

9.1.1 Legal Systems

Most of the world's legal systems fall into three general categories: civil, common, and Islamic law.

9.1.1.1 Civil Law

Civil law, which was inspired by old Roman law, is based on the principle of codified law. Laws are written into a collection, codified, and not determined, as in common law, by judges. Citizens have an accessible and written collection of the laws, and judges must follow these laws.[1]

Civil law countries operate on legal principles of free introduction and free evaluation of evidence. The process in these countries is investigative, as opposed to adversarial in common law countries. In civil law countries, the judge can consider all types of evidence and then decide whether they are trustworthy and/or relevant.[2]

9.1.1.2 Common Law

Common law, the legal system in force in England, Canada, and the United States, is law that is "made by judges." The law exists on the basis of historical legal precedents that have evolved over hundreds of years. To arrive at a judgment, judges are empowered to apply the legal precedents to the facts of a case.[1]

Common law countries operate on legal principles of oral and adversarial procedure. In this system witnesses generally offer information based on their personal knowledge, and their statements can be tested or verified by adversarial cross-examination and coordination or rebuttal by other evidence and other witnesses.[2]

9.1.1.3 Islamic Law

Islamic law, which prevails in countries all over the Middle East and elsewhere, applies to about 20% of the world's population. The basis of the Islamic criminal system is deterrent punishment, and there is no separation of church and state.[1]

In Islamic law countries, computer crimes are considered "taazir" offenses, and rules of evidence are identical to those of civil law. Thus the principles of free introduction and free evaluation of evidence apply.[2]

9.1.2 Legislation

Statutes, which are written by the legislative arm of government, codify the legal rules that define crime or criminal activity. The following statutes are pertinent to intrusion detection and other areas of computer security.

9.1.2.1 Computer Fraud and Abuse Statutes

In the United States, the statute governing computer crime is 18 U.S. Code (USC) 1030, as amended by the National Infrastructure Protection Act of 1996.

The Computer Fraud and Abuse Act, passed by Congress in 1984, defined 18 USC 1030, which criminalizes activities involving unauthorized access to, theft of, or modification of computer systems. The statute was modified in 1994 and again in 1996, in each case extending the description of activity considered illegal and modifying the penalties to adapt to the changing threat environment.

Statute 18 USC 1030 criminalizes certain activities that affect computer systems. These activities include

- Unauthorized access to computer systems

- Theft of the information contained in computer systems

- Unauthorized modifications of the computer system or its contents

The intent of the computer fraud and abuse statute is to allow society to deal with modern threats that cannot be adequately prosecuted under other criminal statutes. For instance, although common law criminal mischief statutes cover damaging property, these statutes do not adequately cover threats such as network worms and macro viruses, which can produce massive damage to systems and information. Furthermore, the statute seeks to accommodate societal shifts driven by the widespread adoption of computer and network technologies, acknowledging that many traditional statutes simply do not apply to modern crimes carried out on computer networks.

The U.S. Department of Justice's Computer Crime and Intellectual Property Section (CCIPS) handles prosecutions of computer-related crime. It publishes legislative analyses of the federal statutes affecting computer crime cases, which offer considerable insight to those who deal with computer crime, such as security managers, systems administrators, information technology (IT) managers, and the lawyers who counsel them. Appendix C, "Resources," lists pointers to the CCIPS Web site, as well as other sources of legal information.

The law governing computer crime is dynamic because it must adapt to the changing threat environment. There have been two major overhauls in the federal computer crime statutes in the last 15 years, and the legislative analyses published by the Department of Justice indicate that this high rate of change is likely to continue as new technologies are introduced and people exploit them for criminal purposes.

Although the computer crime statutes at the federal level are improving, many problems still plague legislation and legal processes.

- Federal statutes are good, but they are not enough. In fact, the vast majority of criminal statutes that affect our daily lives are not federal, but state or local. An expert in state and local computer crime law asserts that well over 90% of all law enforcement and most prosecutable computer crime takes place within the jurisdiction of one or more states.

- Although many states and municipalities are taking on the task of writing state and local computer crime legislation, few are able to provide the resources for enforcing those laws.

- Both state and local judiciary are poorly trained to handle computer crime cases and few have expertise with complex civil litigation involving computer evidence, computer network resources, and valuation of information or services.

- Victims are reluctant to report computer crime, fearing loss of customer trust, bad publicity, expensive loss of system access and staff time, and loss of trade secrets or other intellectual property as part of the discovery or trial process.[3]

9.1.2.2 Electronic Communications Privacy Act

The most important statute that affects how intrusion detection can be done is the Electronic Communications Privacy Act (ECPA), 18 USC s. 2510—the revised federal wiretapping statute. The ECPA strictly regulates the ability of persons to monitor the communications of another party. Section 2 of the act provides an exception for system operators and their employees that allows them to monitor, disclose, or use the communications of users in the normal course of performing system administration or protecting the rights of the service providers. However, this exception doesn't allow a service provider to conduct random monitoring unless it's for the purpose of conducting routine quality control sampling.

The ECPA is complicated, but profoundly affects those responsible for securing computer systems and those building security tools to support them. I delve into particular provisions of this act later.

9.1.3 Civil Litigation/Tort Law

Tort law (also known as *civil litigation*) enables an injured person to obtain compensation from the person who caused the injury. Tort law is, in the tradition of common law, "judge made" law, with decisions based on prior case law. Torts are motivated by the fundamental expectation that people will conduct themselves in a manner that does not injure others. When people cause such injury, be it by negligence or intentional action, the court can require them to pay damages to the injured party.

This is done for two reasons: to allow the person who caused the injury to suffer the pain associated with his or her action and to send a message to the community regarding what is unacceptable conduct, thereby serving as a deterrent to future injury.

9.1.3.1 Tort Law and Computer Security

Some legal experts believe that the current wave of business activity moving to the Internet combined with the increase of damages due to intrusions and other computer crimes will produce a large amount of civil litigation. Certain differences in legal process between criminal and tort law make this outcome likely.

First are the fundamental differences in the nature of proof required for criminal convictions versus damage awards. Criminal proceedings call for proof "beyond a reasonable doubt," reflecting a desire to avoid false imprisonment. Tort action only requires proof "based on the preponderance of evidence." Therefore, in some cases tort action produced awards of damages in situations where criminal action resulted in acquittal. A well-known example of this is the O. J. Simpson civil trial in which a jury found that he was liable for the death of Ronald Goldman and the battery of Nicole Brown Simpson. The jury awarded a sizable judgment to the survivors of Goldman and Brown Simpson, despite the fact that O. J. Simpson had previously been acquitted of murder in a criminal trial.[4]

Second is a reluctance to report computer crime to authorities, because of concerns regarding negative publicity and endangerment of customer and stockholder trust. Furthermore, in those few criminal cases that have been successfully prosecuted so far, sentences have been light, and deterrence effects limited.

Legal experts have pointed out that in the arena of economic crime, criminal proceedings have always been secondary to administrative, regulatory, and civil legal proceedings as the preferred means of conflict resolution among businesses and consumers. Therefore, it is reasonable to expect that this will apply to economic crimes committed over computer networks.

9.1.3.2 Open Season on Service Providers?

Some concerns in the civil liability arena apply to those who deal most with intrusion detection systems: system owners, system administrators, and incident handlers or investigators. The first concern is the possibility of civil litigation targeting those who use intrusion detection systems in an unsuccessful attempt to secure commercial systems. Customers relying on the system being secure and who lose services, access, or intellectual property due to these breaches may seek damages from the system administrators and the system owner.

A second scenario of concern is that of *downstream liability*. This situation involves a system that is not properly secured, which is the target of an intrusion. The intruder then utilizes the system as a platform for attacking a second system, inflicting damages and denial of service. The concern is that the owner of the second system might seek damages from the owner of the first system, asserting that the security problems in the first system enabled the attack on the second system to take place. This case becomes increasingly worrisome when the first and second systems are connected by a trust relationship, such as those that might exist in the context of a strategic partnership. The liability exposure could also apply to situations in which employees use company resources to attack third parties.

A third concern, demonstrated already by a case, is that of system management taking action against a user on the basis of a false positive result from the intrusion detection system. In one case, a customer sued an Internet service provider (ISP) for terminating the customer's service during an alleged spamming incident. The termination of service was based on a false report that the customer was the source of the spamming. The customer claimed business damages due to the mistake and asserted that the ISP did not properly conduct a due diligence investigation before taking the drastic action of terminating access.

9.1.4 Complications in Applying Law to Cyberspace

The application of the law to cyberspace has provoked a great deal of interest from technical experts and legal scholars. The mutability of digital evidence, the time-space warp introduced when utilizing the Internet to conduct business and social transactions, and the complete inability to enforce national borders on the Net are but a few of the issues facing those who would apply traditional legal measures to this network frontier. In this section, I discuss a few issues that can affect the use and function of intrusion detection technologies.

9.1.4.1 Legal Precedents

The rule of law comes into being through two general mechanisms. The first, legislative process, allows the government to make certain rules of law. However, the bulk of the legal rules of society are established by legal precedent and are found in *jurisprudence*, or *case law*.

Legal precedent establishes legal principles by asserting a set of facts, using those facts to reach a certain conclusion, and then instantiating that combination of facts and conclusion as a rule of law to be followed whenever a similar set of facts comes before the court. This system allows the body of legal principles to grow by building on decisions already made. It gives practitioners and citizens some faith that a consistent set of legal solutions is applicable to particular scenarios.

The process of establishing legal precedent for a new set of scenarios takes a great deal of time and resource. Given the relative youth of computer technology and the statutes establishing the legal baselines for this area, the number of cases is still small. The number of cases has been suppressed by the reluctance of victims of computer crime to report their problems to law enforcement and the deficiencies in investigative expertise necessary to establish proof beyond a reasonable doubt. Only time and actual cases carried to judgment and through appeal will provide precedents. Until the body of case law grows, however, we will all suffer from lack of consistency of legal solutions applicable to problems that occur in cyberspace.

9.1.4.2 *Jurisdictional Issues*

Another major issue in applying traditional legal process to cyberspace is that of jurisdiction. Jurisdiction is the definition of a court's judicial authority, usually defined by

- The *territory*—the physical location of the criminal act(s)

- The type of cases—for instance, the jurisdiction of small claims courts is limited to cases asking for damages that do not exceed a particular amount

- The personnel status—for instance, a military court has jurisdiction limited to military personnel

The question of territorial jurisdiction is of great interest when dealing with law in cyberspace. This challenge is colored by questions of *sovereignty*, the principle that dictates that a country is independent and free from outside political authority or control over judicial decisions.

When intruders utilize the Internet to attack systems in another country, they may decide to "jurisdiction shop." That is, they deliberately take a path through a country in which computer crime statutes are lenient or nonexistent, in hopes that the laws of that country will shield them from legal action. This practice makes tracing and apprehending computer criminals much more difficult and makes prosecuting them much more of a challenge. In Section 9.4, I discuss a case in which this situation occurred.

9.1.4.3 *Constitutional Issues*

In the United States, constitutional issues are often associated with investigating and prosecuting computer crime.

The two most often cited amendments in relation to computer intrusions are the First Amendment, the right to free speech, and the Fourth Amendment, the right to be free of unreasonable searches and seizures.

The Fourth Amendment is of particular interest to those in the intrusion detection and investigative realm because it has been interpreted by the courts to strictly limit all searches and seizures unless a warrant has been obtained. Consequently, some or all evidence gained by an unlawful search and seizure in violation of the Fourth Amendment may not be admissible in a court of law.

Constitutional issues that surround the entire process of intrusion detection and investigation of computer crime are subjects of considerable debate. Privacy advocates are critical of many techniques used, citing concerns that monitoring technologies might be used to squelch free speech, that broad-scale monitoring violates the privacy rights of network users, and that tracebacks of hackers constitute questionable activities under the Fourth Amendment or the ECPA.

9.2   Rules of Evidence

Evidence is defined as the proof of facts presented at a trial. In a court of law, the judge or jury is expected to start off with no preconceived idea or knowledge of the facts of a case. This presumption of no prior knowledge represents a blank canvas upon which you paint your case, using the evidence you possess. Evidence does not have to be perfect; however, opposing parties (in a criminal case, the prosecution and the defense) present their evidence, and the best or most compelling evidence (usually) wins.

9.2.1   Types of Evidence

Several types of evidence can be brought before a court. These include the following:

- Real objects that can be deposited with the court and examined by the fact finder.

- An oral (also testimonial) eyewitness account of a witness who was present.

- Circumstantial evidence that allows a judge or jury to deduce a fact from other facts that have been proven. For instance, a fingerprint can be used to establish the presence of a person at a particular location or to establish that the person was in contact with a particular object, even when no witness can attest to that fact.

- Expert opinions rendered by an expert in a particular field, especially after that person has carried out a specific investigation. Readers who may be called as expert witnesses may be interested to learn that an expert witness *cannot* be asked whether the defendant is guilty![5]

Note

Given the relative obscurity of the technical issues encountered in dealing with network intrusions, many network security professionals are likely to be called on to serve as expert witnesses. Two Supreme Court decisions serve to define the admissibility of expert scientific and technical opinions. The first is *Daubert v. Merrell Dow Pharmaceuticals, Inc.* (509 U.S. 579, 125L., Ed.2d 469,113 S. Ct. 2786 [1993]). In *Daubert,* the Supreme Court defined four criteria for the trial courts, acting as "gatekeepers," to use in determining the admissibility and reliability of expert testimony based on a particular scientific technique or theory. These four criteria are

- Whether the theory can be and has been tested

- Whether the theory has been the subject of peer review and/or publication

- Whether there are known or potential error rates

- Whether the technique or theory is acceptable to the "relevant" scientific community

Daubert also requires the court to determine whether the expert testimony is relevant to the facts of the case (that is, whether the testimony "fits" with the facts presented). A subsequent decision, *Kumho Tire Co. v. Carmichael* (1999 U.S. Lexis 2189 [March 23, 1999]), clarifies the scope of *Daubert* and establishes that the four tests called for in *Daubert* should be applied to any expert testimony regardless of whether it is scientific, technical, or based on experience. *Kumho* reiterates the gatekeeper role of the trial court in determining the admissibility and relevance of expert testimony as evidence. If you are called as an expert witness, you may be asked to provide information addressing these four points.[6]

9.2.2 Admissibility of Evidence

The value of evidence is determined by two factors: *admissibility* (that is, it must comply with certain traditional rules or prerequisites to be considered by the fact finder) and *weight* (that is, if it is ruled admissible, it must be comprehensible and persuasive to the judge or jury). The tenets governing admissibility in common law countries include, as general rules:

- A witness testifies about his or her personal knowledge only and shall be subject to cross-examination.

- No secondary sources (other persons, books, or records) for this knowledge can be used. Such secondary information is considered *hearsay* and is disallowed. For instance, suppose my colleague tells me that a second colleague has admitted to hacking the Pentagon. Suppose that the second colleague is subsequently arrested and tried for the hacking offense. This principle means that I cannot testify about the second colleague's confession to my first colleague to prove the hacking offense unless there is an exception to the hearsay rules.

- A document, in order to be admissible, should be authenticated, where possible, by the witness who was responsible for generating it.

- Originals, not copies, of any documents must be introduced as evidence before the court. This tenet, known as the rule of *best evidence* is meant to mitigate the risk of fraud and error.

9.2.3 Restrictions and Exceptions

There are important exceptions to these general rules of evidence. The *business records exception* to the hearsay provision allows a business record created as a part of everyday commercial activity to be introduced as evidence even if no person can testify about the contents of the record from personal knowledge. This exception covers business records such as ledgers and account statements. In addition, the *photographic copies exception* allows copies of certain types of records to be admitted as evidence if certain prerequisites are met.

Other restrictions apply to the collection of evidence. Information that is acquired unfairly or illegally (in violation of the Fourth Amendment of the U.S. Constitution, for instance) may not be admitted at all or only for restricted purposes such as impeachment of a witness.

The topic of computer records as evidence is still extensively debated in many countries. The courts in some countries have accepted them as falling within the business records exception. Other countries have introduced new laws that prescribe conditions that, if met, allow the introduction of computer records as evidence.[2]

9.2.4 Provisions for Handling Evidence

Several strategies for collecting evidence are important to consider to ensure admissibility and persuasiveness.

First and perhaps foremost is having an indisputably strong *chain of custody*. In other words, you should be able to clearly describe how the evidence of the crime was found and be able to provide a comprehensive accounting for everything that has happened to the evidence from the time it was found until it is presented in court.

The Federal Bureau of Investigation recommends that victims of computer crime identify one person to serve as the custodian of all potential evidence, who actively gathers the information from the appropriate people, arranges to secure the information in a safe place (such as a safe deposit box or other secure container), and minimizes the number of people who have access to the information.[7]

A log should be kept of all who have access to the information. Other experts recommend that where possible, the information should be secured using cryptographic measures or written to CD-ROM or similar nonerasable media.

The next requirement is that the methods used to gather the evidence should in themselves be *transparent*. No obstacles should prevent making the methods freely testable by an independent expert. A violation of this requirement is cited as a problem in the Rome Lab case I discuss in Section 9.4.2. In short, if you are not willing to publicly divulge the method you used to gather evidence, you may not be able to use the evidence that method produces.[5]

When records or statements (such as those that might be produced as reports from an intrusion detection system) are introduced as evidence, asserting that something happened, they must be accurate. Proving accuracy is a two-part process: proving the accuracy of the content of the record and proving the accuracy of the process that produced the content.

9.2.5   Rules of Evidence as Applied to System Logs and Audit Trails

Although system logs and audit trails are, in strictest terms, *hearsay* evidence, ordinarily they should fall under the *business records* exception, provided that they are generated as part of your normal business operations. Therefore, you can't decide on a whim to collect audit trails or cobble together an ad hoc monitoring system in order to produce evidence, especially if you can't demonstrate that you trust the output of the audit mechanism enough to use them in the day-to-day conduct of your business.

Part of demonstrating that the audit log generation is part of your business process is a system logging or monitoring policy that clearly articulates what is to be logged and why.

System logs and result logs produced by intrusion detection systems are a special case of circumstantial evidence. They require proof of authenticity, usually provided by testimony of the personnel responsible for setting up and operating the log generation and intrusion detection systems. They may also require an expert to explain the contents of the logs with regard to context, explanation, and interpretation.[5]

From an evidentiary perspective, you should attempt to design security monitoring systems so that redundant event record streams are generated. Whereas a single stream of evidence might be considered too weak to support a conviction on its own, multiple event logs that corroborate one another help build a strong case in court in much the same way that multiple corroborative eyewitness accounts are considered much stronger than a single witness's testimony.

9.3 Laws Relating to Monitoring Activity

What determines whether you can monitor connections and data on your systems? This question has two facets: criminal and civil. Civil liability may hinge upon several issues, including

- Do users of your system have a reasonable expectation of privacy?

- Is a business justification associated with the monitoring sufficient to outweigh the user's right to privacy?

Courts considering questions of civil liability for inappropriate monitoring have considered mostly cases involving employers monitoring employee email, focusing on issues of privacy in the workplace. Most cases so far have decided in favor of employers, upholding employers' rights to monitor their employees' computer files, messages, and history of usage.[8]

Illegal monitoring can also be criminal and is governed primarily by the ECPA. The exact provisions for monitoring depend on whether the monitoring is performed by the system operators, their employees, and their agents or by law enforcement entities. As mentioned earlier in this chapter, monitoring computer systems is regulated by ECPA, 18 USC s. 2510. In general, the act makes most acts of monitoring the voice and electronic communications of another person illegal. Many other countries have similar restrictions on wiretaps and communications monitoring as well; however, this information is outside the scope of this book.

9.3.1 When a System Administrator Monitors a System

The Electronic Communications Privacy Act is the U.S. criminal statute that strictly regulates the ability of a person to monitor the communications of another party. Section 2 of the act provides an exception for system operators and their employees that allows them to monitor, disclose, or use the communications of users in the normal course of performing system administration or protecting the rights of the service providers. This exception allows a service provider to conduct random monitoring only for the purpose of conducting routine quality-control sampling.

Additional exceptions are provided to system operators by the ECPA when

- The monitored message is clearly intended for public access.

- One of the parties involved in the communication (that is, the sender or intended recipient of the message) gives consent.

- The message is being forwarded to another service provider en route to its final destination.

- The system operator obtains the message inadvertently, and the message appears to indicate criminal activity.

9.3.2 When Law Enforcement Agents Monitor a System

When the person(s) seeking to monitor activity are law enforcement officers or their agents, the ECPA's provisions for monitoring are quite different from those applicable to the system operator. For law enforcement agencies to intercept electronic communications, they must first obtain a search warrant. Exceptions to this rule cover emergency situations such as endangerment of life or limb, imminent threats to national security, or activities indicative of organized crime. These exceptions allow the officer to monitor first and then file, within 48 hours, for the warrant. To utilize this provision, the officer must determine that the grounds for the warrant exist and follow up with a proper application to the court for an intercept authorization.

The statute differentiates between monitoring the content (that is data or voice) of the communications, and the context (for example, the phone numbers used by the target of the monitoring) of the communications. It also allows law enforcement officers to use *pen registers* and *trap-and-trace devices*, telephone switch mechanisms that allow investigators to determine the lines used and other such contextual information once they file a proper application for authorization.

9.3.3 Notification of Monitoring

Both law enforcement authorities[7] and many security experts recommend that system operators use login banners and other messaging techniques to notify system users that, while they are logged in to the system, their actions are subject to monitoring. Such notification banners might include information that the monitoring is for system administration purposes and for enforcing security and use policies of the system and that use of the system comprises consent to the monitoring. Notification to system users of monitoring should also be included in documents such as employee handbooks or other such information distributed to users. It should also be publicized as part of the system security policy.

9.4 What Real Cases Have Taught Us

Some of the first Internet hacker cases resulted from the use of intrusion detection research prototypes. The cases themselves have been instructive to those with an interest in intrusion detection and system security.

Two cases illustrate many of the legal issues associated with monitoring computer systems for intrusions and establishing accountability for the intrusion.

The first case is the 1995 intrusion by Kevin Mitnick in which he targeted Tsutomu Shimomura's system at the San Diego Supercomputing Center. This incident, published in the book *Takedown,*[9] culminated in Mitnick's arrest by the FBI in February of 1995.

The second case involves the 1994 attacks on the U.S. Air Force Rome Labs, for which Richard Pryce (using the hacker handle "datastream cowboy") and Matthew Bevan (using the hacker handle "Kuji") were apprehended and charged in England.

Although both cases are interesting from a technical perspective, my intent in this discussion is to highlight some of the legal debates that ensued in the course of these incidents. As you will see, although they both involved intrusions from the Internet, the outcomes of the investigations were affected by the legal rules and procedures that were applied in two different legal systems.

9.4.1   The Mitnick Case

Dr. Andrew Gross, at the time a graduate student at the University of California in San Diego (UCSD), was tracking accesses to the systems assigned to Tsutomu Shimomura, a computational physicist at the San Diego Supercomputing Center at UCSD. On Christmas Day 1994, Gross noted that Shimomura's system had been compromised.[10]

The analysis of the intrusion logs suggested that an IP spoofing attack had been used to compromise the system. This was of interest because the IP spoofing attack had been theorized, but never observed in network intrusions.

Shimomura reported the incident and analysis to a research workshop in Sonoma, California, in mid-January 1995, at which time other experts, including the author, reviewed the log files and agreed with his suspicion that an IP spoofing attack had been used. The report was picked up by the *New York Times* and published the following week.

9.4.1.1   The Investigation

In the meantime, an account holder at the San Francisco–based ISP, the Well, received notification from the ISP that his account had surpassed its quota of allotted space. He investigated and found several large files, some of which had Shimomura's name on them. Recognizing Shimomura's name from the news accounts, he contacted Shimomura and Gross. Gross and Shimomura spoke with the systems administrator and the legal counsel at the Well about the situation. On the advice of legal counsel, the Well hired Gross and Shimomura to investigate. They were given access to system logs, as well as other system information sources (such as account activity) in order to perform the investigation. They found evidence of log tampering and of credit card information that appeared to have been taken from another ISP. They also found collections of electronic mail messages from well-known computer security professionals and copies of files taken from Shimomura's machines at SDSC.

Shimomura and Gross decided to take a proactive monitoring strategy to isolate further activity from the hacker, believing that the hacker would return to the Well account. They were able to ascertain from system logs that the file tampering and illicit accesses were mapped to IP addresses assigned to another ISP, San Jose–based Netcom. Therefore, they placed a packet capture tool on the port connecting the Well to the Internet, configuring the tool to capture and log packets that came from the IP addresses assigned to Netcom.

In the meantime, when Shimomura and Gross first identified some of the files as belonging to Netcom, they contacted Netcom's management. The management at Netcom offered to cooperate and formally requested assistance. Netcom also assigned its system administrators to work with Shimomura and Gross in the investigation.

The investigators and Netcom's system administrator ran a shell script to catch all logins from the username "Joeblow," the account being used to access Netcom's service. When the login occurred, the script automatically dialed the system administrator's pager. A logging script that placed all the access logs in a file and then chronologically ordered them allowed the investigators to perform pattern matching and correlation of the access logs with other login and phone records. This matching enabled the investigators to trace the intruder's path.

With the chain of accesses now established from Netcom to the Well, the investigators turned to the task of finding the source of the intruder's access to Netcom. Netcom's system administrator logged in to the terminal server when the intruder was logged in, and determined the port number being used for the access. With this information, the investigators called on the U.S. District Attorney in San Francisco, who obtained a Trap-and-Trace order on the number associated with the access. Three IP addresses were used, one each from Denver, Atlanta, and Raleigh. Ironically, the Raleigh Trap-and-Trace order was the only order completed.

By this time, the FBI was involved in the investigation and contacted the local carrier that controlled the phone switch in Raleigh (Southern Bell). They also received a Trap-and-Trace order on that site. Working with logs collected at Netcom and logs collected at the Raleigh POP, Shimomura and Gross performed pattern matching to correlate accesses made to Netcom from Raleigh and those going out from Raleigh, matching times, dates, and duration of connections.

At this time, the Trap-and-Trace order on the Raleigh phone switch produced a phone number that was not correct. Based on a series of clicking noises heard when the number produced by the Trap-and-Trace order was dialed, Shimomura and Gross realized that the telephone switch itself had been hacked. Therefore, they repeated their technique of correlating incoming and outgoing call logs, matching times, dates, and call durations. This process produced the location of the incoming call, another phone switch, this one cellular.

At this point, the intruder's calling pattern changed (the activity at the cellular phone switch abruptly stopped), so the investigators relied on the fact that only two cellular service providers were in the area to narrow their search, allowing them to pick up the trail again. When Shimomura and Gross gained access to the second cellular phone switch, they found the intruder and were able to retrace his access from the cellular phone switch, through the Raleigh phone switch, through Netcom, and finally to the original hacked account at the Well. This trace was done by correlating the call data records from the cellular phone switch to the logging mechanisms at Netcom and the Well.

Because the call data records provided the cell site, sector location, and electronic serial number of the phone used by the intruder, Shimomura and Gross determined that they could electronically track the intruder to a narrow search area (to a particular cell, which is 3 to 5 miles in diameter). This information, in combination with their suspicion that the phone had been cloned (that is, it had been illegally reprogrammed with the purloined electronic serial number and mobile identification number from a legitimate subscriber) meant that Shimomura and Gross did not need information about the specific subscriber assigned to the phone account.

Shimomura and Gross decided to wait until the intruder was online and then used triangulation to locate the source of the signal emitted by the cellular telephone. To do so, they drove around the cell with specialized radio direction-finding equipment that tracked signals to a specific location. Once the location was established, the FBI drafted a warrant, executed it on the location, and apprehended the intruder, Kevin Mitnick.[11]

9.4.1.2 Points of Interest

Several legal points of interest appear in this account of the investigation and traceback of Mitnick.

- The monitoring software that detected the original Christmas Day intrusion ran continuously on Shimomura's systems as part of the ongoing operation of the systems. The logs were written to a protected location where they could not be tampered with.[10]

- The Well engaged Shimomura and Gross to assist in investigating the intrusion. This detail is important because under the provisions of the ECPA, a service provider is allowed to protect itself with reasonable precautions, including hiring a security expert to assist in determining whether it is under attack. As Shimomura and Gross were therefore acting as private security consultants to the Well and later to Netcom, they were arguably not required to obtain a court-ordered wiretap to collect the logs as evidence. Had they been public law enforcement officers, such court orders would have been absolutely necessary in order to perform monitoring.

- Cooperating with law enforcement (such as the FBI) does not necessarily make one an "agent" of the government (and therefore subject to the requirements for court-ordered wiretaps) if the activity conducted is within the realm of the "service provider" exception to the ECPA. Dealing with systems anomalies and security incidents is well within the activities allowed system administrators and other employees of service providers while rendering service or protecting the provider. (Note: The determination of "agency" is currently undecided and requires expert legal advice before a decision is made by a service provider or security consultant.)

- Tracebacks were done with the permission and full cooperation of the ISPs involved. Had the tracebacks been done without the involvement of the ISPs management and legal counsels, these actions would likely be considered violations of the Computer Fraud and Abuse Act or the ECPA.

- When the need for a Trap-and-Trace order was established, the investigators involved the appropriate law enforcement personnel who promptly sought Court authorization.

- When the cellular phone switch was identified as the source of the intruder's access, no subscriber data was requested. Had subscriber data been needed, a subpoena or court order would have been required.

- When the intruder's location had been established, the investigators contacted the FBI, which then obtained the necessary warrant and executed it.

Under the terms of a plea bargain agreement signed in March 1999, Mitnick pleaded guilty to seven counts of wire and computer fraud and admitted to penetrating computers at several major corporations and downloading proprietary source code.[12]

9.4.2 The Rome Lab Case

The series of 150 intrusions that targeted the U.S. Air Force's command and control research facility, Rome Lab, from March 23, 1994, to April 16, 1994, has frequently been cited as a harbinger of information warfare. Using sniffer programs and trojaned versions of UNIX login programs, two teenage hackers compromised several Air Force research systems, used these systems as platforms to attack foreign Internet systems, and controlled laboratory support systems.

9.4.2.1 The Incident and Investigation

The Air Force Information Warfare Center deployed a response team to Rome Lab on March 29, after an operator noted a sniffer log and discovered other signs of intrusion on March 25. The team found that intruders had installed numerous sniffers and trojan horses on the systems at Rome Lab and logged in often to check the sniffer logs and launch further attacks on other Internet sites.

The response team decided to pursue three goals: to establish point of origin for the intruders, to establish virtual identities of the intruders, and to monitor their activities while on Rome Lab systems. The team used various approaches, ranging from using the Network Security Monitor, a network-based intrusion detection system that monitored and logged activities, to designing and building two custom tools, one to trace the connection back to the Internet host from which it originated, the other to perform context monitoring on a commercial ISP system that was between the intruders and their victims.

The traceback tool was used for fewer than three days because little to no legislation governed this type of enforcement activity. Because the traceback tool was intrusive (to perform the traceback, it actually did a "hackback" through the systems, gaining user-level access and then using `netstat` and other queries to isolate the path of the intruder through the system), using it required exceptional legal provisions. In fact, the Justice Department Computer Crime Unit granted incremental verbal permission as the team proceeded with the traceback.

The context monitoring tool was very interesting because it contained some attributes that are necessary for monitoring software used in investigative contexts. For instance, it was designed expressly to monitor silently; to generate, log, and filter streams of context information; and to reliably signal the incident team when an attack was detected.

Operating through two ISPs, Cyberspace and Mindvox, the intruders attacked several Rome Lab research systems (all of which were being monitored by the team at the time) and used them as launching points for attacks on several other systems on the Internet, including NASA Goddard, Wright Patterson Air Force Base, and the Korean Atomic Energy Research Institute.[13]

The hackers were eventually apprehended, thanks to more classic law enforcement investigative techniques.

After the hacker handle for Richard Pryce (datastream cowboy) was identified, the Air Force Office of Special Investigations determined Pryce's identity and telephone number. New Scotland Yard was called and after an investigation in which the agency correlated Pryce's telephone connections with the Rome Lab intrusions, agents apprehended Pryce in his parents' home and charged him with 12 different offenses under the British Computer Misuse Act.

During investigation of Pryce's computer, New Scotland Yard investigators found a telephone number for Matthew Bevan (hacker handle "Kuji") and apprehended him as well.

However, prosecutors determined that they had insufficient evidence with which to try Bevan and released him without trial.

Pryce was tried and fined 1,200 pounds for offenses related to the Rome Labs incidents.[14]

9.4.2.2 Points of Interest

Points regarding this case include

- The targets of the attack were military systems of national security importance.

- The attack was discovered after the fact, not as a result of ongoing monitoring or intrusion detection.

- The incident handling was carried out by a team of military computer scientists, supervised by law enforcement personnel from the start.

- The information allegedly taken by the intruders included sensitive information that the government believed could not be publicly disclosed.

- The techniques used by the investigative team were deemed sensitive technologies, not suitable for public disclosure.

- Because of the concerns regarding a possible threat to national security, the Justice Department allowed the military incident-handling team to perform hackbacks to trace the origin of the attackers.

- The jurisdictional issues for this case were a nightmare, crossing several territorial boundaries (with attackers in England and victim systems in the United States, England, and Korea) and organizational boundaries (with victim systems controlled by military, government, commercial, and educational entities). The cooperation between the United States and United Kingdom in investigating and adjudicating the case was noted as extraordinary and commendable.[5]

9.4.3 Lessons Learned

Obviously these cases are instructive to those who want to provide features in intrusion detection systems that support the legal process of apprehending intruders. Some of the lessons learned in these cases follow.

- At times, the goals of intrusion detection (detecting, responding to, and establishing accountability for the intrusions) are at very definite odds with legal restrictions on intercepting or tracing criminal attacks.

- When law enforcement agencies rely on technical experts to support investigations of computer intrusions and misuse, the alliance should continue until the matter is settled. The technical experts may need to provide evidence that the mechanisms used to generate logs and other evidence are accurate and trustworthy. The experts might also need to explain the content of the logs and other evidence to the prosecutor, defense attorney, judge or jury.[5]

- The entire question of investigating intrusions and other incidents is fraught with legal pitfalls and blind alleys. You should involve legal counsel early in the course of incidents and rely on ongoing legal advice to conduct the investigation competently.

- Provisions should be made in your security program to allow for the production and control of evidence in a fashion that maintains integrity, redundancy, and chain of custody.

- Do not use mechanisms to generate logs or information you need as evidence if you are not prepared to allow free access to those mechanisms. Furthermore, do not allege theft of information from your system in connection with a non-intellectual-property criminal case unless you are willing to allow the defense to examine that information. The unwillingness of the U.S. Air Force to allow free access to mechanisms or data was considered in itself a death knell for the prosecution of the Rome Labintruders.[5]

- Ongoing legal training should be included as a standard part of training your systems security and operational staff.

- Monitoring and the traceback of intruders *are not* do-it-yourself projects. Should such measures be necessary, seek expert legal advice and law enforcement assistance early on. Should you fail to do so, you are likely to corrupt your ability to seek legal recourse later for the damages inflicted upon you by the intruder. Worse, you could conceivably face criminal charges or civil liability yourself!

9.5 Conclusion

In this chapter, I've tackled the awkward marriage between legal and network security principles, focusing on rules and procedures that are relevant to the task of designing, developing, and using intrusion detection systems in the real world.

This discussion gives some indication of the frequency with which serious legal considerations arise in the course of network intrusion incident investigations. I hope that this impresses upon you the need to include knowledgeable legal counsel on your team as you design, develop, deploy, and use intrusion detection systems and new system-oriented investigative techniques.

Endnotes

1. Duhaime, L. *Duhaime Legal Dictionary*. World Wide Legal Information Association, Victoria, B.C., 1994–1999.

2. United Nations Committee on Crime Prevention and Control. "International Review of Criminal Policy—United Nations Manual on the Prevention and Control of Computer-Related Crime." revisions 43 and 44, 1999.

3. Smith, F. C. "Some Unintended Legal Consequences of Intentional Technological Disasters." Second Pacific Institute of Computer Security Workshop, San Diego, CA, February 1999.

4. Petrocelli, F. and P. Knoebler. *Triumph of Justice: Closing the Book on the Simpson Saga.* Crown Publishing, 1998.

5. Sommer, Peter. "Intrusion Detection Systems as Evidence." First International Workshop on the Recent Advances in Intrusion Detection. Louvainla-Neuve, Belgium, September 1998.

6. McElroy, K. "*Kumho Tire Co. v. Carmichael* Clarifies Scope of *Daubert,* The Admissibility of Expert Scientific Opinions." available at `http://www.nhdd.com/hot/wh60.htm`, March 1999.

7. Federal Bureau of Investigation, Infrastructure Protection and Computer Intrusion Squad. "If You Become a Victim." available at `http://www.fbi.gov/programs/ipcis`.

8. Dichter, M. S. and M. S. Burkhardt. "Electronic Interaction in the Workplace: Monitoring, Retrieving, and Storing Employee Communications in the Internet Age." American Employment Law Council, Fourth Annual Conference, Asheville, NC, October 1996.

9. Shimomura, T. and J. Markoff. *Takedown.* Hyperion Press, 1995.

10. Gross, A. personal communications, 1995–1999.

11. Smith, F. C. and E. Kenneally. "The Ties That Bind and Set Them Pleaing— Testimony from the Envisioned Trial of Kevin Mitnick." National Fraud Prevention Coalition, to be published December 1999.

12. Thomas, D. "Mitnick Sentenced to 46 Months." *Wired News,* March 29, 1999.

13. "Rome Lab Attacks, Final Report." Air Force Information Warfare Center Countermeasures Engineering Team, January 1995.

14. Smith, G. "U.S. InfoWarriors Fall Short in United Kingdom Hacker Case." *Crypt Newsletter,* November 1997.

CHAPTER 10

For Users

The users of an intrusion detection system hold the keys to the ultimate success or failure of the technology. Knowledgeable users can compensate for the inherent weaknesses of a particular package, whereas inept or hostile users can nullify the value of even the best system design and implementation.

Depending on the functional role of the user, she or he can be called on to perform intrusion detection system selection, integration, use, and follow-through. Because use of the system is extremely product specific, we will focus on the rest of the user's roles in this chapter. These discussions are provided in the hopes of assisting a user who has been assigned responsibility for intrusion detection for an operational system.

10.1 Determining Your Requirements

In this section, a quick questionnaire is provided that allows you to itemize the requirements that are likely to drive your selection of an intrusion detection system. Some of the questions can be answered off the top of your head; others take more thought.

10.1.1 Your System Environment

First, obviously, look at the systems environment you're trying to protect. This environment consists of the technical, political, and physical surroundings of the system and the organization to which it belongs.

- **System configurations**   This aspect includes the technical details of the system environment such as network diagrams, the number and types of hosts, and the operating systems and application software running on those hosts.

- **Security configurations**   This aspect of the environment includes other security mechanisms (both software and hardware) running within your enterprise. These can include firewalls, encryption devices, virtual private networks, and authentication devices. Document the locations of each on the network diagram.

- **Goals of the enterprise** These goals are the primary functions your organization hopes to perform in using its systems. Such functions might include accounting, process control, maintenance of scientific or business databases, or communications.

10.1.2 Goals and Objectives

Knowing what you want the system to do for you is helpful when determining what features you need. You should be able to articulate the concerns that are foremost in your organization in which intrusion detection might play a role.

- **Protect against outsiders** Is the primary concern of the organization intrusion from the Internet or from a dial-up connection? If the system isn't connected to a network or modems, this question may be moot.

- **Protect against insiders** Is your organization concerned about a rogue authorized user overstepping his or her permissions? (This area might be of great concern to public agencies in which employees have access to individual tax and earnings records.) Does your organization also want to detect errors introduced by authorized users?

- **Determine new needs** A commonly stated goal of monitoring system usage patterns is to determine when a change in technology or business objective drives a new need for connectivity or bandwidth. Such needs can show up as anomalous levels of user activity. Though these goals are not abjectly security relevant, they are of interest when configuring monitoring and detection rules.

- **Maintain managerial control** Another goal that doesn't fit entirely in a security-centric category is that of maintaining managerial control over systems use. In some organizations, such management goals include things like monitoring employee performance or policing employee use of the Internet.

Note
When management wants to police and restrict employee access to certain Internet sites, a separate category of software product, called Secure Internet Filtering Technologies (SIFT) is usually applicable.

10.1.3 Reviewing Your Policy

Here you review your security policy with an eye to determining who requires what accesses or permissions, which accesses might be required, and which accesses should be avoided at all costs. For instance, it is difficult to think of a situation in which any customer should have access to employee payroll or other personal information.

- **Goals** Articulate the goals of the security policy, both in terms of standard security goals (integrity, confidentiality, availability) as well as in terms of more generic management goals (privacy, protection from liability, manageability).

- **Job descriptions** List the general job descriptions of system users (along with the accesses each user requires to system assets).

- **Use standards** Does the policy include use standards? What are their tenets (for instance, no access to porn sites during business hours, no rude email to executives or customers)?

- **Formality of practice** Organizational styles vary widely, depending on the type of business and the organizational culture. Organizations that have more-formal practices often require certain system operations to take place in a particular fashion. For example, a high level of formality is found in a military site that handles classified materials.

10.1.4 Requirements and Constraints

These articulate common requirements and constraints that might affect the selection of an intrusion detection system. For instance, some subcontracting arrangements that involve network access to a customer's system require the subcontractor to use a specific set of security mechanisms.

- **External requirements** This area covers requirements for intrusion detection that are levied from outside the organization. The preceding example (subcontractor agreement) is an external requirement. Another example is a government contract requiring certain levels of protection of private data.

  - **Customer access** These include SEC requirements for customer access to financial institutions.

  - **Accreditation** This includes requirements for intrusion detection to be *accredited* to run in multilevel secure mode or at a high level of trust. *Accreditation* is an official approval of a particular system to operate in a specific mode, using a particular set of protections. Accreditation demonstrates due diligence with regard to security.[1] An example of an accreditation process that might include such requirements is the Department of Defense Certification and Accreditation Process (DITSCAP).

  - **Due diligence/best practice** This includes legal or internal audit requirements to maintain some standard level of security management.

- **Investigative support**   Investigative support includes requirements to maintain audit logs and trails to support law enforcement investigations. This requirement may include embedding integrity assurance mechanisms, utilizing media that is not rewritable, and documenting the chain of custody of logs.

- **Resource constraints**   Resource constraints are often the greatest limiting factor to implementing security in a major system. These constraints can include limitations on funding available to purchase security system software, funding for people to run that software, and funding for system resources such as processors and storage.

  - **Technology budgets**   Can you afford to purchase, maintain, and operate an intrusion detection system? It is also fair to ask whether you can afford not to. A risk assessment can help answer these questions by articulating the answers in terms of cost-benefit trade-offs.

  - **Staffing**   Do you have the staff to monitor an intrusion detection system full time? How about around the clock, seven days a week?

  - **Control**   Does your organization have sufficient managerial clout to instigate changes in response to an intrusion detection system finding?

10.2   Making Sense of Products

When you purchase and install an intrusion detection system, you're entrusting the security of your organization's computing resources to the designers and developers of that product. Here are some questions that can help you determine whether that trust is warranted. These questions should start you thinking about your set of requirements for intrusion detection as well, helping you become a savvier consumer.

10.2.1   Understanding the Problem Space

An intrusion detection product is only as good as the designer's vision of the intrusion detection solution space. A product designer who has spent time studying intrusion detection, as well as the operational practices that affect intrusion detection capabilities (such as system and network management, network and computer security, design of fail-safe systems), is likely to design a system that offers features that actually help you manage the security of your system.

You also have the option to purchase several systems, each optimized to a function you have decided is important to you. As product interconnectivity improves, a building-block approach to intrusion detection capability should be more feasible.

10.2.2 Is the Product Scalable?

As discussed in Chapter 7, "Technical Issues," scalability of intrusion detection systems is one of the most pressing technical issues for this generation of products. This issue should be of interest to you if you are managing a large, complex system (say in the thousands or tens of thousands of hosts) or a geographically distributed system (such as that in a multinational corporation with numerous branch operations).

Some products assume that you will utilize their intrusion detection product in a piecemeal fashion, with a separate system running on each host or network segment. Others were designed from the outset to accommodate a hierarchical reporting and alerting infrastructure.

If you are planning to implement intrusion detection on your systems and require scalability, look for a product that was designed with scalability in mind and ask vendors for worked examples that demonstrate successful installations in systems similar to yours. Ask for customer references if you have any doubts.

10.2.3 How Did You Test This?

Your intrusion detection system is one of the most important protections for your system and is likely to be a target of attack at some time. As such, investigate to what degree the vendor has anticipated this possibility of attack and determine how the vendor has addressed this risk.

First, look for signs that the vendor understands the need for hardening the intrusion detection system against attack. At least two levels of hardening should be present in a product. First is the hardening of the system on which the intrusion detection system will run. When the intrusion detection system is sold as an integrated unit (that is, when you buy a system, you get both the software and the hardware on which it runs), ask for information about the configuration of the operating system and hardware configuration. Ask also about provisions for ongoing security management of the intrusion detection host system. When the intrusion detection system is sold as a software package, check to see whether the vendor has included instructions (or embedded tools) for security hardening the host on which you will install the software. Again, look also for provisions for ongoing security management of the host.

Second, look for signs that the vendor understands the need for hardening the intrusion detection application itself. Look for signs of extensive quality assurance testing. Look for evidence of secure programming practices. Look for vendor assurances of appropriate security measures taken in the design and development of the systems. (Does the firm do background checks on its developers to minimize the possibility of subverted software in the product?) Also, look for signs of security-savvy design. Examples include the following:

- Encrypted communications between sensors and control consoles

- Encrypted license keys restricting the hosts that can be scanned by the product

- Support of token-based or other strong I&A of those configuring the system

- Logging mechanisms for the intrusion detection system itself

10.2.4 Is This Product a Tool or Is It an Application?

There is a functional break point in intrusion detection products that is based on the product vendor's assumptions regarding the user's level of expertise. Some systems (I think of them as "tools") assume that users have a great deal of hands-on experience in using and administering TCP/IP networks. These tools are usually marketed as network-based intrusion detection products and characterize activity of interest in terms of connections, services, and port numbers. These tools are extremely powerful in detecting many of the infrastructure attacks that are common today but are likely to mean little to users who conceptualize security in terms of subjects, objects, and access control.

Other systems (I think of them as "applications")[1] assume no user technical prowess whatsoever. They feature user interfaces with simplistic, intuitively obvious displays, lots of coaching through setup and execution, and extensive report generation features. These products can be a boon to novices and to people who are not accustomed to dealing with packet-level network traffic. However, these rarely have the capability to do the sorts of selective packet capture and fine-grained analysis that "power users" demand.

10.2.4.1 Which Is Better?

Security isn't a one-size-fits-all game! Both tools and applications have their place in a security management strategy. Tools are wonderful in network operations centers or other network management environments where there are security experts who have a good understanding of what constitutes abnormal or clearly bad network traffic. You might argue that the functions provided by the best of these tools could (indeed should) be included as part of a more general network monitoring/management package, not confined to a stand-alone security tool.

Avid fans of the network-based tools often sneer at the novice-oriented applications, asserting that they are so removed from the "real action" of the packet flow that they are of no value. I disagree. One of the attributes of truly effective security management is independent of the technical expertise of the system management. This feature is consistency of process, and it has much more to do with the ability to reliably survey the security state of the system at regular intervals, consistently reporting exceptions to the appropriate people, than it does with being able to tell that an FTP session is running on the wrong port number.

Therefore, my answer to the question "Which is better?" is as follows: The best security solution is the one that is used and continues to be used over time. Furthermore, the best solution is the one that best fits the user's needs and capabilities while yielding a measurable improvement in security. The fit will vary over time, as user's expertise levels change with experience and as the solutions and the systems they protect evolve with the rest of technology.

10.2.4.2 What Is Optimal?

My answer to this question is in some ways the same. An intrusion detection system should be easy to use, well fitted to the capabilities of the user, and well fitted to the needs of the customer organization.

Products should be designed to grow with the user's capabilities or the customer's needs, without requiring a total replacement of the system. Supporting this could be as simple as providing a user interface that can be tuned and configured to meet the needs of the user. Defining and implementing an industry-wide interoperability standard that allow customers to select security system components and combine them to meet their specific needs could also satisfy this goal.

10.2.5 Buzzwords versus Wisdom

Intrusion detection is considered a hot product area and many product vendors are entering the market. Some of these vendors have an excellent grasp of intrusion detection, whereas others do not. Here are examples of products and vendors you might want to avoid:

- Your entire dialogue with the vendor is conducted in buzzwords, and upon further investigation you find that the vendor has no expertise or understanding of the fundamental concepts of security or intrusion detection.

- The product itself is a collection of functions just thrown together with little sense of how they might be applied in operational use. For instance, if best practice outlines a sequence of steps for securing a system asset, does the product guide you through the steps in appropriate order? Or does it present functions to you with no sense of proper sequence?

- When you try contacting the vendor for specific product information, no one is available to discuss technical issues associated with integrating the system into an operational network.

- Major portions of intrusion detection capability are missing, making the system a repackaged network sniffer or firewall.

- No provisions are made for information updates, bug fixes, or operating system support.

- The vendor has no sense of the importance of hardening the intrusion detection system or the system on which it runs against attack.

10.2.6   Anticipated Life of Product

Given the dynamic nature of the security products industry, ask hard questions of any product vendor regarding future plans of the company and the contractual commitments made by the company to support the products it sells. Installing and configuring intrusion detection systems for a large enterprise is a nontrivial investment—before you select a product, get some assurance that you won't be left without support for a reasonable product life.

10.2.7   Training Support

Good security staffers and system administrators are hard to find. Therefore, you should determine how much help your intrusion detection product vendor is willing to provide to help you train your staff on the use of the vendor's equipment. Does the vendor offer formal courses? Better yet, does it offer training packages as part of the product? The vendor deserves brownie points if it offers Web site or other online training that encompasses principles of security management beyond intrusion detection. Some vendors have done an excellent job here, with extensive Web-based communities in which vendor experts provide coaching and classes in related subjects.

10.2.8   Prioritized Goals of Product

Intrusion detection systems, though commonly thought to have a limited function, actually serve several critical functional goals in system security management. Designers often optimize a system to meet one functional goal and then add functions to meet market demands. For instance, a system designed to be a simple network packet monitor and logger may not be designed to handle the rigor of performing up-the-stack analysis of traffic. At the same time, if your needs are for a network monitor and nothing else, this system might be the best fit for your needs. Look again for the designer's bias in prioritizing functions. A close match between this set of priorities and your needs bodes well for your happiness in using the product to protect your systems.

10.2.9 Product Differentiation

A common product marketing strategy used in intrusion detection systems (as in other products) is to invent a new feature. The vendor then asserts that the product does something unique and therefore stands out from the rest of the field. Whether this is good for you depends on a couple of factors. First, does the feature actually solve a problem or increase usability? Beware of features borrowed from other areas of security (firewalls, encryption systems, virus detectors) that may not be a good fit for intrusion detection systems. Beware even more of features said to indicate product superiority if you do not understand how the feature would help you and your organization meet your security goals. When someone attempts to sell you an intrusion detection product, using feature names that are unfamiliar to you, ask for an explanation—and continue asking until you have a clear idea of what the feature offers and whether it is of value to you. Don't hesitate to ask for additional evidence that the feature operates as billed and that it is integrated with a product that reflects a sound approach to managing the security of a system.

10.3 Mapping Policy to Configurations

Once you've acquired your system and pulled together your goals and requirements for operating the system, it's time to consider the conversion of your security policy to a form that makes sense to your intrusion detection system. This section will outline a set of processes that can help.

10.3.1 Converting Policy to Rules

As a first step to tackling the task of converting your security policy to a form that you can use to configure your intrusion detection system, review your security policy. Remember from the discussion of security policy in Chapter 2, "Concepts and Definitions," policy should be organized in three sections. First, the overall *policy* states a philosophy of protection. This philosophy drives a second-level *procedure*, which states the specific goals that are associated with the philosophy of protection. This procedure, in turn, drives a third-level *practice*, which states the specific task that accomplishes the goal, along with the responsible party, the time interval, the reporting requirement, and the means of enforcing compliance.

If these practices aren't in place in your organization, then the task before you is to come up with this hierarchy. When you have practices, you have the basis for making up rules.

10.3.2 Subject-Objects to Real World

Most rules for configuring intrusion detection systems to enforce security policy can be formulated by using a simple security model. Note that in each case, the attributes can be grouped or generalized.

In short, ask these five questions of your security practices:

1. What is the subject? (The subject is the entity, such as a user of process, that initiates an action.)

2. What is the object? (The object is the entity, such as a file or device, that is affected by the action.)

3. What is the action? (You want to identify the action, such as a read or write, that connects the subject and the object.)

4. What are the constraints? (These restrictions apply to the subject-action-object operation.)

5. What are the responses? (The responses are the actions that should result when the constraint has been violated— reporting the violation, disabling access, or taking other actions.)

Take for instance the practice:

Jane Smith is responsible for maintaining the corporate calendar. Only she is allowed to modify it.

Subject = Jane Smith

Object = Corporate calendar file(s)

Constraints = Read, Write

Responses if someone else (user X) modifies Jane's calendar:

1. The modifications performed by user X should be reversed.

2. Jane Smith should be notified that user X attempted to change her calendar files.

3. User X should receive an email message that notifies her that the access has been noted and that she shouldn't touch that file.

4. User X's boss should be notified if user X is an insider, or user X's IP address should be placed on a firewall filter list if user X is an outsider.

Note

The response portion of this section is actually a form of contingency planning or damage recovery, standard practices in most commercial organizations. Double-check your organizational policies to make sure that your planned responses are compatible with these practices in your organization.

10.3.3   Monitoring Policy versus Security Policy

A lot of confusion frequently occurs when organizations convert security policy to monitoring policy. *Monitoring policy* is the statement that is actually implemented in an intrusion detection system.

For instance, this security policy statement:

Access to patient financial information is restricted to the accounting clerk.

translates to the following monitoring policy statement:

If patient financial information is accessed and subject is not a member of the group "accounting-clk," then generates an alert message.

10.3.4   Testing Assertions

Whenever you are translating regulatory statements in natural language to rules, the possibility exists that what you said (and converted to monitoring rules) wasn't really what you meant. Therefore, the steps of any configuration operation for intrusion detection should include verifying and testing the signatures you entered. The owner or person charged with managing the resources being protected should verify the intrusion detection rules applicable to his or her resources. In some cases, you might want to get a sign-off from the owner before proceeding. A variety of strategies are available for testing, including automated test scripts.

10.4   Show Time! Incident Handling and Investigation

So you've done your job and done it well. Your trusty intrusion detection system has just notified you that an intruder has attacked your system in a fashion that requires a manual response. Now what?

With the knowledge that your site has been the target of an intrusion, you enter the realm of incident handling, an entire security specialty in itself. Lest you be tempted to panic in the face of this scenario, you can take certain steps to make incident handling and investigation far more productive. This section addresses some of them, gleaned from seasoned experts who have worked in this area for years.

10.4.1 Scout's Honor

At the risk of sounding like a Boy Scout, the key to optimizing incident handling is simple: Be prepared. This means including incident-handling policies, procedures, and practices in your organization's security policy. Preparedness also means performing a need assessment within your organization to determine whether you have the personnel who can perform incident handling and to establish the limits of those personnel, in expertise as well as workload. Other preparation includes determining in advance when to bring in outside assistance and establishing relationships with the sources of that assistance before the need arises.

An absolutely critical part of this preparation is establishing secure, out-of-band communications for the incident-handling team members. Most hacker tradecraft includes capturing email and other online messaging as a routine part of conducting intrusions; if you use these channels to notify incident handlers, you also notify intruders that they have been discovered and furthermore inform them of the countermeasures you plan to take. This action places your team at a strategic disadvantage and jeopardizes the effectiveness of the incident-handling operation.

10.4.2 Best Practices

If writing incident-handling procedures and practices sounds like a daunting task to you, you're absolutely correct. Navigating the labyrinth of concerns associated with incidents is a task requiring a great deal of forethought.

Fortunately, some excellent resources are available that you can utilize in adding incident-handling procedures and practices to your organizational security policy. My favorite, The Internet Engineering Task Force's RFC 2350, "Expectations for Computer Security Incident Response,"[2] is a wonderful reference for this area. The document provides a generic framework for articulating the topics you should address in defining and fielding a security incident-handling team. It provides a road map for organizations building a new team, with reporting and informational templates that can be customized to your environment. Use it!

Other resources are also available. The Carnegie Mellon Computer Emergency Response Team (CERT) maintains a variety of online and manual resources for security professionals, with a focus on security vulnerability reporting and incident handling. The CERT also conducts training for incident-handling teams, which is excellent. If your organization requires a major, dedicated, incident-handling team, consider enrolling in the Forum for Incident Response and Security Teams (FIRST), the international consortium of incident-handling teams. FIRST conducts an annual conference featuring tutorials and presentations on security and incident handling.

Finally, if you do not have suitable personnel to perform incident handling, you might consider outsourcing this function. Several major corporations offer incident-handling as part of their security consulting services. I include some of these in Appendix C, "Resources."

10.4.3 When the Balloon Goes Up

Incident handling, especially in cases when the intrusion is ongoing, can be a frantic, adrenaline-laden operation. If you have done your homework and your incident-handling plan and procedure is in place, it's time to place your focus on the situation at hand.

First, don't panic! Incidents are an unfortunately common occurrence. Assemble your team (specified in the incident-handling plan) and start working the procedure. Don't forget to note the detection of the intrusion and the start of your incident-handling team in your incident log—it'll save you a lot of grief when doing your final report of the incident.

The challenge for security managers facing an incident response and investigation is mounting an appropriate response while sparing the members of the team. Indeed, many who have worked on major incident-handling episodes tell horror stories of teams sleeping under desks in network operations centers and working 48-hour shifts.

Although this scenario might happen, it's not a model to emulate! Pace your team, reminding people to take breaks for meals and rest. Doing so may be difficult in the heat of the moment, but the team needs to remain alert and think clearly to respond to intruder challenges. It's difficult to maintain an edge in the face of eyestrain, fatigue, and falling blood-sugar levels! If you are faced with an unusually persistent or malevolent intruder, you should consider escalating the response effort and calling in some outside help.

Part of managing the process in a staff-sparing fashion requires some order and discipline. Prioritize every task that arises in the course of incident handling. Some tasks are indeed time critical and must be done immediately. Others, however, can just as easily be scheduled to occur after the incident has been resolved. You should consider postponing any comprehensive report writing or other paperwork (aside from logging events in the all-important incident log!) until your team has handled the incident.[3]

> **Note**
>
> Network forensics is the investigation and analysis of the artifacts of network intrusions. This is a relatively new area, with few citable references. If you are interested in network forensics, I recommend that you read Andrew Gross's dissertation on the topic.[4] Klayton Monroe has developed an advanced suite of tools (called BlackLab™) for use in evidence gathering, computer forensics, intrusion analysis, and intrusion detection.[5]

10.4.4 Dealing with Law Enforcement

You've assembled your team, worked your incident-handling procedure, and things haven't gotten better. In fact, they've gotten worse and appear to be on a downhill slope. Now what?

In extreme cases, you may find yourself and your site under siege. You may have an unusually malicious or stubborn adversary on your hands who is attacking critical systems. Or your investigation may have discovered signs that you're dealing with something that requires additional intervention. For instance, you may have found files on your system that are clearly marked classified military documents, credit card records, child pornography, or other indicators of criminal activity.

These situations require assistance from law enforcement agencies. Your incident-handling plan should include a clear idea of whom to contact at the appropriate agency. In some organizations, the director of corporate security or other such corporate official should make the call. If your organization is under contract to certain government organizations, the contract may dictate which law enforcement agency is involved. Finally, law enforcement agencies at local, state, and federal levels handle certain sorts of computer crime. Again, your director of corporate security or corporate legal counsel can assist you in determining which agency to contact.

In most cases, you will find law enforcement to be courteous, responsive—and nontechnical. Lest you be tempted to use the latter as reason not to involve them in solving your problem, let's also take into account what they can do!

First, law enforcement personnel are likely to know the criminal laws that can be applied to help terminate the incident—it is my experience that many officers have a better practical understanding of the criminal statutes than some attorneys!

Second, law enforcement officers have the power to seek and execute search and arrest warrants and the legal authority to do many things that you simply cannot do (without running the risk of facing criminal charges yourself). These actions include gathering information from the sites from which your intruder is coming (by obtaining and serving subpoenas for system logs and user records). In other cases, law enforcement agencies can enlist the help of international authorities to isolate the source of your intruder. Finally, law enforcement agencies can perform investigations that are both effective and in compliance with complex and often arcane rules of evidence and procedure, so that the intruder can be tried in a court of law.

You may be called upon to support law enforcement in the investigation of your incident. Depending on your organization, you'll probably want to involve your corporate legal counsel as well as your corporate security director in this process. Introducing law enforcement agencies can complicate your incident-handling operation, but in extreme cases you need the full force of the legal process they can exert on your behalf. Refer to Chapter 9, "Legal Issues," for more information about legal issues and intrusion detection.

10.4.5   Expectations

Another element of managing incident handling is that of interacting with your corporate management. Many in corporate management have unrealistic expectations of system security staffs. One of these expectations is that the mere presence of a security staff ensures that no incidents will ever take place. Another is that if the organization ignores security incidents, they'll magically go away. These wishes, in combination with the perception that security represents a fiscal black hole, not a legitimate cost of doing business, can make life very difficult for you.

The best defense in this situation is a clear statement of the facts. Draw up documents outlining the goals, functions, powers, and scope of the security function, including intrusion detection and incident handling, and have them signed off by the management chain. As part of this task, articulate the trade-offs and potential problems, giving management the opportunity to think about resolution strategies. Doing this sort of preparation will save you a lot of headaches when you're in the heat of handling an intrusion or other security problem.

10.4.6   Damage Control

You've performed incident handling and have taken it to resolution. It's time to clean up the systems. First, consider which elements of the system may require replacement, even on a temporary basis. If, for instance, the incident resulted in legal action, you may need to remove hard drives or other evidence sources to preserve the chain of custody.

Again, some proactive measures can make this resolution phase much easier. For instance, if you used an integrity checker to compute checksums for your critical system files, you have the perfect means to isolate exactly which files the intruder might have altered.

In cases where budgets allow it, a "hot spare" (a system that is complete with preloaded software) can allow you to take a corrupted system offline without sacrificing customer access to your systems. This step is absolutely critical if the attacked system is your company's Web server, especially if it is used for electronic commerce. I assert that hot spares should be maintained for any system used for primary customer access to the organization.

After the systems have been restored to normal operation, write a full accounting of the incident. Outline the events and the actions taken by the incident handling team. This report and others like it will serve you well when accounting for the results your security team accomplished in protecting the corporate systems. Furthermore, use these results to train users, staff, and management on security threats and the measures that you need to take to deal with them.

10.4.7   Dealing with Witch Hunts

The entire premise of incident-handling procedures is that the person driving the investigation of the intrusion represents the victim of the attack. What about the situation in which you or one of your users is accused of being the source of an attack against another site? This situation levies its own requirements on intrusion detection systems. As in classic law enforcement and criminal investigations, the objective is not only to identify those accountable for the incident but also to exonerate those who are not.

Situations have already occurred in which one site running an intrusion detection system accused another site of launching an attack. This accusation was based on the intrusion detection system's findings. In some cases, the intrusion detection system's detection signature was found to be imprecise, necessitating the manual review of system logs and raw packet traffic for the time in question. In other situations, intrusion detection systems have deemed activity as clearly corresponding to attacks when, in fact, the user was performing legitimate job functions on the system.

One good way to protect yourself from accusations of being the source of attacks or problems on other sites is to capture raw log or packet data at various points within your network enclave. From the discussion of the legal process in Chapter 9, remember that the best defense against false accusations is your own set of evidence. If you have audit logs to show that the problems did not come from your site, chances are that you can derail trouble of this sort before it starts.

10.5   Conclusion

The user of an intrusion detection system determines whether the system functions at optimum levels; indeed, the user determines whether the system functions at all! This chapter covered material to assist the user of a system in determining need, selecting a product, placing the product, configuring it, and handling incidents that the product detects.

Endnotes

1. National Computer Security Center. "Glossary of Computer Security Terms." NCSC-TG-004-88, 1988.

2. Brownlee, N. and E. Guttman. Request for Comments: 2350, "Expectations for Computer Security Incident Response." The Internet Society, June 1998.

3. Gula, R. personal communication, July 1999.

4. Gross, Andrew H. "Analyzing Computer Intrusions," PhD thesis, University of California, San Diego, San Diego, CA, 1997.

5. Monroe, Klayton. *BlackLab*ᵃ : *A Workbench for Forensic Analysts,* Area Systems, Exodus Communications, Inc., Columbia, MD, December 1999.

CHAPTER

For Strategists

One of the most critical players in security management is the security strategist, the person who makes the decision to deploy intrusion detection as a part of a security program in corporate system environments. In the best of worlds, the security strategist is the CEO or someone who reports directly to the CEO. As such, he or she has independent funding authority, as well as sufficient influence on corporate processes that are critical to achieving security goals. I propose this view while realizing that less-optimal scenarios are much more common. In all too many situations, the strategist is asked to address security problems in the organization, but is given no resources to devote to the task. Even when the need is compelling, few strategists have the requisite information and expertise to build a strong case for incorporating sound information security practices in the corporate process.

In this section, a road map is outlined for those tasked with improving security in corporate systems. Also included are discussion points for building the case for security, advice for building a strong security program, and a set of questions that should be asked of product and service vendors who propose specific solutions.

11.1 Building a Case for Security

In a global economy, your competition may not think twice about enlisting the help of hackers—or other computer criminals—to steal information and gain the competitive edge. Given the almost daily news reports of computer and network security breaches occurring in public systems, the need to argue for computer security seems redundant. However, many organizations do not view themselves as being targets. These organizations do not have sound system security practices and supports in place. Given an organization with no existing program in this area, where does one begin? Let's take this problem step by step and lay the groundwork for an appropriate systems security program.

11.1.1 Assembling Information

Before you start developing a security strategy, take some time to review the issues, the current best practices, and your environment. Many books and other information sources on computer security can guide you. A comprehensive list of these references is included in Appendix A, "Resources." I've flagged the references that are especially well suited to readers who are new to security. These sources can serve to answer specific questions that arise along the way.

At this point, gather information on your organization and its information systems. To understand what needs to be done, you need to understand each system, its purpose, and the policies and practices that govern its operation. This overview will allow you to better gauge the impact of various security measures on current operations. The information that you gather should include the identities of those responsible for the operation of these systems. Convincing them of the necessity of the security process will be critical to your success.

Consider placing this information in a location where you can access it easily as you work on your case; you are likely to need your data for everything from meetings to security plans and policies. Spreadsheets or databases can be excellent repositories. Remember to hold this information securely. Consider using encryption tools to protect its integrity and confidentiality.

11.1.2 What Is the Organization Trying to Accomplish?

After you gather and review the information, it's time to articulate the security goals and objectives for your organization. This can start as a philosophical statement (something akin to a security-specific mission statement), but you'll eventually want to flesh it out to include specific security goals. One way of jump-starting this process is to interview the heads of the organizational elements that use the systems. Ask these people to list their primary security concerns, both general and specific. Take this list of concerns, augment them with those concerns that apply to the entire organization, and combine them—identifying sources for each. This list will be of value when you get around to performing risk assessment.

11.1.3 How Does Security Fit Into Overall Business Goals?

An often-neglected part of building a management case for systems security is establishing the impact of security on the goals of the business. To do so, you need first to document these business goals. The information you collected in the first step of this process should help here. Augment it by meeting with executive management and other parties who are charged with determining corporate business strategy. Most will have either quantitative models or personal expertise that outline general rules of thumb.

For instance, many corporate financial managers know exactly how much the organization spends to generate a dollar of revenue. Marketing managers often know what portion of the organization's income comes from a particular customer or market segment. Sales management often knows how much it costs to generate a single customer, and what impact losing a customer or group of customers has on the corporate bottom line. In these discussions, focus on those portions of the business process that most heavily depend on the corporate computing and networking infrastructure. Also, focus on those corporate assets that are developed and maintained in the corporate network.

11.1.4   Where Does Information Security Fit Into the Corporate Risk-Management Program?

Now that you are equipped with background information, an understanding of the business goals of your organization, and the security goals of your organization, it's time to pull it all together. In most cases, this procedure involves a systematic risk-assessment process, in which you organize information about the mission of the business, the assets, the culture, and the operational tenets. You outline concerns in each of those areas, and then consider the impact of security measures on those concerns. This routine will allow you to create a set of cost-benefit assertions, with a valuation assigned to each system component and a corresponding cost for securing that asset.

In most corporations, risk management is a standard business practice with benefits quantified as a return on investment (ROI). This process is much the same, with a focus on assessing those returns on investment relevant to information security. Some excellent risk-management software packages allow you to perform exhaustive information security-risk assessments. If you are functioning in a large organization, it is to your advantage to use such software.

In building this cost-benefit model, be absolutely certain to include the following items:

- The ROI associated with protecting the corporate reputation. For instance, what is the business impact of hackers taking over the corporate Web site, substituting pornographic images for corporate logos, and posting text full of racial slurs and slanderous remarks about the firm's largest customer?

- The ROI associated with keeping the corporate stockholders happy. For instance, what is the stock price impact of a succession of security incidents, all publicized on the front page of a major national newspaper?

- The ROI associated with maintaining continuity of system service. Here's a test question: What is the business impact of a denial-of-service attack that takes all of your systems down for a day? A week? Longer?

Risk assessment provides critical input for your security strategy: a rough idea of what information security is worth to the organization. Now move on to the next step, in which you look at security needs.

11.1.5   What Do We Need to Secure the System?

Now that you have an understanding of the system and organization, a sense of desired goals, an understanding of the business process into which your security strategy must fit, and the valuation of the system elements you're going to protect, it's time to get down to specifics. The next step in the process is to specify the necessary elements of an information security infrastructure.

The foundation of any security infrastructure is a set of three documents:

- Information security policy

- Information security procedures (also called standards)

- Information security practices (also called guidelines)

These documents are arranged in a hierarchy, with more dynamic elements placed lower in the hierarchy. Figure 11.1 shows an example of the linkages and differences among the three. These three documents contain information that defines and describes the information systems of your organization, the security goals and issues associated with each system and organization using the system, and other information that drives security requirements.

As a first step, you need the security policy and the security procedures. You are likely to find that you already possess much of the information needed to prepare these two documents, thanks to the steps you've already taken. The third document, the practices or guidelines, will be completed later as measures are implemented and responsibility assigned to specific personnel.

After the policy and procedures are complete, you should develop an information security architecture outlining a plan for implementing the measures contained in the procedures. This architecture should specify the hardware, software, and communications links making up the systems environment, outlining the information stored or handled by each, the threats applicable to each, and the corresponding level of protection desired for that information. After you have established the architecture, a process should be defined for handling the selection, integration, and ongoing maintenance of each protection.

Figure 11.1   Examples of Information Security Policy, Procedure, and Practice

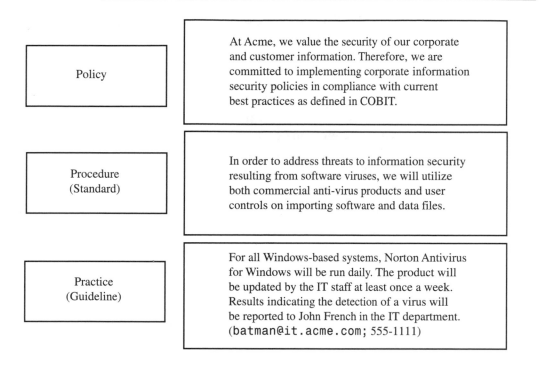

Next, all organizational personnel should be trained. This training (which should be on-going, and targeted to the technical level and functional role of the user) should cover the corporate policy and procedures for information security, outlining the rationale driving the policy and procedures. Information security awareness training should also be provided to all personnel. This training will include information to heighten user sensitivity to new threats or noted problems.

Appendix A, "Resources," contains information about commercial sources of security training and materials for that training.

Given clear marching orders and well-trained personnel who understand the why and wherefore of security policy, it's time to address specific security technologies and products.[1]

11.1.6   Finding Allies

In major organizations, technical concerns associated with information security are certainly of importance. However, decisions regarding funding and management support for security are often driven by political considerations. Given this fact, you should seek out those whose interests are likely to be compatible with yours. In particular, two functional elements found in many large organizations are likely to understand and appreciate your interest in securing the corporate information assets. Use them as a starting point for a corporate-wide, consensus-building exercise. Everyone has a stake in information security.

11.1.6.1 Internal Audit

Internal audit departments are charged with performing ongoing independent examinations of business processes within corporations and other organizations. Auditors perform these appraisals to examine and evaluate the effectiveness of the internal management controls. The appraisals also measure the adequacy of the controls, and the organization's overall quality of performance. Internal audits are a requirement for most public corporations, and their reports and recommendations to officers of these corporations are considered ironclad.

Internal auditors cover several items in their examinations that coincide with information security goals: reliability and integrity of information, the safeguarding of assets, and compliance with policies and regulations. In particular, intrusion detection systems can provide internal auditors with information that allows them to perform their appraisals faster and more accurately. Because a goal of internal audit is to protect the owners and stake-holders of corporations from fraud and mismanagement, a logical and mutually beneficial relationship exists between internal audit and information security.

11.1.6.2 Marketing

Marketing departments of major corporations are concerned with matching the products produced by the organization to the needs and wants of customers. Marketing departments are considered the primary income-producing elements of commercial organizations. Customers expect and value the trustworthiness of an organization with which they do business, so marketing departments are solicitous of any threats to the organization's reputation. Because many major customers make their initial approach to organizations via the Internet, threats to the corporate Web site represent quantifiable and potentially disastrous threats to the corporation's reputation.

Imagine the horror within a major online stock brokerage when a user reported an unauthorized transfer of $40,000.00 from his trading account to a Latvian bank. The customer's brokerage account was secured by using a password-based authentication mechanism, a mechanism considered weak by security professionals. Fortunately, the loss was discovered and traced quickly enough to allow recovery of the funds from the Latvian bank, but news of the incident represented bad publicity for the firm, creating serious trust issues between the stock brokerage and both current and prospective customers.[2]

Astute marketing managers realize that good system security protects the corporate image and goodwill, eliminating a major threat to the corporate revenue levels. Furthermore, protecting systems from denial-of-service attacks addresses another marketing nightmare: lack of customer access to the organization. Tales abound of unfortunate organizations that lose untold income due to Web ordering sites that do not work; or, even worse, they crash, and then drive customers to buy elsewhere. Marketing interests are served well by strong information security, so this can be another set of valuable allies.

11.1.7 Overcoming Management Resistance

Two issues typically arise in the course of discussing a strong security program. First is that of cost. Security is never a profit center, and there is often resistance to expending funds on what is commonly considered a bottomless pit. The second issue is that of balancing security with operational need.

The key to resolving cost-related resistance is to demonstrate a return on security investment. This presentation can be based on the risk assessment you conducted. Although the time and effort required to build a strong information security program is not trivial, it pales in comparison to the time and effort required to deal with even one catastrophic attack. You might point out that insurance policies require funds, too, but few organizations would choose to forego those costs!

For smaller organizations there is an additional argument for establishing an information security program. Many contractors levy requirements for information security programs on small businesses, as a prerequisite to bidding on certain contracts. This practice is especially common when dealing with intellectual property belonging to customers—for example, contracts for hardware or software design services.

Another strategy for addressing resistance is to present the cost estimates corresponding to the protections you defined as necessary. In these cost estimates, you should demonstrate that each protection addresses a specific category of threat.

Addressing the concerns regarding conflicts between security and operational goals requires an emphasis on planning and ongoing process. An integral part of any effective security policy is a procedure for resolving conflicts. This procedure is akin to an arbitration process, in which each party presents its case to a knowledgeable and impartial decision-maker. Corporate management needs to understand that security is a dynamic process. It is meant to guide and control activity that goes on in a fast-paced, complex environment. The activity involves constant interaction with a number of parties, often with conflicting interests. When the system environment changes in any way, so must the security measures protecting that system.

11.2   Defining Requirements for IDS

After you obtain initial management buy-in for establishing a new information security program, it's time to take a closer look at intrusion detection. In this section, we step through determining goals and objectives for the functions and consider the factors that govern the selection of a particular solution.

11.2.1   Revisiting Goals and Objectives

As a first step toward determining which intrusion detection system is best for you and your organization, it's helpful to ask again: What do we hope to gain by running an intrusion detection system? The more finely-grained these goals and objectives are, the better. As discussed in Chapter 2, "Concepts and Definitions," intrusion detection systems have two primary goals: accountability and response. Accountability is the capability to assign responsibility for a particular system event to a person. Response is the capability to recognize an attack and block it from accomplishing its ultimate goal, thereby shielding the target of the attack from a security breach.

In many organizations, accountability is sufficient, especially if the provisions for taking corrective actions against the responsible party are established and well publicized. These corrective actions run the gamut from legal remedies (civil or criminal process) to reprimand or dismissal. Accountability is also preferable in situations where the risk of repeated attacks originating with the same party is high. In military circles, reliable establishment of accountability is preferred in cases when tactical systems are under hostile attack because repeated attacks can be addressed through the use of deadly force.

In other organizations, where extracting retribution from users is not as feasible, response may be of greater appeal. An example of such a situation is the case of a strategic partner. In that case, the strategic partner is vital to your business and, as such, is permitted access to your corporate systems to do business with you. How do you handle the situation in which an attack appears to originate with a user coming from your strategic partner's network?

These concerns should be articulated as part of the partnership agreement. However, an intrusion detection system can provide a means of enforcing that agreement. In some cases, both accountability and response might be desirable. However, because each goal has unique requirements for support, it is helpful if you have an idea of which one is more important to you and your organization.

11.2.2   What Are the Threats?

Numerous threat models describe the security problems that are likely to arise in your systems. We can use several schemes to classify these problems. Following are some possible approaches:

- **Internal versus external** In this case, the relevant boundary defining internal and external is the security perimeter of the organizational system. Most threat models define these perimeters as existing at network interfaces such as firewalls, modems, routers, or other such boundary devices.

- **Authorized versus unauthorized** In this case, the threat is classified as involving theft or bypass of system access controls or exceeding authorization.

- **Goals of intruder** In this category, the goals are characterized as violations of the three security properties: confidentiality, integrity, and availability. Confidentiality breaches usually involve surveillance attacks or access control violations. Integrity breaches usually include unauthorized alteration of data, software, or system configuration information. Availability breaches include many network attacks, including packet floods and denial-of-service attacks that trigger system crashes.

- **Intentional versus inadvertent** For purposes of pursuing legal remedies, it's helpful to distinguish threats resulting from deliberate actions on the part of an intruder from those resulting from human error or acts of God. Making this distinction can require additional detection capabilities on the part of an intrusion detection system.

11.2.3 What Are Our Limitations?

Because organizations do not often have unlimited information technology (IT) budgets, or unlimited computing or network bandwidth, it's important to define the limitations to which an intrusion detection installation is subject. For instance, what is the maximum network bandwidth hit that your organization can accommodate. Virtually none? That's important to know. Is sufficient equipment funding available to absorb the cost of a dedicated workstation for running an intrusion detection system? If so, what are the performance characteristics of that system? Will someone be assigned to the care and feeding of the IDS, or will it be responsible for finding and notifying the responsible person when it detects problems? Does the primary user of the system have any special needs (for example, is the person vision- or hearing-impaired?).

11.2.4 Considerations in Adopting Intrusion Detection and System Monitoring

Several issues might arise as you proceed toward installing intrusion detection capability on your systems. First is the issue of user privacy.

The courts have ruled that businesses have the right to monitor all employee communications that occur on corporate systems. As a matter of principle, you should take steps to assure tight control over the information collected in the course of intrusion detection-related monitoring.

This procedure is simply a matter of sound information management policy. A great deal of critical information passes over the network, much of it is monitored by the intrusion detection system. If a person has no legitimate need to review the information, it should not be reviewed. This approach is not only privacy sparing, which is increasingly important to users, but also mitigates risk associated with loss or divulgence of critical corporate information.

Legality is another concern. Certain information (for instance personal information contained in human resources files) is protected by the Privacy Act, and divulgence of this information can leave the organization subject to fines and other legal penalties.

Another consideration is that of archiving the information collected by intrusion detection systems. The raw information should be archived to media, and stored under lock and key. If there is any allegation of criminal activity, the archived information could be admissible in a court of law as evidence. For the information to retain its evidentiary value, you must be able to demonstrate that you've maintained a clear chain of custody (that is, you handled and stored the information in a fashion that protected it from alteration).

Perhaps more important, the information could also be needed if someone accuses your corporation of being the source of a security incident or illegal activity. Again, the system logs can be admissible in court, this time to exonerate your organization.

11.3   Marketing Hype versus Real Solutions

Congratulations! You're close to the end of this process. You've gone to bat for information security, and you've been successful. You used an orderly process to decide that the system is ready for intrusion detection and, furthermore, have a concise description of your functional requirements. Now, it's time to shop for a specific solution. Every salesperson for every intrusion detection system vendor is calling on you, each asserting that his or her employer's solution is the only suitable one for you and your needs. In this section, a set of questions is provided that allows you to rank the various commercial solutions as you work toward an optimal selection.

11.3.1   What Product Is Best Fitted to Us and Our Goals?

Thanks to all the work you've done in isolating your requirements, you have a set of selection criteria for your intrusion detection system. So use them!

Work, step by step, through the list of criteria, asking the vendor for information. Beware of proprietary hype and terms—ask for explanations until you're comfortable that you understand exactly what the vendor's product is offering.

11.3.2   How Painful Is This Product to Install?

Your installation experience is a good gauge of how the rest of your experience with the product will go. If you're functioning in an environment in which one harried system administrator is responsible for installing and maintaining security software for several hundred systems, a system that requires five people and three weeks to install and tune might not be an optimal choice for you. A system that requires a UNIX wizard to install and run it might not be the best choice for a Windows NT shop staffed by temporary employees. If a vendor asserts that the product is a turnkey product that even a novice could install, ask for a hands-on demo!

11.3.3   How Painful Is This Product to Run?

Even if the product installs easily, the evaluation task isn't over. Check out the run-time features of the product. Is it stable for nontrivial periods of time? Can you make it crash (especially by exercising the user interface or increasing its monitoring load by generating network traffic or auditable events from another system on the network)? How does the product respond to increasing the set of detection scripts? How easy is it to change the detection scripts? Can you change the scripts in run time, or must you bring the system down and do it offline? How are alarms reported? Is there a way to cut them off?

Here's a cautionary note about assessing the coverage of a particular system. Sales and marketing departments are always tempted to inflate the number of attack signatures that a product can recognize. Beware of detection signature bloat! Many products artificially inflate the number of scenarios they recognize by including irrelevant signatures (for instance, recognizing the same network attack from a variety of operating system platforms; an Internet Protocol (IP) spoof looks the same regardless of whether a Sun Solaris, Windows NT, or Linux system sees it) or variations of the same signature. (Is exercising a finger attack using one set of characters to overflow the buffer different from exercising the same attack using another?)

Another worthwhile question about the usability of intrusion detection systems regards distributing bug patches and additional attack signatures. Ask the vendor about the frequency of such updates, the form of those updates, the effort required to install and activate those updates, and the measures taken by the vendor to protect your system in the process of making those updates. For example, could an adversary readily trick your personnel into installing malicious software by pretending to be the vendor distributing updates?

11.3.4   What Are the Expectations of the Personnel?

A useful but seldom-used product differentiation is the distinction between tools and applications. The difference between the two in the security technology world is the level of expertise expected of the user. Intrusion detection products address a wide range of user experience and skill levels. Some products ("tools") are well suited for use by network management staff with years of experience managing high-speed networks. These users can often decode packet traffic in real time, visually spotting malformed packets and other anomalies that are incomprehensible to other users.

Other products ("applications") offer clear, simple displays and control consoles that generate management summaries of detection results, complete with explanations of any alarms triggered. Involve the person who will use the product in your buying decision, making sure that the product is a good match to that person's skills and preferences.

11.3.5   Who Was the Dream Customer for Whom This Product Was Designed?

Perhaps the best of all possible worlds is one in which you find a product that appears to have been designed especially for you. Unfortunately, unless you are part of a larger, extremely well-standardized market, this scenario is unlikely. Still, when a product appears to have a strange or illogical set of system features, you should ask for which market the product was originally developed. This question allows you to spot products that were actually developed for non-intrusion detection purposes, but retrofitted to take advantage of the growing intrusion detection market. In this case, you should check the capabilities of the product against your goals and objectives for an intrusion detection system to confirm that the product meets your needs.

11.4   Integrating Security Into a Legacy Environment

The preceding questions are also applicable when you are not starting from scratch. How does the process of selecting an intrusion detection system work when the organization already has a security infrastructure in place?

Actually, this situation is common. The decision process and requirements for this path to security are much the same as the process of building from scratch. However, when the legacy security measures are effective and the need is simply to augment them, additional considerations come into play. In this section, we address some of those issues and suggest possible strategies for resolving them.

11.4.1 Assessing the Existing Systems

As in the case of building a security infrastructure from scratch, the first step in working with an existing system is to perform a needs assessment, identifying the needs as well as the existing protections. It's impossible to predict what you'll find in this assessment. In years of performing this sort of evaluation, I've found a wide range of existing conditions: from 10-year-old security policies that have been stashed in a file cabinet (and never used) to ancient systems with excellent security infrastructures that are well-fitted to the system environment and goals.

In performing the systems and needs assessment, one critical difference arises between assessing needs for a legacy system versus assessing needs for a new infrastructure.

In the legacy case, you must evaluate every system and protection against the question: Does this work? This process actually represents an opportunity to improve the odds of securing the organizational systems because you have some sense of whether a protection strategy will be effective.

11.4.2 Leveraging Investments in Security

Only rarely will organizations have the IT security budget to provide all the protections they want, regardless of need. For the remaining cases, you must do some critical analysis of the payback associated with various investments in security mechanisms.

When IT protection budgets are severely constrained, some rules of thumb apply. Let's travel through one such approach to applying protections on the basis of ROI, starting from the lowest investment and working to the highest. First, let's address those protections that come "for free."

For instance, a review of system documentation can often yield instructions on using protections that are already provided as part of operating systems and application software. An example of such a protection is the userid/password challenge utility, provided as an integral part of most modern operating systems. Many of these utilities are not particularly strong; few can stand up to rigorous attacks from intruders. However, for curbing threats arising from less-expert or persistent intruders, these built-in tools offer some protection. This protection can be augmented at low cost by enacting user regulations that require users to generate and use strong passwords that are not easily guessed.

If your organization runs on Windows/DOS-based systems, the next investment in protection technologies should be a commercial virus detector. These security packages are usually low-cost and easy to use, and they protect you from attacks that can inflict great damage to systems and data files alike. Because the latest round of macro viruses proved to be especially disruptive, the ROI associated with virus detectors is especially high.

If your organization is connected to the Internet, the next investment in security should probably be a firewall. Although the most popular firewalls are commercial turnkey systems, lower-cost options are available, although these may require some outside assistance to set up. Firewalls can filter out some of the nastiest network attacks and eliminate a significant portion of threats coming from the Internet.

Educating users about the security benefits of a firewalled network is challenging. Users are apt to install tunnels or backdoors to continue to network as they always have. Analyze that usage, and make provisions for user comments and suggestions. For example, you can allow streaming audio and video into the network so that employees can listen to newscasts, or you can permit after-hours network gaming.

Next on the list are vulnerability assessment products. These range from the freeware (for example COPS, SATAN, Tiger, and ISS-freeware) to commercial packages, some of which are easy to use. These products allow you to spot problems and correct them, and deliver significant improvements in security for the funds expended.

Don't forget other components of the communications infrastructure that are not usually considered information systems (such as the company PBX, wireless paging services, or fax devices). These require scanning and monitoring for vulnerabilities as well. Although some freeware exists for performing vulnerability assessment for these devices (for instance, "war dialers"), some of the tools are of questionable quality. Fortunately, excellent commercial products are now available for this purpose.

At this point, it's finally time to consider adding intrusion detection products to your protection suite. These products will capture problems that the rest of the infrastructure simply can't address.

11.4.3   Dealing with "Wetware"—the Humans in the System

Perhaps the most critical system components in securing a system are the humans involved in administering and using the system. In some cases, user compliance with security policies is the biggest determinant of the ultimate success or failure of a system's security effort. Well-trained, motivated, and security-aware users are rare, but can make critical contributions to any system security program.

11.4.3.1   Attitudes about Finding Problems

Unfortunately, managers do not always recognize security-reinforcing behavior as such, and often discourage the very attitudes and activities that reinforce strong security. This condition develops because of corporate management cultures that favor short-term tranquility over longer-term results. Such an environment represents absolute disaster when it comes to security.

For instance, many organizations actively discourage users from reporting security problems they find on corporate systems. In extreme cases, those who conscientiously report problems are dismissed or otherwise penalized for bringing those problems to the attention of others.

As a security manager, I groan when I hear these accounts because I believe it is far preferable to learn of problems early from a trusted insider and to correct or monitor them. It is far worse to learn about them later from a hacker group that publishes to one of the security newsgroups (especially when that newsgroup posting not only announces the problem, but also announces the release of an attack tool to exploit the problem!).

11.4.3.2 Hackers as Security Experts

Another worrisome management trend in corporate life today is the tendency to consider current or reformed hackers as "security experts." Although many issues are associated with this practice, one fact should be taken into account by anyone considering hiring a hacker.

The skills necessary to exploit security vulnerabilities in systems are quite different from those required to design and build trustworthy systems to begin with. As Gene Spafford of Purdue University's CERIAS security center says, "By analogy, stealing cars and joyriding does not provide one with an education in mechanical engineering, nor does pouring sugar in the gas tank." Hiring someone from "the other side" to protect your system makes about as much sense as hiring the Medellin cartel to protect your child from drug dealers!

11.4.4 Handling Conflicts

Many of the problems that involve system misconfiguration are the result of a conflict between security and performance goals. A classic example of this situation is the following: A security staffer installs a firewall to protect the corporate systems from Internet attacks. The staffer configures the firewall by using the time-honored policy rule: Block all connections and then enable only those you believe are absolutely necessary. The network administrator sets up the same firewall. But the administrator configures the firewall by using another and equally time-honored policy rule: Allow all connections, blocking only those you know to be bad. In this situation, who is right? A standard information security answer is that the security staffer is correct. In fact, both approaches are correct, but each serves a fundamentally different organizational need. So, how does one resolve this conflict in organizational needs?

This situation demands a corporate information security policy. The policy should state the management-sanctioned organizational priorities, with provisions for resolving conflicts between security and operational needs. When these conflicts cannot be settled locally, someone in management should be empowered to make the determination of appropriate risk.

There is a technical solution strategy, too. Intrusion detection systems allow one to construct control points that are more flexible than those provided by firewalls alone.

11.5   Dealing with the Effects of Corporate Transitions

The corporate world today is absolute quicksilver. Major corporations swallow smaller competitors at a dizzying pace, often demanding drastic transitions in corporate cultures and operational priorities. Many of these corporate transitions carry security impacts with them. Because many of them drive changes in security policies and practices, I mention them here. However, because each situation is so unique, I do not recommend solutions to the issues. Solutions are left to those better acquainted with the specific situations.

11.5.1   Mergers and Acquisitions

Mergers and acquisitions represent special security challenges. These challenges are driven by two factors. The first is the combination of previously separate corporate network environments, often introducing heterogeneity of system platforms, both hardware and software.

The other is that a significant difference often exists between the security stances of the constituent organizations, as reflected by the different cultures. In some cases, an organization that operates at a high level of security finds itself forced to connect to a network enclave that is riddled with security problems, thereby compromising the original security state.

11.5.2   Strategic Partners

Another modern corporate phenomenon is that of strategic partners. These partners can sometimes include former or current competitors. Strategic partners present special challenges to those who manage security for organizations, for a variety of reasons. These issues are associated with a compelling need for network connectivity that does not bring with it any commitment subject to local control. Thus, people who are not compelled to adopt your security policies are nevertheless authorized to access your system.

A recent incident highlights the security issues associated with strategic partners. A corporation had two strategic partners who were fierce competitors: company A and company B.

Company A discovered that its systems had been hacked, compromising a critical new product design specification. Upon investigation, company B was found to have been responsible for hacking company A's systems, using the strategic partner's corporate network as a path to company A!

Intrusion detection systems can be a solution that allows the access required by a strategic partner, while preventing that partner from using your system as a launching pad for further attack.

11.5.3   *Globalization*

One effect of the Internet has been to shrink the business world, encouraging an unprecedented expansion into global markets. As this expansion occurs, it brings with it additional security issues. The geographical distribution of corporate satellite offices necessitates the distribution of critical corporate information across a large number of networks. Each of these networks, as well as the paths between them, require security.

There are issues arising from the political and legal perimeters that result from operating across multiple legal jurisdictions, each of which may have widely differing regulations and statutes governing computer security. Investigating and seeking legal remedies for computer crimes is especially problematic, given certain countries' tolerance for hacking.

Another factor that often affects security managed at a global level is that of export controls on cryptography. Because a common way of connecting satellite offices to headquarters is to use encryption-based products, such as link encryptors and encrypting routers to secure transactions, the export control restrictions can affect the protections available to you.

Appendix A includes references and pointers to information about export restrictions and other factors affecting security strategy for global business. Because this area is politically volatile and several court challenges are in progress, you should check the current status of these restrictions as part of your security planning.

11.5.4   *Expansion and Contraction*

As corporate organizations adapt to a more competitive global marketplace, many use mergers and acquisitions to grow, and then downsize to reduce personnel costs. This activity has had profound side effects on employees and associates of the organizations involved. These trends lead to a perception on the part of employees that the organization is not trustworthy and that employee loyalty to organizations is no longer appropriate.

The dissolution of trust relationships may elevate the risk of insider abuse. The measures adopted by some organizations to deal with the increased costs of full-time employment (such as outsourcing, using temporary or contract labor) also serve to reduce the traditional trust relationship between employee and employer.

These changes in the dynamics between employer and employee drive a need for increased user monitoring and policy compliance measurement. Intrusion detection systems can support these needs, as can improved personnel security practices for critical systems personnel.

11.5.5   Going from Private to Public

Finally, a set of problems arises as firms go from private to public funding. This event shifts the security threat picture in a couple of ways. First, the publicity associated with an IPO, especially that which associates the corporation with some astronomical number of dollars raised, places the organization on the public's radar screen. Some people will simply be curious, and will access the corporate Web pages to acquire additional information about the corporation. However, others will use their awareness of the corporation in a much less innocent fashion. Some will be interested in determining the vulnerability of the organization's systems. Others may attempt to hack the site, and then report the incident to the press in hopes of manipulating stock prices.

Stock price concerns also produce a side effect that represents a real loss to security professionals. Due to the sensitivity of stock prices to press reports of security breaches, many public corporations prohibit systems security personnel from divulging security incident information to colleagues in the community. This posture makes the task of tracking security threat trends much more difficult for security managers, and ultimately leads to poorer system security for everyone.

11.6   Conclusion

You should now have some ideas about how to build a case for integrating information security into corporate business process. You should also know how to make that case to corporate management to obtain resources and authority to implement the information security process. After you have management commitment, you also have ideas on how to deal with the two common scenarios: building information security infrastructures from scratch, and extending and upgrading existing infrastructures to use improvements in security technology. Finally, you have guidance on ways to select the best intrusion detection system for your environment, complete with a set of scenarios in which intrusion detection may help you deal with common corporate transitions.

I have two final reminders for those tasked with determining security strategy. First, security is a continuous process, requiring a constant flexing and adaptation of the protection envelope to accommodate system growth and change in the environment. Many of the steps outlined in this chapter should be repeated at regular intervals, as well as when major changes occur in the system or its environment.

Second, although most of the examples and references are drawn from commercial organizations, the same strategic process applies to nonprofit organizations, which need security, too. Although risk management might not be characterized in terms of ROI, security measures can be expressed in simple cost-benefit terms. Here, "cost" can be expressed in terms of labor or availability of systems resources, and "benefit" can be expressed in terms of improved access.

Endnotes

1. Although many security books outline processes for building programs similar to those I have covered in this chapter, I especially recommend: Garfinkel, Simson and E. H. Spafford. *Practical UNIX and Internet Security.* O'Reilly and Associates, Sebastopol, CA, 1996.

2. Abramson, L. "E-Commerce Fraud." *Morning Edition,* Washington, DC, National Public Radio, June 4, 1999.

CHAPTER 12

For Designers

Intrusion detection systems (IDS) present an appealing vision to those charged with managing systems security. System managers who are already stretched to their limits dealing with nonsecurity issues welcome the possibility of an omniscient, intelligent, tireless security oracle that can spot signs of security problems, notify those responsible for handling them, and take action to block the attacks before they inflict any lasting damage.

Fulfilling this vision represents a tall order for product designers. To design useful intrusion detection systems, a designer must understand, and preferably master, the following:

- The principles of security management

- The principles of operating systems, network protocols, and major applications

- The range of acceptable security policies for customer environments

- The legal limitations placed on monitoring and encryption

- Threats and vulnerabilities, including attack scripts, typical policy violations, and symptoms of both, for all major commercial operating systems and applications

- Optimization schemes for data and memory-intensive processing

- A wide range of algorithmic approaches for performing pattern matching and statistical anlysis

- Principles for testing and assuring both robustness and trustworthiness of system software

- The ability to track research, isolating those results that are applicable to the task at hand

Some of these topics are covered elsewhere in the book. Others have been saved for this chapter.

This chapter provides some principles and discusses general rules that are and will continue to be applicable regardless of the specific intrusion detection project at hand. The following sections are peppered with information and advice gleaned from those who designed and developed some of the first-generation research and commercial intrusion detection products. Finally, we will discuss the specific issues that differentiate security tools from other sorts of software products and examine some principles for dealing with these issues.

12.1 Requirements

There are a lot of "security experts" around these days, many of them proclaiming that they alone know the composition of the "best" intrusion detection system. This is akin to a baker claiming that she or he alone knows the recipe for bread! The truth of the matter is if you know the definition of bread, the main components, and the rules of chemistry that make it all work together, you can devise your own bread recipe that may in fact be better than anyone else's!

Previous chapters have provided descriptions of the components required to build intrusion detection systems. As with bread recipes, your design determines which components your system will include, how those components work together, and in what proportions. Perhaps most important, the quality of your design determines whether the combination forms a coherent suite of capabilities that are meaningful to the users of the system.

In this section, we will discuss some of the security "fixtures" from which you'll need to leverage key capabilities. This chapter will take you through some ongoing philosophical discussions regarding the nature of network security, hoping that the insight these discussions can provide might allow you to approach some of the perpetual problems from a fresh new angle. Finally, we will explore some factors affecting requirements for intrusion detection systems, focusing on those attributes that drive design decisions. Because network security in general and intrusion detection in particular are inherently reactive technologies, many of these requirements will evolve or flex with the systems they protect.

12.1.1 Good versus Great Intrusion Detection

As you review the existing information on intrusion detection, including this book, you'll see some common features that define intrusion detection. Although you should have a clear understanding of these features, the ultimate success of your system will hinge on your ability to package these features in a way that maximizes their value to a customer.

So let's get down to cases. What makes a good intrusion detection system? A good system is

- **Effective** Effectiveness is the most important requirement of all. Intrusion detection systems must be able to accurately and consistently detect attacks or other predefined usage patterns of interest.

- **Easy to use** Ease of use is also important. Security experts are scarce and expensive. A well-designed tool that can enable a non-security expert to reliably perform routine security-related tasks can help customers deal with this scarcity.

- **Adaptable** The system should be adaptable to the host platforms, the targets, the threat environment, and the customer's policies. Few customers run homogeneous system environments; the system must accommodate input from each of the different platforms and make sense of all of them.

- **Robust** The system should run reliably with provisions for redundant or other fault-tolerant features.

- **Fast** The system should be able to perform the monitoring tasks for the target environment without falling behind.

- **Efficient** The system should make optimal use of computing, storage, and communications bandwidth so that it minimally affects the target environment that it monitors.

- **Safe** The system must have features that prevent unauthorized persons from using it as a vehicle for attacking others.

In addition to these primary requirements, a second level of requirements can create an intrusion detection system that is an irreplaceable part of system security management. A great system is

- **Accommodating** An accommodating system enables users to fit the intrusion detection system to their needs over time. Such adaptability allows the system to evolve to fit the needs of users as they become more adept at using the system. Such a system should also accommodate special needs of physically challenged users (in keeping with such features provided by commercial systems vendors).

- **Security enhancing** This feature means that the system automatically gravitates to settings and modes that reflect sound security practice. For instance, this environment includes such rules of thumb as making default settings extremely conservative so that users have to take deliberate action to enable risky functions.

- **Scalable** In a scalable system, components should be designed with standard or well-documented interfaces. These interfaces, in keeping with the requirement to be security-enhancing, should support appropriate authentication mechanisms.

- **Realistic** A realistic system allows users to balance needs for manageability with needs for security.

- **Hardened** A hardened system is designed to withstand deliberate attacks and furthermore generates an event log or other audit trail of its own operation.

12.1.2 Different Approaches to Security

At times you may review some classic references on security and wonder what you missed. The principles might appear sound in theory, and the terminology makes sense, but you can't understand how to translate the formal structures and stilted language into a realistic approach to securing systems in this chaotic world of network technology.

First, don't panic. Many classic approaches to security originated as physical security tenets and were ported to the network world. This port, for many reasons, doesn't always work.

Given this fact, it is sometimes helpful to explore several approaches to security, drawn from the real experiences and observations of others. Each approach contributes some insight that can help you take security from a dry bookish topic to an internalized compass that provides guidance to you as you design tools that enable the protection of systems in the real world.

12.1.2.1 Security as a Control Function

Classic approaches to security are tightly bound to the notion of control. In this realm, security is the state of being protected against uncontrolled losses or other ill effects. This view of security is often marked by the assumption that absolute security is attainable. It furthermore implies that this level of absolute security can be preserved. This is done by transitioning from an absolutely secure state to other absolutely secure states, using only operations proven to preserve security.

The absolute approach to security is actually applicable when the environment being protected is simple, relatively static, and well-defined. This viewpoint implies that the threats to the security of the entity are also simple and well-defined. The monolithic view of security also implies that the control domain of the entire environment is the same as the security domain.

Clearly, none of these conditions apply to modern computer systems. Furthermore, as systems technology effects changes such as telecommuting and distributed workforces, many of the assumptions of organizational control over environments will become even rarer with the passage of time.

12.1.2.2 Security as Risk Management

When you acknowledge that monolithic security is probably not a realistic expectation in today's system environments, it's time to consider another model. In most commercial circles, this quest has culminated in defining meaningful security in terms of risk management. Risk management takes a more process-oriented view of security, defining processes that allow you to identify threats and risks, then eliminating those that you can, and minimizing the rest. This approach acknowledges from the outset that security processes are not ever likely to provide perfect protection and takes steps to deal with the cases in which security fails. Risk management is the prevalent approach to computer security today.[1]

12.1.2.3 Security as Ecology

Some security experts argue that even risk management is an unrealistically linear characterization of security. Several propose another approach to security: to view it as a sort of ecology. *Ecology* is defined as the study of the relationships between organisms and their environment. In drawing an analogy between the two realms, note that both deal with complex entities that function in a nondeterministic fashion. The environment is composed of both other organisms (users, systems, subnets) and nonorganic entities (special-purpose devices, hardware, safes, fences, guards, guns). Ecology also comprises notions of boundaries (ecological boundaries, security perimeters, control perimeters) and change drivers (evolution, upgrades and new products/platforms).

What does this analogy buy you with regards to new insights on security? First, it gives you an appreciation of the complexity of the problem you have to tackle. The ecological aspects of security assert that you cannot afford to focus on one portion of the system without keeping track of the impact of each decision on the health of the ecosystem. Each additional network connection and user session adds to the complexity of the fray.

Furthermore, you must be constantly aware of the trade-offs each design decision requires of the system environment. Monitoring can have profound effects on performance if implemented inappropriately. Bad user interfaces can lead to efforts to bypass or nullify portions of the intrusion detection system to preserve the function of the target system. You must be aware at every juncture of the impact your design decisions have on the utility of the intrusion detection system, on the one hand, and the performance and reliability of the target system, on the other.[2]

12.1.2.4 Security as Transfer Function

Yet another approach to security that yields a great deal of practical insight comes from the cryptographic systems community. This approach was articulated in a review of the failure of cryptographic systems in commercial transactions. It asserts that one cause of ineffective computer security systems is the failure of designers to understand the practical but undocumented goal of security in the commercial world. Most acknowledge and understand that commercial security systems are designed to manage risk. In addition, they also need to support the goal of transferring liability.

In practical terms, if the security system fails, for whatever reason, the customer organization wants the system to support the transfer of liability (in intuitive terms, blame) to another party. That other party can be an account holder (in the case of a financial payment system), an insurer (in the case of a business computer system), or the government/taxpayer (in the case of criminal charges brought). I must point out, in a scenario that might be alarming to vendors and consumers of security technologies alike, that the liability can just as easily be transferred to service providers, product vendors, and consultants!

To a degree, this approach to security is an extension of the "security is ecology" approach. In this case, the legal system is just another part of the ecosystem in which you're planning to insert your intrusion detection system. From a systems design perspective, the effect of adding liability transfer to the ecosystem is to add goals and constraints to your systems requirements.

What goals and constraints are added? The following nine principles are provided:[3]

Principle 1   Security systems that are to provide evidence must be designed and certified on the assumption that they will be examined in detail by a hostile expert.

Principle 2   Expect the real problems (security system failures) to come from blunders in the application design and in the way the system is operated.

Principle 3   Before setting out to build a computer security system, make sure you understand its real purpose (especially if it differs from the advertised purpose).

Principle 4   Understand how liability is transferred by any system you build or rely on.

Principle 5   The judicial treatment of new types of technical evidence may take years to stabilize and may not converge to anything consistent.

Principle 6   Computer security legislation is highly likely to suffer from the law of unexpected consequences.

Principle 7   Don't rely on engineering standards to solve legal problems.

Principle 8   Security goals and assumptions should be based on industry practice in the application area, not on general "computer" concepts.

Principle 9   A trusted component or system is one that you can insure.

12.1.3   Policies—One Size Does Not Fit All

Most security experts consider security policies to be the Rosetta Stone for an organization's security program. When consultants are hired to assist an organization in starting a security program, the first task usually includes writing such a policy.

Because many designers of intrusion detection systems come from the ranks of security consultants or from other security disciplines, these people design systems with the assumption that an organization has a security policy and that, furthermore, the security policy is structured in a particular fashion. Although this assumption may have been true for the first wave of customers buying commercial intrusion detection systems, it may not apply to customers who function outside large organizations (and who do not have the resources that a large organization might have to devote to the writing of a security policy).

Policies vary widely from organization to organization, ranging from well-structured, extremely current working documents to ancient legal boilerplate stuck in the back of a file cabinet in the president's office. In any event, as the intrusion detection system that you design will likely be expected to accommodate detecting non-compliance with security policies, you should become acquainted with a plethora of real policies.

There are several possible sources. If you are planning to target government or military markets, their security policies are sometimes public record. Appendix C, "Resources," includes at least one book that provides policy templates for organizations to use in building their own. Searching for appropriate policy sources is also a request you might make of your marketing department, who may be able to find such information in its initial market research.

As part of your review of policies, you might look at some of the policy-building advice contained in network security texts and manuals and other references. You'll want to take note of the policies, both as they exist in your customer organizations and as they should exist in order to be effective, well structured, and complete.

This background research will serve you well. Depending on your target market and the state of security in that market, you may need to include a policy-builder front end with your product. This policy builder could, for instance, ask the customer a series of questions. Depending on the answers, the policy builder could then generate a customized security policy template for use by the intrusion detection product and generate a security policy document for the user. If you follow this approach, be very clear about the sorts of policies your intrusion detection system can enforce. To reduce legal liabilities, the sales process for your product should reflect this clarity.

If you assume that customers already have a security policy, you should perform a thorough check of your requirements for the configuration interface design. Make absolutely sure that your configuration front end allows the customer to easily specify any pattern required to detect noncompliance with the policy.

If the target market is an area with special legal requirements for monitoring activity, you may find that inserting policy rules to cover these requirements makes good business sense.

Again, if the legal requirements are subject to change, make sure that your configuration interface allows a user to readily accommodate these changes.

12.2   Security Design Principles

I've already emphasized the need for fail-safe measures in intrusion detection and other security products. In my opinion, providing such measures is one of the most critical needs in security management technologies today.

Much of what we know about correcting software flaws and errors that lead to vulnerabilities was documented more than 20 years ago. The Multics project was a landmark computer system initiative that started in 1965 as a collaboration between Bell Telephone, General Electric, and the Massachusetts Institute of Technology. This effort represents one of the most extraordinary projects in the history of computer technology, affecting almost every major computing system that came after it. Although the Multics effort produced numerous noteworthy advances in computer technology, it also produced an unusually secure system. Many of the titans of computer science and computer security were involved in the project. Among them are Peter Neumann, one of the principal architects of the IDES intrusion detection model and system; Roger Schell, former director of the National Computer Security Center; and Robert Morris, designer of the UNIX password protection algorithm and former chief scientist of the National Computer Security Center.

Multics was the first computer system to pass a Department of Defense Trusted Systems evaluation at the B2 level. Multics featured a sophisticated mechanism for implementing Mandatory Access Control (MAC), one of the cornerstones of trusted systems.[4] Jerome Saltzer and Michael Schroeder, both members of the Multics security design team, wrote a landmark paper in 1975 outlining the basic principles of information protection. These principles continue to serve as a valuable road map to designers of secure systems. Of particular note to those in the security product arena are the security design principles for protection mechanisms. These principles are described in following sections.[5]

12.2.1   Economy of Mechanism

The first principle, economy of mechanism, encourages simplicity. The old KISS maxim (Keep It Simple, Stupid) applies here. KISS is a common theme in security (it is one of the cornerstones of the reference monitor model) for an excellent reason. Protection mechanisms are effective if they are error free. Period. Furthermore, the errors that affect the effectiveness of protection mechanisms usually don't show up in normal use. Normal use doesn't usually include attempts to bypass or otherwise subvert the mechanism. Therefore, the mechanism must be simple enough to evaluate manually, by inspection, by mathematical proof, or by other means. To be capable of performing these evaluations, the protection mechanism must be small and simple.

12.2.2   Fail-Safe Defaults

The second principle of fail-safe defaults has been promulgated as a security rule of thumb for years. This principle states that access privileges should be denied by default and that part of the protection design should articulate the specific conditions under which access is allowed. Again, the rationale for this principle is intuitively clear. If a protection mechanism designed with fail-safe defaults fails, it denies access that should be permitted. This failure mode is obvious and easily detected, especially when those affected are users! On the other hand, if a mechanism designed to permit everything by default fails, the failure allows access that should be denied. The latter problem is much more likely to go unnoticed than is the former (until someone uses the illicit access as an avenue for attack!).

This principle should be applied to the protection mechanism at all points, both internally at the interprocess level as well as externally at the interface. Thus at every point in the implementation, every decision to grant access should require a deliberate action to enable it.

12.2.3   Complete Mediation

The principle of complete mediation means that you should check every access to every object to make sure that the accessing entity is properly authorized for the access. In other words, you should check for access authority at every read, write, open, and so on operation for every file or other system object.

Such vigilance mitigates some of the most common security vulnerabilities, such as race conditions. Saltzer and Schroeder assert that this principle, systematically applied, comprises the most critical foundation for a protection mechanism.

This principle also introduces another secondary need for protection mechanisms. If you check authorization at every access, you must have a strong authentication mechanism in place! This principle reinforces the importance of strong identification and authentication for the entire system.

12.2.4   Open Design

The next principle, that of "open design," states a lesson we've learned repeatedly in the security world: Don't depend on security by obscurity! The design of the protection mechanism should not rely on attackers being ignorant. To assume that this ignorance would endure the wide distribution of the protection mechanism is foolhardy at best.

Other excellent rationales exist for this principle, among them the need to allow constituencies (that is, those designers of systems that depend on the protection mechanisms) to review the protection mechanism design to determine to their own satisfaction that the mechanism is trustworthy. This practice also allows extensive peer review as a means of bolstering the testing and quality assurance process for the mechanism.

Another secondary but important need for protection mechanisms is introduced as part of this principle. If you do not rely on the ignorance of potential attackers to enable the protection mechanism, on what do you rely? Here the concept of protection credentials, such as keys or passwords, is introduced. The rationale is that keys or passwords are easier to protect than the entire protection mechanism. These credentials need to be provided and handled in a fashion that doesn't subject them to capture or replay attacks.

12.2.5 *Separation of Privilege*

Separation of privilege is the description of a principle that many of us have seen applied in everyday life. Do you have a safe deposit box? The bank probably uses a two-key system for locking the box so that your key alone is not sufficient to open the box. Another example of this principle in action is the missile arming and firing system that must have the participation of two people with proper credentials to operate.

In the protection mechanism realm, separation of privilege means that you shouldn't enable access decisions based on only one condition being met. Require that at least two conditions be met before access is allowed. This practice eliminates a bevy of spoofing attacks.

12.2.6 *Least Privilege*

The principle of least privilege asserts that every entity on the system, be it user or process, should operate with no more than the minimum level of privilege it requires to complete the task at hand. The privilege should be elevated at the time it is needed and downgraded at the instant it is no longer required. This principle limits the window of opportunity for an attack. This strategy has several second-order benefits, including limiting the opportunity for problems associated with interaction between privileged processes. The principle also limits the interval you have to audit when attempting to investigate an incident involving privileged access.

The technique of "privilege bracketing," used in many trusted systems development environments, supports this principle of secure design. Because the ability of an attacker to use the intrusion detection system as a vehicle of attack likely involves exploiting privilege, this technique is one you should master and utilize.

12.2.7   Least Common Mechanism

The principle of least common mechanism is subtler than the rest of the principles and a bit more difficult to implement. It states that you should minimize the amount of mechanism that is common to more than one user (in this case, a user is an IDS operator or controller) and relied upon by all users. Therefore, you should minimize the sharing of channels or resources. The primary problem addressed here is that of the inadvertent leakage of information between two users of a common resource. A secondary concern is that additional size or complexity results from attempting to serve all users with a common application, thereby exposing all of them to the ill effects of an error or flaw in that application.

12.2.8   Psychological Acceptability

Were I prioritizing these principles of protection mechanism design, I'd rank this principle first because, in my experience, the security product world ignores it. Ironically, psychological acceptability is a vision we can readily tackle and fulfill. This principle asserts that the human interface with the protection mechanism must be easy to use. Furthermore, it should be designed so that the required interaction is intuitively obvious to the user. The best of protection mechanisms are totally worthless if users do not use them. Good interface design removes an obstacle to someone's using the protection correctly and consistently.

12.3   Surviving the Design Process

As you travel down the road toward a complete intrusion detection system, you'll find a lot of diversions. Because this area is currently an interesting and high-visibility market niche, many parties will be interested in your design effort, some offering advice by the truckloads. I'm offering some here—your success requires you to establish clear goals and priorities from the beginning of your process and then to maintain your focus! Doing so is difficult, especially when everyone is interested in looking over your shoulder and critiquing your work. In this section, I provide some advice, gleaned over the last 10 years, on surviving the design and development process. Although it targets designers in commercial organizations here, the advice also applies to other environments.

12.3.1   Establishing Priorities

Establishing clear goals and priorities is critical to your ultimate success, as well as to your continued sanity along the way! Assuming that you have at least general marching orders ("Hey you! Go build an intrusion detection system!"), it's time to do your homework, tracking down the information that will tell you the state of the world and where you want your product to fit in it.

First, determine the resources that you have available to conduct your background research. You need to answer two questions at the outset: What products are out there, and what features do they offer? If this information is provided to you as part of your tasking, great! If not, you may have to hunt it down yourself. Because this project is a market survey, you may be able to get the information, or at least some assistance, from your marketing department. It may also help you answer two other important questions: Who are the customers for this product, and how much are they willing to pay and for what specific capabilities?

At the same time, start establishing other specifics, such as the platform(s) your intrusion detection system is to run on and monitor and organizational preferences with regard to development environments. At this time you should also identify any experts whose participation you will require.

I hope by now that you have the answers to these questions:

- What are the goals for this product effort?

- Who determines success?

- Who will use the system, and what are their needs and capabilities?

- What are the resource and other constraints placed on me?

- In what system environment will this system run?

- In what threat environment will this system run?

- Which specific capabilities must this system have?

- Who are our competitors, what capabilities do their products have, and what deficiencies?

From this information, compile a list of resources, capabilities, and constraints.

This data should give you the basis for developing initial system descriptions against which you can play what-if test cases. After a few rounds, you'll probably have some notion of your product architecture; then you're ready to march!

12.3.2   On Threat Curmudgeons

When conducting the market and customer needs assessment, include several questions about the threat environment and the customer's assumptions about the threat environment. This environment drives one of the first critical junctures of an intrusion detection (indeed any security system) design. Some product designers assume that the primary function of their system is to be a security administration tool, not a system protection tool. This outlook profoundly colors the look, feel, and capabilities of the system.

For instance, if you design a host-based intrusion detection system that depends on Windows NT event logs as information sources, does your threat model include the possibility that an adversary might tamper with the event logging mechanism? If so, you need to include both information sources aside from the event log and rules to check those sources against what the event logs tell you. On the other hand, if you do not believe that any adversary would tamper with the logging mechanism, you may choose to focus your efforts on assisting and advising the intrusion detection customer in managing the event logging mechanism and then organizing the information provided by the event log in various ways.

If you want your systems to accommodate a full range of threat environments, you must devote some time and energy to becoming a threat curmudgeon. Search the available references for published hacks that might affect the operation of the system components, on which your system will rely. Then determine how to mitigate these vulnerabilities. Check your system design against the security design principles, screening for violations of those principles. Subject the design and subsequent implementations to penetration testing. Traverse all major interfaces in the system, systematically asking questions about the trustworthiness of every data exchange. (For each data exchange ask: Who does this come from? How do I know that it's really coming from them? Are they authorized to receive this information? How do I know that?) At every point where the answer is "I don't know," consider using cryptographic measures to strengthen identification and authorization.

Extend this process to the host on which your system is to run. As part of your design, include a process for hardening the operating system platform on which your system will run. This effort may mean stripping an operating system down to bare bones, eliminating any superfluous utilities and applications. In extreme cases, this approach may mean altering hardware or physical configurations (for instance, switching to non-flash BIOS, recommending physical security measures as part of installing your system, or inserting tamper-resistant hardware devices).

12.3.3 Striking and Maintaining Balance

To be successful, your system needs to be both correct, in a security sense, and usable, in an operational sense. Striking this balance, especially if you've never worked in the operational areas is a real challenge. Even if you've worked in some of the operational roles, you are likely to need some additional input or a second opinion in some areas.

One way to satisfy this need is to convene an advisory team of experts from functional areas that are affected by your system. These would obviously include security but could also include system administration, network operation, and incident investigation staff. Ask this team to participate in a peer review process, reviewing your system design from time to time. This participation of operational personnel is extremely valuable because they can point out problems that might arise when your system is placed into operational use. Team members can also offer advice on how to deal with such conflicts, suggesting alternatives or workarounds.

12.4   Painting the Bull's Eye

With the first crop of commercial intrusion detection products have come the arguments over determining which system is best. Part of this debate involves settling on metrics for assessing performance. Metrics allow designers, developers, and customers to make intelligent determinations of what works best in meeting a particular set of goals. Unfortunately, all metrics are not equal, and a strong temptation exists, while marketing a particular intrusion detection product, to focus on metrics that may not be the best indication of a product's worth.

This section will discuss the area of measuring performance of intrusion detection systems, outlining various schemes for structuring your testing and benchmarking. We will talk about how some vendors have misused metrics in their marketing campaigns and how you as a designer can encourage your organization to focus on metrics that actually mean something to customers and other interested parties.

12.4.1   Gauging Success

This discussion of intrusion detection system metrics focuses on issues of performance, although the user interfaces and management aspects of the system are also important. However, customers and other users of the technology who interact with the user interfaces and management features can easily judge the quality of those items. But these users cannot always judge the performance of the monitoring and detection engine.

The five general areas of interest in assessing the performance of an intrusion detection system are accuracy, coverage, speed, efficiency, and robustness.

- **Accuracy**   Does the system correctly and consistently detect intrusions? Does the system detect normal activity as indicative of intrusion? Does the system detect intrusion activity as normal?

- **Coverage**   Exactly what proportion of known intrusions does the system detect?

- **Speed**   How quickly can the system find problems and report them to the user?

- **Efficiency**   How greedy is the system in terms of computing, network, and storage resource?

- **Robustness**   How often does the system fail? How does it function under stress, and how gracefully does it fail and recover from that failure?

Now let's look at how NOT to gauge performance!

12.4.2   False Starts

Almost anyone who has dealt with the commercial security products market can tell you stories of ineffective products sold by bending the truth about performance metrics. Some of the most common offenders include the following:

- Vendors who inflate the number of attack signatures by assigning multiple names to a single attack. One typical case involved a vendor who counted a single attack as three separate signatures by using different names for the attack.

- Vendors who assert that their network-based intrusion detection system is best solely because it can capture a large number of packets per minute.

- Vendors who inflate the number of attack signatures by counting network-based attack scenarios for every operating system platform they support, even though the packet-level signature on which the detection is based is identical for all of the platforms.

- Vendors who inflate the number of attack signatures by including archaic or downright nonexistent bit patterns as legitimate signatures.

I predict that as intrusion detection products grow to include anomaly detection features, this sort of weirdness will increase!

12.4.3   Testing Approaches

The first rule of testing intrusion detection is to withstand the temptation to oversimplify performance measurement. Intrusion detection systems are complex systems, usually running in somewhat chaotic environments. Thus to accurately measure their effectiveness, the systems need to be tested against a lot of criteria. Although using simplistic measures to demonstrate product superiority is considered a marketing necessity, that oversimplification applied to the design realm dooms you and your system.

You can use a variety of processes to test your system. Most involve placing the system into a test environment, instrumented with systems that are programmed to alternate "normal" or benign operations with intrusions or misuse scenarios. An early research effort dealing with testing intrusion detection systems outlined a "basic" testing procedure:

1. Create and/or select a set of test scripts.

2. Establish the desired conditions. (This step accommodates a second/third round of testing in which you add various levels of background activity.)

3. Start the intrusion detection system.

4. Run the test scripts.

5. Analyze the intrusion detection system output.

This basic testing procedure was used to run three rounds of testing, each round characterizing a performance attribute:[6]

1. **Accuracy**   Did the system correctly identify all of the intrusion activity staged? Did it misidentify normal activity as intrusion?

2. **Resource usage**   How much storage space does the intrusion detection system use per active user per hour (or other time interval)? How much memory and processor does the system consume? What is the latency between the staging of an intrusion and the system's notification of the user? Does the system become backlogged? If so, at what level of network or target system saturation?

3. **Stress testing**   How do various system stressors affect the performance, reliability, and accuracy of the intrusion detection system? If the system fails, how gracefully does this occur?

The researchers utilized the `expect` tool, based on the TCL/TK system, to stage the intrusions and the "normal" background activity.

12.4.4   Measuring Network-Based Performance

In network-based intrusion detection systems, you should place many conditions and provisions on the performance testing and measurement process. In benchmarking a network-based monitoring system, keep the following factors in mind:

• The packet capture and filter performance will vary greatly, depending on the sort of processor used.

• You should differentiate between "hard" limits, dictated by the system's design and implementation (for example, the size of state tables), and "effective" limits (the CPU, memory, and storage bandwidth).

- Packet capture rate alone is not a meaningful measure of performance. It needs to be qualified with the analysis the system performs on the packets. Some products simply count the packets. Others perform "up the stack" IP processing (in which the packets are reassembled into TCP/IP sessions), which take more time and resources but also provide much more accuracy in detecting intrusions and other problems.

- The speed of the network media on which a system can operate is also not a meaningful measure of performance. Having a system that "works on 100Mbit LANs" is not nearly as meaningful as having a system that "works on 100Mbit LANs under full traffic loads"!

- In calculating packet capture rates, you must measure packet drops and missed packets; to do otherwise is to "cook" the metrics regarding the speed and the accuracy of the intrusion detection system.

- When calculating performance, you should expect to see delays associated with record storage and retrieval, especially in systems on which large disks have been installed to accommodate stateful analysis and database features.[7]

- All signatures are not equivalent. In fact, some of the best systems have far fewer detection signatures because the signatures they do provide detect multiple instances of a common attack form.[2]

12.5 Advice from the Trenches

Because I believe that some of the best advice for new designers comes from those who precede them, to wrap up this chapter, I asked a number of designers of early intrusion detection systems and vulnerability assessment systems to offer their lessons learned. In particular, I asked them for surprises that they encountered in the course of designing their first products and for their advice to those who are designing new products.

12.5.1 Use Good Engineering Practices

To build good intrusion detection systems, you have to do high-grade design and engineering and do it even better than in other places. It's a tricky area to develop in because the people most interested in security are typically those who are the least disciplined, least likely to practice decent software engineering techniques, and the most individualistic and quirky.[2]—Steve Smaha, designer of Haystack, DIDS, Stalker, Net Stalker, and Web Stalker

12.5.2   Secure Sensors

Attack sensors should be placed on physically secure systems! In one case, a site wasn't getting any alerts because—the designers discovered much later—the person's system was being shut down every night when the user went home. In another, the user knew he wasn't supposed to turn off his system, but "borrowed" the Ethernet cable for another computer on his desktop.[8]—Mike Neuman, designer of TCP Watcher, IP Watcher, T-Signt, and UNICORN

12.5.3   Pay Attention to Correct Reassembly

Lots of the network-based products out there don't actually reassemble TCP/IP sessions correctly. Consequently, a tool like fragrouter can go right past them! Products that don't reassemble correctly are doomed when hackers start using tools like BONK and fragrouter against them.—Marcus Ranum, designer of Network Flight Recorder

12.5.4   Don't Underestimate Hardware Needs

The packet reassembly issue raises another critical issue nobody seems to think of: RAM. To do reassembly in our product (and our code is very efficient), we need about 128MB of RAM to handle a saturated FDDI (17,000 packets per second). That's buffer space for packets that are even slightly out of order. Many folks are waiting/looking to the router/switch makers to sell switches/routers that do IDS. But can you see the major router manufacturers adding 128MB of RAM to a router any time in the near future? No way. I'm concerned that they'll do no TCP reassembly and will sell products that a hacker can blow right past.[9]—Marcus Ranum

12.5.5   Don't Expect Trusted Sources of Attack Data

Eliciting attack details from either official or unofficial organizations remains exceedingly difficult. No one is forthcoming with details about even four-year-old vulnerabilities, and most residents of the security mailing lists are too young to remember four years ago! This situation is more than frustrating.

We have institutions with perfect recall of old vulnerabilities that are unwilling to release details. How will programmers ever improve their practices if they don't know what the bad ones are? At least these attacks should be released after a couple of years! How danger-ous is a four-year-old hack? Who is using the same system, same operating system version, same services, and so on that they were using four years ago? Releasing explicit details on how to hack ancient operating systems isn't going to affect anyone; however, not releasing these details will inevitably result in hackers being able to recycle old attacks, targeting new, naive victims.—Mike Neuman

12.5.6   Think Through Countermeasures

Be a little more intelligent about countermeasures. One company detects denial-of-service attacks and shuts off the attacked service in response. Isn't that a denial-of-service attack itself? Another logs all alerts to a file, and then a separate response process reads the file to act on any alerts. One portscan generated more than 30,000 lines of "attacks," which caused the firewall to shut itself down. The administrator then reenabled the firewall, which caused the response daemon to read the next line of the file, which caused the firewall to shut down. After 10 iterations of turning on the firewall and it shutting down, the administrator had to delete the attack log.—Mike Neuman

12.5.7   No Support for Forensics

Absolutely no one (else) is putting money into intrusion investigation and response tools for good reason—very few customers want or care about additional capabilities. Customers want an IDS to detect all hackers and cut them off. That's it. This situation is analogous to a corporate security system that detects people trying to break into the company and locks the doors. What about identifying the intruders? What about trying to put them in jail? Yes, companies will have to hire investigators, but computer security is no different from physical security in that respect.—Mike Neuman

12.5.8   Support Modern Security Features

Build your product with support for multiple forms of encrypted traffic. Windows 2000 is going to ship with an IPSec stack. NetBSD, FreeBSD, and Linux have reliable IPSec stacks as well. Given access to the key authority (or the raw key database), decrypting these and detecting attacks on the fly will not be difficult. Doing the same for Kerberos is possible, too.[8]—Mike Neuman

12.6   Conclusion

I've taken you on a tour of design issues associated with intrusion detection and other security management tools. We've covered some topics in requirements and reviewed the timeless security design principles with which you can build a hardened system. We've also talked about some things you can do to survive designing your system and about measuring whether your system works and how well it works. Finally, I provided some advice from developers of the early products in this market space, eliciting advice and opinions on issues involving intrusion detection design and development. I hope that now you're all charged up and ready to build a spectacular intrusion detection system!

Endnotes

1. Geer, Daniel E. "Risk Management is Where the Money Is." Presentation to the Digital Commerce Society of Boston, Boston, MA, November 3, 1998.

2. Smaha, S. E. personal communication, August 1999.

3. Anderson, R. J. "Liability and Computer Security: Nine Principles." Third European Symposium on Research in Computer Security (ESORICS), Brighton, U.K., pp. 231–245, November 1994.

4. Van Vleck, Thomas H. "Multics Home—General Information." available at `http://www.multicians.org`.

5. Saltzer, Jerome H. and M. D. Schroeder. "The Protection of Information in Computer Systems." Proceedings of the IEEE, 63(9): 1278–1308, September 1975.

6. Puketza, N. F., K. Zhang, M. Chung, B. Mukherjee, and R. A. Olsson. "A Methodology for Testing Intrusion Detection Systems." *IEEE Transactions on Software Engineering*, v. 22, no. 10, pp. 719–729, October 1996.

7. Ranum, M. J. posting to IDS mailing list, July 1999, available at `ids@uow.edu.au`, used by permission of the author.

8. Neuman, M. C. personal communication, August 1999.

9. Ranum, M. J. personal communication, August 1999.

Future Needs

"Any sufficiently advanced technology is indistinguishable from magic."
—Arthur C. Clarke
The Lost Worlds of 2001

Now that you understand the fundamental tenets of network security and the role that intrusion detection can play in protecting systems, it's time to look toward the future.

I say this knowing that even attempting to predict the future is a risky proposition. In the years I've worked in this area, time and time again I've seen security strategists blindsided by major technological or cultural developments. For instance, in 1990 Microsoft, although considered a major influence, was considered to be strictly an operating system vendor and only for a minor proportion of systems. Its dominance of the computing industry was considered unlikely. The notion that any firm, let alone a personal computer clone manufacturer, would acquire Digital Equipment Corporation was heresy. And the World Wide Web was considered an interesting idea out of the ivory towers of CERN, but nothing more. Few in security seriously considered the security impact of any of these influences, as they were considered such long shots. And yet they are integral parts of our landscape today.

Security has also gone through major change. Computer security was still very much a military and government issue into the 1980s, and those interests promoted a view of security as a software engineering issue, with formal methods considered to be the only path to "real" security.

In this chapter, I do my share of crystal ball gazing (with a little help from my friends). I outline various social, technological, and security trends and discuss the effect they are likely to have on intrusion detection functions of the future.

13.1   Future Trends in Society

The effect of the Internet on society is positively revolutionary, and that revolution has only begun. The Internet has served to compress time and space with incredible ease. Let's take a look at several trends that are likely to directly affect security and intrusion detection.

13.1.1   Global Villages and Marketplaces

In many parts of the world, the Internet has touched almost everyone and has had profound effects on commercial activity. Television programs and print advertisements display URLs for Web sites, and Internet commerce sites routinely advertise in mass media. Schoolchildren use the Internet to communicate with peers on other continents. Even young children now understand how to surf the Web for the newest information on their favorite television stars, books, and school assignments. Homebound senior citizens utilize Internet chat groups and interactive game sites to provide needed social interaction and entertainment. In the commercial realm, many retail outlets have migrated to the Internet, and the number and valuation of e-commerce sites balloon with no end in sight.

13.1.2   Privacy as an Economic Driver

However, as more everyday activity takes place on the Internet, the public is painfully aware of and concerned about violations of privacy. Privacy implies protection of a variety of types of information. First, people want to protect the data that belongs to them. In addition, they want to protect data about themselves, as well as information about their activities (for instance, what information they access). Although many security specialists consider the primary threat to privacy to be criminals, surveys of Internet users indicate that they are as concerned about privacy violations at the hands of government officials and corporations. Online banking and other scenarios in which financial assets are manipulated on the network only serve to heighten these concerns.

Privacy issues, though they have been debated in political and ideological circles, have significant commercial impact, too. The European Community's Privacy Directive includes regulations that could serve to prohibit U.S. firms from conducting electronic commerce in European markets unless the firms demonstrate that they can protect personal information at the level mandated by European law.[1] Even in the United States, commercial surveys indicate that security and privacy are considered the major obstacles to the growth of e-commerce. The financial incentive associated with privacy protection will drive many security markets.

13.1.3   A Different Kind of War

The reach of the Internet has not been limited to commercial entities. The networking of government has allowed more efficient and responsive interactions between citizens and their elected representatives.

Unfortunately, the networking of government also provides access to adversaries, which run the gamut from terrorist groups to military forces of other countries. Their network access can allow them to easily and effectively disrupt some critical operations of government. The buzzword *information warfare* was coined to describe this threat, and a great deal of attention has been given to it in military and civilian circles alike.

A secondary effect on classic models of warfare has also occurred, although it has not generated nearly as much media attention. That is the realization that, given the Internet, one can relatively easily shift the objective of war from military to economic dominance. Access to information enables even small countries to have a significant impact on the political titans of the world. Just as terrorism has allowed obscure political elements to affect the political decisions of major nations, economic information warfare can provide similar access and leverage to a small but knowledgeable adversary.

13.1.4   Sovereignty

As mentioned in Chapter 9, "Legal Issues," as the world becomes interconnected, the traditional concept of national sovereignty is placed in jeopardy. Its reliance on boundaries that are physically circumscribed dooms it, especially as network topologies become more and more estranged from physical configurations. This softening of national borders will have profound effect on governmental powers and functions such as law enforcement and the court system.

13.2   Future Trends in Technology

The network environment that enables such change in society is subject to massive change itself. Many trends in technology are likely to affect the environment intrusion detection monitors.

13.2.1   Changes in the Network Fabric

In networking we've already seen switching replace broadcast topologies to a large extent. As we've already noted, this change represents a current issue in network-based intrusion detection. However, developments in networking technology continue to affect the environments in which intrusion detection systems and functions reside.

As fiber-optic networking technology realizes incredible increases in network bandwidth (more than a millionfold in the 10 years from 1989 until 1999[2]) and the advent of products that enable the universal network, the difference between the network access provider and the telephone carrier will continue to blur.

The concept of the *universal network* is that all existing networks (voice, Internet, cable TV, data, and video broadcast networks) can be integrated into single, packet-switched, fiber-optic networks, with vast improvements in performance and manageability. This process would use specialized network switches that utilize wave-division multiplexing to accomplish multigigabit switching speeds.[3] This merging of network streams will drive access costs down. In some countries, Internet service providers have provided public access at no charge, with subsidization of charges by government and business. With low cost or free access, connection models shift to continuous access (instead of the traditional dial-up models of networking that use a modem to make sporadic connections to the network). When network access is continuous, the opportunity for attack skyrockets. This environment brings a much more apparent need for security.

13.2.2 Open Source Software

The UNIX world has already seen the effect of open source software with the proliferation of Linux. Although many assert that open source software can improve security (because it allows reviews of source code that can uncover security vulnerabilities), this environment also drives further change. Business models in which software and network access are provided at no cost to the user call for changes in traditional approaches to management and security. This change in business model continues to shift value from the system itself to the information residing on the system. Businesses understanding that information represents a critical asset will seek ways to protect it. This will drive the need for security products and services.

13.2.3 Advances in Wireless Networking

Along with the merging of household network access may come centralized data management services, utilizing thin clients, specialized single-purpose systems. These services include centrally managed applications (in which the price of access includes the ability to use a variety of software applications, all of which are managed by the access provider) and seamless access (in which you can utilize your data from your cellular phone or handheld personal digital assistant as easily as from your desktop system).

Seamless access will be driven by the growth in high-speed wireless networking. Four major contenders in wireless networking are offering data rates ranging from 1.6MB per second to 46MB per second. These networks will be coupled with various device control protocols to enable intelligent houses with remote control appliances and communications devices and truly integrated personal digital assistants that handle everything from screening telephone calls and email to managing financial accounts and transactions. This growth in wireless networking will serve to enable another trend, ubiquitous computing.

13.2.4   Ubiquitous Computing

The first wave of computing is defined as many users utilizing one computer. The second wave is defined as one computer per user. The third wave of computing, ubiquitous computing, calls for many computers for a single user and is likely to change the experience of computing for much of the population. The concept of ubiquitous computing is that computers are everywhere—transparent yet available throughout the physical environment. Furthermore, these computers are interconnected by wireless networks and therefore able to coordinate their activities, exchanging information and adapting to environmental cues.

This ubiquity of computing has interesting consequences, as do many of the other advances in technology. Many of these affect security as people who have lived for years with the assumption of privacy and control over their physical environment suddenly find that they are vulnerable to access by adversaries utilizing network connections. Just as telemarketers and prank callers have changed peoples' attitudes about telephone service, abuses of ubiquitous computing and unfettered network access may well change attitudes about network services.

13.3   Future Trends in Security

Each technological advance in combination with the proliferation of those advances (as the reach of the Internet grows) brings with it corresponding security issues. The complexities of modern systems challenge us to devise revolutionary approaches to dealing with this environment.

13.3.1   Management

In the early days of computer security, different ideological camps were vigorously debating the true nature of computer security. One camp argued that computer security was clearly a technical problem, which could be surmounted by rigorous software engineering practices, with software evaluated to determine whether certain assurances and features were provided.

The other camp argued that computer security was clearly a system management problem because users and administrators were at that time and would continue to be the primary source of most computer security problems regardless of the technical quality of the system.

The subsequent evolution of the software industry and associated computer security problems prove that whereas neither camp is totally correct, neither is totally wrong, either![4]

If you speak with the security experts charged with protecting systems of any large organization, chances are that the first complaint they have about existing security measures, intrusion detection among them, is that they are not manageable. *Manageability* is the use of technologies and products to achieve two goals: increase usability of systems and reduce costs associated with acquiring and operating them.

What will it take to make future security products manageable, even as the environments they protect are not? Several tenets are often utilized by system manufacturers; as eventually it would be nice to integrate security into their management platforms, you might want to think in the following terms:

- Manageable systems are simple. They utilize technical means and good design practices to eliminate as much complexity as possible.

- Manageable systems can be remotely accessed. This requirement obviously introduces additional requirements for security products but can actually work to the benefit of security. Certain sorts of broad-scale attack strategies are more apparent when analysts have a similarly broad view of the system events.

- Manageable systems are designed to be easy to use. This requirement means that even when the system is complex, the presentation of the information about the system allows the users to access a view of the system that is meaningful to them.

- Manageable systems are reliable and are designed so that even when things go wrong, it is easy to rectify the problem.

- Manageable systems assume that changes will be made and are designed to accommodate them.

In addition to these tenets, the following truisms have come to light in the management of security in complex systems:

- Where possible, security should be transparent to users. This practice can eliminate issues associated with user ineptitude or other errors in using security mechanisms.

- Where they can't be transparent, security mechanisms should be extremely simple to operate. Simple to operate can mean token- or biometrics-based. It does not mean multiple, machine-generated, 11-character passwords changed every 10 days!

13.3.2 Privacy-Sparing Security

As mentioned in the section on social trends, the interconnectivity that the Internet represents has driven and will continue to drive issues associated with individual privacy rights. In so doing, it compels security professionals and policy makers alike to take another look at issues that were previously lumped together as common entities. These issues are anonymity, privacy, and security.

According to Webster, *anonymity* is "the quality or state of not being named or identified." *Privacy* is defined as "freedom from unauthorized intrusion," and security is defined as "freedom from danger."[5] Some organizations on the Internet claim that anonymity and privacy are equivalent. Others assert that although security is necessary to assure privacy, it can also represent a risk to both privacy and anonymity.

The following balance must exist: Anonymity is not always required to enforce privacy. Perhaps the operative concept here is for privacy to represent control over one's anonymity, not the absolute assurance of anonymity. After all, to enforce security, anonymity directly countermands concepts of accountability that are necessary, under some schemes, to protect against unauthorized access. On the other hand, security should be designed to be privacy sparing; that is, a fundamental goal of security should be to preserve the privacy of users, divulging identity only when permission is sought and obtained in advance.

Part of this privacy-protecting process can be accomplished by using a broker or other mechanism to grant authorization without identifying the user. (As you may recall from Chapter 2, "Concepts and Definitions," *authorization* is defined as "the granting of access to users, objects, or processes.") Decoupling authorization from identification and authentication commonly occurs in cash transactions. The possession of cash serves to authorize the user to acquire goods and services without requiring the user to divulge his or her identity to the merchant conducting the transaction. Electronic commerce will always have a significant demand for commercial transactions that support authorization without I&A.

Some approaches to intrusion detection make the balance between security and privacy much easier to strike. For instance, focusing on the *context* of transactions (that is, traffic patterns and other information that do not reveal the content of communications) instead of *content* (the actual message conveyed) allows you to determine when certain sorts of problems occur without sacrificing the privacy of users.

13.3.3   Information Quality versus Access Control

I am hopeful that another change will occur in the security world, dealing with the handling of vulnerability information. The longstanding tradition of many who are charged with handling security incidents is to tightly control and never divulge information about vulnerabilities, lest it tell attackers how to intrude upon systems. This practice has driven the growth of many hacker sites that traffic in such information. This situation might be fine except that

- The quality of the information from hacker sites is unknown.

- Given the growth in data-driven attacks, there is little assurance that the sites do not prey on those who visit them for information.

I am among a growing community of security professionals who believe that reliable technical information about past attacks must be available from a trusted source. This approach not only provides a necessary repository for information needed by security managers, researchers, and developers but also mitigates the risk of attackers recycling old attacks.

13.3.4   Crypto, Crypto Everywhere . . .

Encryption, the bastion of classic information security, will also become more common in the form of virtual private networks, hardware-based link encryptors, smart cards, and media encryption software. Several recent operating systems included virtual private network features. As mentioned before, this technology will change the face of network-based intrusion detection, nullifying the value of content-based network packet analyzers and other stream-based information sources.

Although widespread use of encryption may solve some important problems in network security, attack tools to target the encryption software and hardware are likely to evolve. Such attacks would collect information, especially keys, from the endpoints of transactions, the points at which data is not encrypted. Monitoring for such attacks may require different information sources than those currently utilized by intrusion detection systems. Protecting the endpoints of cryptologic operations may grow to be one of the most important functions of intrusion detection systems.

13.3.5   The Erosion of Perimeters

One tenet of security best practice that appears to be in danger with the expansion of the Internet is the establishment of crisp security perimeters. Perimeters define the area of coverage for security policy, so this change in perimeters also brings a change in fundamental concepts of policy. The problem is analogous to the problems associated with jurisdiction and legal systems on the Internet. On the network, the classic definition of these perimeters (that is, in terms of geography) is irrelevant. So what takes their place in the network world? Ironically, some suggest that the only real boundaries on the Internet are cryptographic boundaries. Within such a definition, the sovereignty or rights of control belong to the entity that possesses the cryptographic keys.[6]

13.3.6   *Liability Transfer versus Trust Management*

Finally, as mentioned at several points throughout the book, the use of the Internet for commercial purposes will emphasize the role of security mechanisms as liability transfer agents, not as trust management mechanisms. This reinforces the need for strong identification and authentication, anonymity-preserving authorization mechanisms, and protected audit trails and other transaction logs. It also affects the content of detection rulebases because commercial regulations will certainly dictate certain classes of activity that must be detected and blocked. This trend suggests that the commercial insurance industry will at some point become involved in establishing security standards, at least for commercial activities carried out on the Internet and in other systems environments.

13.4   A Vision for Intrusion Detection

Within the maelstrom that comprises system security of the future, let's consider where intrusion detection and its supporting functions fit. Throughout this book, we've mentioned several persistent roles that intrusion detection (and the monitoring functions associated with it) can play, both now and in the future. Among these are monitoring the health and efficacy of other security mechanisms in the target system, supporting legal and business processes, and providing general system management support.

In this final section of the book, let's go further afield and talk about the things we'll need to optimize intrusion detection systems of the future.

13.4.1   *Capabilities*

In the best of worlds, what would intrusion detection systems do? I posed this question to experts in intrusion detection and network security and found a variety of items on wish lists of customers and system designers alike. Some of these focus on the analysis capabilities of the systems, whereas others address the management and interaction of the detection system itself.

Optimal intrusion detection systems would perform detection based on descriptions of event semantics, independent of syntax. This approach bridges the current gap between security policy and monitoring policy. For example, given a semantics-based detection engine, you would tell the intrusion detection system to "detect all access control violations" and it would do so for the systems monitored regardless of platform, protocol, or data type. This type of operation would be a vast improvement over the current state of detection, in which this detection goal requires complex, specific, operating-system-dependent detection signatures.

Another benefit of this capability is that, in cases involving attacks that "morph" or "mutate" (as do polymorphic viruses), the detector would recognize the mutated attack as well as the original, establishing an evidentiary and accountability trail linking the two.[7]

Another optimal feature is tighter integration of intrusion detection functions with general network management. Tighter integration would allow the intrusion detection system to perform improved trends analysis, possibly predicting impending attacks in time to block or otherwise impede their progress.[8] It is apparent from discussions with law enforcement officials and incident-handling experts that future intrusion detection systems must include features that support investigation of intrusions.

Given the nuances of legal processes worldwide, monitoring functions must be able to collect information that is reliable, protected from alteration and destruction from the time of generation until the time it is used as evidence for legal proceedings, and comprehensible to nontechnical jurors and investigators who may be called on to make decisions based on that information.[9]

Improved usability and manageability of intrusion detection systems, especially in large (more than 10,000 host) facilities is often mentioned as a need in future intrusion detection systems. Such new systems would be designed with an understanding of which detection functions can be fully automated and which should involve a person in the decision process. They would also include a rich set of interface options to allow users to view event patterns from a variety of perspectives to spot items of interest.

13.4.2   Highly Distributed Architectures

A trend that will grow in the future is the use of highly distributed monitoring architectures for intrusion detection. This approach could utilize a number of autonomous agents with variable targeting strategies. For instance, each agent could target a specific event type, signature type, platform, or process, depending on the strategy used, and various strategies could be available for governing the location of the analysis and response functions. Most likely, such agents would coexist with other information sources (logging mechanisms in operating systems and infrastructure devices) and would be managed by a supervisor process.

This supervisor process could correlate data from agents and other data sensors (for instance, agents collecting information from routers, firewalls, and network switches) to recognize subtle signs of trouble.

Distributed monitoring and analysis architecture is also well suited to implementing some of the immune-system-based intrusion detection approaches. For instance, a group of agents might patrol the system looking for anomalous processes touching critical files. Each agent might measure process activity against a particular attack signature. If an agent finds a match between the process and the attack signature, the agent might modify the process, perhaps impeding its processing speed a tiny bit. As the process triggers more agents, each will slow the process a bit more until it is slow enough to be addressed by a human or some sort of a "street sweeper" agent, who records information about the process and then kills it.

13.4.3 911 for Security Management

Interconnectivity of security devices will continue to be an issue. I believe that such secure connectivity may well be supported with a specialized communications layer earmarked for time-critical functions. This function might mimic the 911 emergency services channels that exist in many community telephone systems. As more critical functions move to the network (for instance, public utilities and health monitoring), they will need a reserved protected communications channel for use in emergencies.

13.4.4 Ubiquitous Information Sources

Given the drastic expansion of current networking bandwidths and nodes, the sources that intrusion detection systems must monitor will also increase. This situation creates a daunting task for collection and analysis components of intrusion detection systems. Sources are likely to exceed the most commonly used host- and network-based information. For instance, information could be logged and consolidated from hardware devices, thin clients, communication links, and other parts of the security infrastructure. Furthermore, the key to supporting business and legal process is collecting information across the network fabric, performing redundant monitoring, and using analysis schemes to identify corroborating information for detected attacks.

13.4.5 Silicon Guards

Another trend that could occur is a hardware version of an intrusion detection system, perhaps as part of an integrated security and networking appliance. This device would be marketed to household and small business markets, in order to allow customers to deal with the security challenges associated with continuous household connectivity to the Internet. The integrated security and networking appliance might include networking-interface hardware (including hubs or routers), a firewall, a link encryptor, a Web server, and other functions needed to allow fast yet safe connectivity.

13.4.6 Emphasis on Service, Not Product

Finally, as in telephony, central communications and network providers may eventually subsume intrusion detection. This change may come with the formation of network service utilities, as discussed earlier in this chapter.

When household network services are provided as part of an integrated network access service package, intrusion detection may well appear in a couple of guises. First, should it be performed at the network level as part of standard network management, intrusion detection will be completely transparent to end users.

Second, if it is provided to users at a household level, intrusion detection can be an optional centralized service (much as call-waiting or caller-ID services are to telephone services today) provided to users as a part of their integrated network access package.

Finally, should the network access utility market be left unregulated (with unfettered competition for customers), the buying decision will probably depend on the ability of utilities to deliver high-quality services at a reasonable cost.

In this case, intrusion detection may be used by the utility to assure the highest quality of service. In any case, intrusion detection will be more tightly integrated with network management facilities, with features that allow network administrators to place monitors and specify detection scenarios as local and global needs require.

13.5 Conclusion

Intrusion detection remains now, as I found it more than 10 years ago, at once a frustrating yet utterly fascinating problem, attracting the attention of some of the most talented people in this generation of technologists. In the opinion of many experts, myself included, computer security is one of the most important technological issues of this era.

The Internet has transformed the experience of community for much of the world. And in this fledgling community, many people believe that certain rights should apply. As in the physical world, users have a right to control their system environments, conducting commercial and other transactions in safety and privacy. And also, as in the physical world, this right is balanced with the responsibility to carry out these transactions in compliance with legal and ethical standards that promote the wise and productive use of the network. This balance of rights and responsibilities will allow us to utilize the power of network collaboration to solve many of the pressing problems of the new millennium.

Endnotes

1. Swire, P. P. and R. E. Litan. "None of Your Business: World Data Flows, Electronic Commerce, and the European Privacy Directive." interim report, Brookings Institution, October 21, 1997.

2. *Gilder Technology Report,* July 1999.

3. Taptich, B. "Photonic Synthesis, Juniper Eyes the Universal Network." *Red Herring,* March 1998.

4. Schaefer, M. personal communication, 1995.

5. *Webster's Ninth New Collegiate Dictionary.* Merriam Webster, Inc., 1985.

6. Geer, D. E. "Risk Management Is Where the Money Is." speech to the Digital Commerce Society of Boston, Boston, MA, November 3, 1998.

7. Schaefer, M. personal communication, June 1999.

8. Ziese, K. personal communication, May 1999.

9. Spafford, E. H. personal communication, September 1999.

Glossary

This list of terms and definitions covers the jargon of computer security and intrusion detection.

A-B

access control: restricting access to objects according to the access rights of the subject. Access control can be defined by the system (Mandatory Access Control, or MAC) or defined by the user who owns the object (Discretionary Access Control, or DAC).

accountability: the ability to map a given activity or event back to the responsible party.

accounting management: in network management, the identification of individual and group accesses to various network resources for purposes of allocating access (for bandwidth management or security reasons) or to properly charge those users for network services.

accreditation: the official approval of a particular computer system to operate in a specific mode, using a particular set of pro-

tections, in order to demonstrate due diligence with regard to security.

active response: a response in which the system (automatically or in concert with the user) blocks or otherwise affects the progress of a detected attack The response takes one of three forms: amending the environment, collecting more information, or striking back against the attacker.

anomaly: unusual or statistically rare.

anomaly detection: detection on the basis of whether the system activity matches that defined as abnormal.

anonymity: the quality or state of not being named or identified.

application based: descriptor for system monitors that collect data from running applications. The data sources include application event logs and other data stores internal to the application.

application log: in Microsoft Windows NT, one of three types of event logs. The application log contains events recorded by applications.

audit: the process of generating, recording, and reviewing a chronological record of system events to ascertain their accuracy.

authentication: the process of confirming the identity of a system entity (that could be a user, a system, a network node, and so on).

authorization: the granting of access to users, objects, or processes.

availability: the security requirement that the information and system resources continue to work and that authorized users be able to access resources when they need them, where they need them, and in the form in which they need them.

Basic Security Module (BSM): Sun Microsystems's security package provided to bring Sun's operating systems into compliance with the TCSEC C2 trusted system rating.

batch mode analysis: analysis that is performed on a periodic basis. Also called *interval-based analysis.*

Berkeley Packet Filter (BPF): a kernel architecture for packet capture, developed by researchers at the Lawrence Berkeley Laboratory.

broker: in software, a suite of programs that convert one program's interface to a form recognized by another program.

C-D

composition: 1. in intrusion detection, the process of combining event records from different sources or perspectives into a coherent event stream. 2. in computer security, combining a set of components into a system to allow you to determine the security attributes of the system from the analysis of the properties of the system's components.

computationally greedy: requiring a great deal of computing power; processor intensive.

confidentiality: the security requirement that access to information be limited to those users who are authorized to access it.

configuration management: in network management, identifying, tracking, and modifying the setup of network devices, such as routers and file servers.

control perimeter: the boundary defining the scope of control authority for an entity. For instance, if a system is within your control perimeter, you have the right and ability to control it in response to an attack.

coverage: the proportion of known attacks detected by an intrusion detection system.

credentialed analysis: in vulnerability analysis, passive monitoring approaches in which passwords or other access credentials are required. This sort of check usually involves accessing a system data object.

data reduction: the processing of data to eliminate redundant or irrelevant information. Data reduction improves the fidelity of the data when used for detection purposes and reduces the amount of storage required to archive the data.

datagram: the data unit in TCP/IP networks that travels between the IP module and the UDP module.

decoy server: a specialized server, established to serve as an environment into which intruders can be diverted. Also known as a *honey pot.*

deterministic: the property of processes that allows one to traverse a process both backwards and forwards, from any entry point within the process.

dynamic analysis: analysis that is performed in real time or in continuous form.

E-H

EDP audit: electronic data processing audit, the adaptation of the classic business process audit procedure and practices to accommodate data processing systems.

encryption: the process of taking an unencrypted message (plaintext), applying a mathematical function to it (encryption algorithm with a key), and producing an encrypted message (ciphertext).

event log: Microsoft's audit mechanism for Windows NT systems.

external penetrators: unauthorized users of a computer system.

fail-safe: describes the design properties of a computer system that allow it to resist active attempts to attack or bypass it.

false negative: in intrusion detection, an error that occurs when an attack is misdiagnosed as a normal activity. Also known as a *type II error.*

false positive: in intrusion detection, an error that occurs when a normal activity is misdiagnosed as an attack. Also known as a *type I error.*

fault management: in network management, identifying and locating faults in the network. This process includes finding the problem, isolating the source of the problem, and repairing (or isolating the rest of the network from) the problem.

firewall: security product that provides a security boundary between networks of differing trust or security levels by enforcing a network-level access control policy.

honey pot: a specialized server, established to serve as an environment into which intruders can be diverted. Also known as a *decoy server.*

host based: descriptor for system monitors that collect information from sources internal to a computer.

I-M

identification and authentication (I&A): a security mechanism that serves to assign a unique identity to each user (identification) and to confirm the user's identity (authentication). For many systems, I&A is implemented as userID (identification) and password (authentication) challenges.

integration: in system engineering, the combination of components into a coherent entity.

integrity: the security requirement that information be protected from unauthorized alteration.

integrity checker: a security mechanism that uses cryptographic message digest algorithms to detect integrity breaches.

internal penetrators: authorized users of a computer system who overstep their legitimate access rights. This category is divided into masqueraders and clandestine users.

interoperability: the ability of a system or product to work with other systems or products without special effort on the part of the customer.

interval-based analysis: analysis of information that occurs on a noncontinuous basis. It covers both noncontinuous collection of information and continuous collection with noncontinuous analysis of information. Also called *batch mode analysis*.

intrusion: any intentional violation of the security policy of a system.

intrusion detection: the process of monitoring the events occurring in a computer system or network, detecting signs of security problems.

intrusive monitoring: in vulnerability analysis, gaining information by performing checks that affect the normal operation of the system, even crashing the system.

manageability: the use of technologies and products to achieve two goals: increase usability of systems and reduce costs associated with acquiring and operating them.

man-in-the-middle attack: an attack strategy in which the attacker intercepts the communications stream between two parts of the victim system and then replaces the traffic between the two components with the intruder's own, eventually assuming control of the communication.

mapping: to draw conceptual connections between two processes or models.

masqueraders: attackers that penetrate systems by using user identifiers and passwords taken from legitimate users.

message digest: a cryptographic function that reliably reveals changes in information objects.

misuse detection: detection on the basis of whether the system activity matches that defined as bad.

monitor: any information-collection mechanism utilized by an intrusion detection system.

monitoring approach: the point at which information is collected.

monitoring policy: the rules outlining the way in which information is captured and interpreted.

N-R

network based: descriptor for system monitors that collect information from network sources, usually using packet capture.

network hop: an attack strategy in which the attacker successively hacks into a series of connected systems, obscuring his or her identity from the victim of the attack.

network management: controlling a network to maximize its efficiency and productivity. The five subcategories of network management are security, fault, accounting, configuration, and performance management.

noncredentialed analysis: in vulnerability analysis, active monitoring approaches in which passwords or other access credentials are not required. This sort of check is usually done by reenacting exploits, provoking a run-time reaction from the system.

nonintrusive monitoring: in vulnerability analysis, gaining information by performing standard system status queries and inspection of system attributes.

nonparametric: statistical techniques that make no assumptions about the underlying distribution of the data.

operating system audit trails: records of system events generated by a specialized operating system mechanism.

Orange Book: common name for the Trusted Computer System Evaluation Criteria, which outlines the properties of systems that can be used to hold classified or otherwise sensitive data. This criteria was developed by the National Computer Security Center.

packet: data unit that is routed from source to destination in a packet-switched network. Transmission Control Protocol/Internet Protocol (TCP/IP) is such a packet-switched network.

passive response: a response option in intrusion detection in which the system simply reports and records the problem detected, relying on the user to take subsequent action.

password cracker: specialized security checker that tests user passwords, searching for passwords that are easy to guess.

performance management: measuring the performance of various components of the network. This action includes using the results of those measurements to optimize the network performance.

polymorphic viruses: computer viruses that change form as they run. This change in form is usually intended to allow the virus to evade detection by a virus detector.

practice: the security policy provision that most specifically states how a particular security function will be carried out.

privacy: freedom from unauthorized intrusion.

privilege: the level of trust with which a system object is imbued.

privilege bracketing: the technique, used in writing secure source code, in which the privilege level of a process is increased to allow the process to run at a high level of privilege, then decreased immediately, once that need has passed.

procedure: the portion of a security policy that states the general process that will be performed to accomplish a security goal.

promiscuous mode: for network interface hardware, a mode of operation that generates an interrupt for every network frame sensed. This approach allows the network interface to display all network traffic on the segment and to capture packets for intrusion detection.

protection domain: the area of the system that the intrusion detection system is meant to monitor and protect.

protection envelope: for systems, the coverage of a set of security protections. Sometimes this area is defined by a security perimeter.

protocol stack: a set of utilities that implement a particular network protocol. For instance, in Windows machines a TCP/IP stack consists of TCP/IP software, sockets software, and hardware driver software.

Rainbow series: the set of documents outlining the Trusted Systems Initiative, a U.S. government program formed to address problems associated with computer security. The name refers to the brightly colored covers of the document set.

real-time analysis: analysis that is performed on a continuous basis, with results gained in time to alter the run-time system.

rulebase: the list of rules and/or guidance that is used to analyze event data.

S-T

scalability: how well a particular solution to a problem works when the size of the problem grows.

security log: in Microsoft Windows NT, one of three event logs. The security log contains events that are defined as security relevant.

security management: 1. the process of establishing and maintaining security in a computer or network system. The stages of this process include prevention of security problems, detection of intrusions, investigation of intrusions, and resolution. 2. in network management, controlling (granting, limiting, restricting, or denying) access to the network and resources, finding intrusions, identifying entry points for intruders, and repairing or otherwise closing those avenues of access.

security perimeter: the boundary that defines the area of security concern and security policy coverage.

security policy: 1. the set of management statements that document an organization's philosophy of protecting its computing and information assets. 2. the set of security rules enforced by the systems security features.

self-contained: refers to audit records that do not require other records for interpretation.

shunning: a response to a detected attack in which the system terminates the current and refuses subsequent TCP connections with the source IP address of the attacker.

signatures: patterns indicating misuse of a system.

sovereignty: power over a political state.

stack smashing: a common attack strategy in which buffer overflows are utilized to alter program execution in a fashion that yields additional privilege to the attacker.

static analysis: analysis of information that occurs on a noncontinuous basis. Also known as *interval-based analysis.*

steganography: hiding information by encrypting it and then using a specialized algorithm to embed it in other information.

STREAMs: a system programming model for writing device drivers.

SVR4++: a proposed standard for the format of operating system audit trails, originally proposed by Stephen Smaha.

system log: 1. in Microsoft Windows NT, one of three event logs. The system log contains events generated by the Windows NT operating system components. 2. in UNIX systems, files of system and application events, which are usually text files written a line at a time by system programs.

Tan Book: *A Guide to Understanding Audit in Trusted Systems,* a volume in the Rainbow series that explains the Trusted Systems audit system criteria, outlining functions of intrusion detection systems.

target based: descriptor for system monitors that use cryptographic hash functions to detect alterations to system objects, searching for unexpected changes.

tcpdump: a network monitoring and data acquisition tool that performs filter translation, packet acquisition, and packet display.

TCP/IP: Transmission Control Protocol/Internet Protocol, the protocol upon which the Internet is based.

TCSEC: Trusted Computer System Evaluation Criteria, the U. S. Department of Defense criteria for specifying the features and assurances suitable for computer systems that are to handle sensitive data. Also known as the Rainbow Series.

thin clients: specialized single-purpose systems.

threat: any situation or event that has the potential to harm a system.

trust: the confidence that what is expected of a system entity corresponds to actual behavior.

trusted processes: processes certified as supporting a security goal.

trusted systems: systems that employ sufficient hardware and software assurance measures to allow their use for simultaneous processing of a range of sensitive or classified information.

type I error: in intrusion detection, an error that occurs when a normal activity is misdiagnosed as an attack. Also known as a *false positive.*

type II error: in intrusion detection, an error that occurs when an attack is misdiagnosed as a normal activity. Also known as a *false negative.*

U-Z

ubiquitous computing: a term describing computing that occurs when computers are numerous, everywhere, transparent, highly available, and heavily interconnected. Furthermore, these computers will be interconnected via wireless networks and therefore will be able to coordinate their activities, exchanging information and adapting to environmental cues.

universal network: all the existing networks (voice, Internet, cable TV, data and video broadcast networks) can be integrated into a single packet-switched fiber optic network with vast improvements in performance and manageability.

vulnerabilities: weaknesses in systems that can be exploited in ways that violate security policy.

vulnerability analysis: analysis of the security state of a system or its components on the basis of information collected at intervals.

war dialer: software package that sequentially dials telephone numbers, recording any modems that answer.

Bibliography

This is a comprehensive listing of papers and other references related to intrusion detection. It is based on a bibliography originally started and maintained by Steve Smaha and his team at Haystack Labs. In more recent years, I've added entries, focusing on new research and technology in the area. I've tried to eliminate any papers that are not technical in focus and to include some papers that, although they are not abjectly intrusion detection papers, deal with topics critical to people working in the area.

Abbott, Robert P., J.S. Chin, J.E. Donnelley, W.L. Konigsford, S. Tokubo, and D.A. Webb, "Security Analysis and Enhancements of Computer Operating Systems." Technical report NBSIR 76–1041, Institute for Computer Science and Technology, National Bureau of Standards, 1976.

Anderson, James P. *Computer Security Threat Monitoring and Surveillance*. Fort Washington, PA: James P. Anderson Co., 1980.

———. "Computer Security Technology Planning Study." ESD-TR-73-51, v II. Electronic Systems Division, Air Force Systems Command, Hanscom Field, Bedford, MA, October 1972.

Anderson, Ross. "Liability and Computer Security: Nine Principles." Third European Symposium on Research in Computer Security (ESORICS), Brighton, U.K., November 1994.

Anderson, Ross, and A. Khattak. "The Use of Information Retrieval Techniques for Intrusion Detection." Presentation, First International Workshop on the Recent Advances in Intrusion Detection, Louvain-la-Neuve, Belgium, September 1998.

Anderson, Ross, and R. Needham. "Programming Satan's Computer." *Computer Science Today,* Computer Science Today, Lecture Notes in Computer Science, Springer-Verlag, Heidelberg, Germany, v 1000: 426–441. Springer LNCS v 1000: 426–441.

Axelsson, Stefan. "On a Difficulty of Intrusion Detection." Proceedings of the Second International Workshop on Recent Advances in Intrusion Detection, W. Lafayette, IN, September 1999.

Axelsson, Stefan, U. Lindqvist, U. Gustafson, and E. Jonsson. "An Approach to UNIX Security Logging." Proceedings of the Twenty-First National Information System Security Conference, Crystal City, VA, October 1998.

Bace, Rebecca. "A New Look at Perpetrators of Computer Crime." Proceedings of the Sixteenth Department of Energy Computer Security Group Conference, Denver, CO, May 1994.

Balasubramaniyan, J. S., J. O. Garcia-Fernandez, D. Isacoff, E. H. Spafford, and D. Zamboni. "An Architecture for Intrusion Detection Using Autonomous Agents." COAST technical report 98/05, Purdue University, W. Lafayette, IN, June 1998.

Balasubramaniyan, Jai S., J. O. Garcia-Fernandez, D. Isacoff, E. H. Spafford, and D. Zamboni. "An Architecture for Intrusion Detection Using Autonomous Agents." Proceedings of the Fourteenth IEEE Computer Security Applications Conference, Tucson, AZ: 13–24, December 1998.

Baldwin, Robert W. "Kuang: Rule-Based Security Checking." Documentation in `ftp://ftp.cert.org/pub/tools/cops/1.04/cops.104.tar.x5.2`.

Baldwin, Robert W. "Rule-Based Analysis of Computer Security." Massachusetts Institute of Technology, June 1987.

Banning, Debra, G. Ellingwood, C. Franklin, C. Muckinhirn, and D. Price. "Auditing of Distributed Systems." Proceedings of the Fourteenth National Computer Security Conference, Washington, DC, October 1991.

Bauer, David S. and M. E. Koblentz. "NIDX—An Expert System for Real-Time Network Intrusion Detection." Proceedings of the IEEE Computer Networking Symposium, New York, NY, pp. 98–106, April 1988.

Bishop, Matt. "A Model of Security Monitoring." Proceedings of the Fifth Annual Computer Security Applications Conference, Tucson, AZ, December 1989.

———. "A Standard Audit Log Format." Proceedings of the 1995 National Information Systems Security Conference, Baltimore, MD, October 1995.

———. "Vulnerabilities Analysis: Extended Abstract." Proceedings of the Second International Workshop on Recent Advances in Intrusion Detection, W. Lafayette, IN, September 1999.

Bishop, Matt, S. Cheung, C. Wee, J. Frank, J. Hoagland, and S. Samorodin. "The Threat from the Net." *IEEE Spectrum* 34, no. 8(1997): 56–63.

Bishop, Matt and Michael Dilger. "Checking for Race Conditions in File Access." *Computing Systems* 9, no. 2 (Spring 1996): 131–152.

Blain, Laurent and Yves Deswarte. "An Intrusion-Tolerant Security Server for an Open Distributed System." Proceedings of the European Symposium on Research in Computer Security, Toulouse, France, October 1990.

Bradley, Kirk, S. Cheung, N. Puketza, B. Mukherjee, and R. A. Olsson. "Detecting Disruptive Routers: A Distributed Network Monitoring Approach." Proceedings of the Nineteenth IEEE Symposium on Security and Privacy, Oakland, CA, May 1998.

Brentano, James. "An Expert System for Detecting Attacks on Distributed Computer Systems." Master thesis, Division of Computer Science, University of California, Davis, CA, March 1991.

Brentano, James, S. R. Snapp, G. V. Dias, T. L. Goan, L. T. Heberlein, C.-L. Ho, K. N. Leavitt, B. Mukherjee, and S. E. Smaha. "An Architecture for a Distributed Intrusion System." DOE Computer Security Conference, Las Vegas, NV, March 1991.

Carrettoni, F., S. Castano, G. Martella, and P. Samarati. "RETISS: A Real Time Security System for Threat Detection Using Fuzzy Logic." Proceedings of the Twenty-Fifth Annual IEEE International Carnahan Conference on Security Technology, Taipei, Taiwan, October 1991.

Cheswick, William. "An Evening with Berferd in Which a Cracker Is Lured, Endured, and Studied." Proceedings of USENIX Security Conference, San Francisco, CA, Winter 1992.

Cheung, Steven, R. Crawford, M. Dilger, J. Frank, J. Hoagland, K. Levitt, J. Rowe, S. Staniford-Chen, R. Yip, and D. Zerkle. "The Design of GrIDS: A Graph-Based Intrusion Detection System." University of California, Davis, Computer Science Department technical report CSE-99–2 1999.

Cheung, Steven and K. N. Levitt. "Protecting Routing Infrastructures from Denial of Service Using Cooperative Intrusion Detection." Proceedings New Security Paradigms Workshop 1997, Cumbria, U.K., September 1997.

Chung, Christina, M. Gertz, and K. Levitt. "Misuse Detection in Database Systems Through User Profiling." Proceedings of the Second International Workshop on Recent Advances in Intrusion Detection, W. Lafayette, IN, September 1999.

Chung, Mandy, N. Puketza, R. A. Olsson, and B. Mukherjee. "Simulating Concurrent Intrusions for Testing Intrusion Detection Systems: Parallelizing Intrusions." Proceedings of the 1995 National Information Systems Security Conference, Baltimore, MD, October 1995.

Christoph, Gary G., K. A. Jackson, M. C. Neumann, C. L. B. Siciliano, D. D. Simmonds, C. A. Stallings, and J. L. Thompson. "UNICORN: Misuse Detection for UNICOS." Proceedings of Supercomputing '95, San Diego, CA, December 1995.

Clyde, Allen R. "Insider Threat Identification Systems." Proceedings of the Tenth National Computer Security Conference, Washington, DC, September 1987.

———. "A Surveillance-Gate Model for Automated Information Security and Insider Threat Identification on Sensitive Computer Systems." Proceedings of the Second Insider Threat Identification Systems Conference, Rockville, MD, April 1987.

———. "Suspicious Event Testing and Weighted Scoring for the Analysis of a Surveillance Data Set." Proceedings of the Third Insider Threat Identification Systems Conference, Rockville, MD, April 1987.

Crosbie, Mark. "Applying Genetic Programming to Intrusion Detection." Proceedings of 1995 AAAI Fall Symposium on Genetic Programming, San Jose, CA, November 1995.

Crosbie, Mark, B. Dole, T. Ellis, I. Krsul, and E. H. Spafford. "IDIOT—Users Guide." Technical report TR-96–050, Purdue University, COAST Laboratory, W. Lafayette, IN, September 1996.

Crosbie, Mark, and E. H. Spafford. "Defending a Computer System Using Autonomous Agents." Proceedings of the Eighteenth National Information Systems Security Conference, Baltimore, MD, October 1995.

D.C.I. Intelligence Information Handling Committee. Proceedings of the 1987 Intrusion Detection Expert System Conference, Vienna, VA, November 1987.

Debar, Herve, M. Becker, and D. Siboni. "A Neural Network Component for an Intrusion Detection System." Proceedings of the IEEE Symposium on Research in Security and Privacy, Oakland, CA, May 1992.

———, and B. Dorizzi. "An Application of a Recurrent Network to an Intrusion Detection System." Proceedings of the International Joint Conference on Neural Networks, Baltimore, MD, June 1992.

Denning, Dorothy E. "An Intrusion Detection Model." Proceedings of the 1986 IEEE Symposium on Security and Privacy, Oakland, CA, April 1986.

————, D. Edwards, R. Jagannathan, T. Lunt, and P. G. Neumann. "A Prototype IDES—A Real-Time Intrusion Detection Expert System." Final report, Computer Science Lab, SRI International, Menlo Park, CA, August 1987.

———— and P. G. Neumann. "Requirements and Model for IDES—A Real-Time Intrusion Expert System." Technical report, Computer Science Lab, SRI International, Menlo Park, CA, August 1985.

de Queiroz, Jose Duarte, L. F. Rust da Costa Carmo, L. Pirmez. "Micael: An Autonomous Mobile Agent System to Protect Networked Applications of New Generation." Proceedings of the Second International Workshop on Recent Advances in Intrusion Detection, W. Lafayette, IN, September 1999.

Dias, Gihan, K. N. Levitt, and B. Mukherjee. "Modeling Attacks on Computer Systems: Evaluating Vulnerabilities and Forming a Basis for Attack Detection." SRI Intrusion Detection Workshop 5, Menlo Park, CA, May 1990.

Doak, Justin. "Intrusion Detection: The Application of Feature Selection, a Comparison of Algorithms, and the Application of a Network Analyzer." Master thesis, University of California, Davis, CA, September 1992.

Dowell, Cheri and P. Ramstedt. "The Computerwatch Data Reduction Tool." Proceedings of the Thirteenth National Computer Security Conference, Washington, DC, October 1990.

Farmer, D. and E. H. Spafford. "The Cops Security Checker System." In the Proceedings of the Summer of 1990 Usenix Conference, Anaheim, CA: 165–170, June 1990.

Farmer, Dan, and W. Venema. "Improving the Security of Your Site by Breaking into It." Internet white paper 1993, available from http://www.fish.com.

Farmer, D. and W. Venema. Security Administrator's Tool for Analyzing Networks (SATAN). Available from http://www.fish.com/zen/satan/satan.html.

Feiertag, Richard, L. Benzinger, S. Rho, and S. Wu. "Intrusion Detection Inter-component Adaptive Negotiation." Proceedings of the Second International Workshop on Recent Advances in Intrusion Detection, W. Lafayette, IN, September 1999.

Frank, Jeremy. "Machine Learning and Intrusion Detection: Current and Future Directions." Proceedings of the Seventeenth National Computer Security Conference, Baltimore, MD, October 1994.

Frincke, Deborah, D. Tobin, and Y. Ho. "Planning, Petri Nets, and Intrusion Detection." Proceedings of Twenty-First National Information System Security Conference, Crystal City, VA, October 1998.

Garvey, Thomas D. and T. Lunt. "Model-Based Intrusion Detection." Proceedings of the Fourteenth National Computer Security Conference, Washington, DC, October 1991.

Gates, James D. "Tools for Identifying the Source of Security Breaches." Proceedings of the Third Insider Threat Identification Systems Conference, Rockville, MD, April 1987.

Gross, Andrew H. "Analyzing Computer Intrusions." Ph.D. thesis, University of California, San Diego, Department of Computer Sciences, San Diego, CA, 1997.

Guha, Biswaroop and B. Mukherjee. "Network Security via Reverse Engineering of TCP Code: Vulnerability Analysis and Proposed Solutions." Proceedings of the IEEE Infocom '96, San Francisco, CA, March 1996.

Gupta, S. and V. D. Gligor. "Experience with a Penetration Analysis Method and Tool." Proceedings of the Fifteenth National Computer Security Conference, Baltimore, MD, October 1992.

Habra, N., B. Le Charlier, and A. Mounji. "Preliminary Report on Advanced Security Audit Trail Analysis on UNIX." Universitaires Notre Dame de la Paix, Namur, Belgium, Research report, December 1991.

————, B. Le Charlier, and A. Mounji. "Advanced Security Audit Trail Analysis on UNIX: Implementation Design of the NADF Evaluator." Research report, Universitaires Notre Dame de la Paix, Namur, Belgium, March 1993.

————, B. Le Charlier, A. Mounji, and I. Mathieu. "ASAXL Software Architecture and Rule-Base Language for Universal Audit Trail Analysis." Proceedings of the Second European Symposium on Research in Computer Security (ESORICS), Toulouse, France, November 1992.

Halme, Lawrence R. and R. K. Bauer. "AINT Misbehaving—A Taxonomy of Anti-intrusion Techniques." Proceedings of the Eighteenth National Information Systems Security Conference, Baltimore, MD, October 1995.

————, and Brian L. Kahn. "Building a Security Monitor with Adaptive User Work Profiles." Proceedings of the Eleventh National Computer Security Conference, Washington, DC, October 1988.

————, and J. V. Horne. "Automated Analysis of Computer System Audit Trails for Security Purposes." Proceedings of the Ninth National Computer Security Conference, Washington, DC, September 1986.

Hansen, Stephen E. and T. Atkins. "Automated System Monitoring and Notification with Swatch." Proceedings of the USENIX Systems Administration (LISA VII) Conference, Monterey, CA, November 1993.

Haskins, Denis H. "Keeping Watch on a VAX." *Digital Review,* December 16, 1988.

Heady, Richard, G. Luger, A. B. Maccabe, and M. Servilla. "The Architecture of a Network Level Intrusion Detection System." Technical report CS90–20, Department of Computer Science, University of New Mexico, Albuquerque, NM, August 1990.

————, G. Luger, A. B. Maccabe, M. Servilla, and J. Sturtevant. "The Prototype Implementation of a Network Level Intrusion Detection System." Technical Report CS91–11, Department of Computer Science, University of New Mexico, Albuquerque, NM, April 1991.

Heberlein, Todd. "Network Security Monitor (NSM)—Final Report." Lawrence Livermore National Laboratory, Davis, CA, February 1995.

———— and M. Bishop. "Attack Class: Address Spoofing." Nineteenth National Information Systems Security Conference, Baltimore, MD, October 1996.

————, K. Levitt, and B. Mukherjee. "A Network Security Monitor." Proceedings of the 1990 IEEE Symposium on Research in Security and Privacy, Oakland, CA, May 1990.

————, K. Levitt, and B. Mukherjee. "A Method to Detect Intrusive Activity in a Networked Environment." Proceedings of the Fourteenth National Computer Security Conference, Washington, DC, October 1991.

————, B. Mukherjee, and K. N. Levitt. "Internetwork Security Monitor." Proceedings of the Fifteenth National Computer Security Conference, October 1992.

————, B. Mukherjee, K. N. Levitt, and G. Dias (with D. Mansur). "Towards Detecting Intrusions in a Networked Environment." Proceedings of the Fourteenth Department of Energy Computer Security Group Conference, May 1991.

Helman, Paul and G. Liepins. "Statistical Foundations of Audit Trail Analysis for the Detection of Computer Misuse." *IEEE Transactions on Software Engineering* 19, no. 9(1993): 886–901.

————, G. Liepins, and W. Richards. "Foundations of Intrusion Detection." Proceedings of the Fifth Computer Security Foundations Workshop, Franconia, NH, June 1992.

Hoagland, James, C. Wee, and K. N. Levitt. "Audit Log Analysis Using the Visual Audit Browser Toolkit." University of California, Davis, Computer Science Department technical report CSE-95–11, 1995.

Hochberg, Judith, K. Jackson, C. Stallings, J. F. McClary, D. DuBois, and J. Ford. "NADIR: An Automated System for Detecting Network Intrusion and Misuse." *Computers and Security* 12, no. 3 (May 1993): 235–248.

Hofmeyr, Steven A., S. Forrest, and A. Somayaji. "Intrusion Detection Using Sequences of System Calls." *Journal of Computer Security* 6, no. 3 (1996): 151–180.

Ilgun, Koral. "USTAT: A Real-Time Intrusion Detection System for UNIX." Master thesis, University of California, Santa Barbara, CA, November 1992.

———. "USTAT: A Real-Time Intrusion Detection System for UNIX." Proceedings of the IEEE Symposium on Research in Security and Privacy, Oakland, CA, May 1993.

———, R. A. Kemmerer, and P. A. Porras. "State Transition Analysis: A Rule-Based Intrusion Detection Approach." *IEEE Transactions on Software Engineering* 21, no. 3 (March 1995): 181–199.

Jackson, Kathleen A., D. DuBois, and C. Stallings. "An Expert System Application for Network Intrusion Detection." Proceedings of the Fourteenth National Computer Security Conference, Washington, DC, October 1991.

———, M. C. Neumann, D. Simmonds, C. Stallings, J. Thompson, and G. Christoph. "An Automated Computer Misuse Detection System for UNICOS." Proceedings of the Cray Users Group Conference, Tours, France, October 1994.

Jajodia, S., S. K. Gadia, G. Bhargava, and E. H. Sibley. "Audit Trail Organization in Relational Databases." Proceedings of the 1989 IFIP Workshop on Database Security, Monterey, CA, September 1989.

Javitz, Harold S. and Al Valdez. "The SRI IDES Statistical Anomaly Detector." Proceedings of the 1991 IEEE Symposium on Research in Security and Privacy, Oakland, CA, May 1991.

Kahn, Clifford, P. Porras, S. Staniford-Chen, and B. Tung. "A Common Intrusion Detection Framework." Submitted to the *Journal of Computer Security,* July 1998.

Kelsey, John and B. Schneier. "Minimizing Bandwidth for Remote Access to Cryptographically Protected Audit Logs." Proceedings of the Second International Workshop on Recent Advances in Intrusion Detection, W. Lafayette, IN, September 1999.

Kerchen, Paul, R. Lo, J. Crossley, G. Elkinbard, and R. Olsson. "Static Analysis Virus Detection Tools for UNIX Systems." Proceedings of the Thirteenth National Computer Security Conference, Washington, DC, October 1990.

Kim, Gene H. and E. H. Spafford. "Writing, Supporting, and Evaluating Tripwire: A Publicly Available Security Tool." Proceedings of the USENIX UNIX Applications Development Symposium: 89–107, 1994.

Kim Gene H. and E. H. Spafford. "Tripwire: A Case Study in Integrity Monitoring." *Internet Beseiged: Countering Cyberspace Scofflaws;* edited by Dorothy and Peter Denning, Addison-Wesley, 1997.

King, Maria M. "Identifying and Controlling Undesirable Program Behaviors." Proceedings of the Fourteenth National Computer Security Conference, Washington, DC, October 1991.

Ko, Calvin C. W. "Execution Monitoring of Security-Critical Programs in a Distributed System: A Specification-Based Approach." Ph.D. thesis, University of California, Davis, CA, August 1996.

———, G. Fink, and K. Levitt. "Automated Detection of Vulnerabilities in Privileged Programs by Execution Monitoring." Proceedings of the Tenth Annual Computer Security Applications Conference, Orlando, FL, December 1994.

———, G. Fink, and K. Levitt. "Execution Monitoring of Security-Critical Programs in Distributed Systems: A Specification-Based Approach." Proceedings of the IEEE Symposium on Security and Privacy, May 1997.

———, D. Frincke, T. Goan, L. T. Heberlein, K. Levitt, B. Mukherjee, and C. Wee. "Analysis of an Algorithm for Distributed Recognition and Accountability." Proceedings of the First ACM Conference on Computer and Communication Security. Fairfax, VA, November 1993.

Kogan, Boris and S. Jajodia. "An Audit Model for Object-Oriented Databases." Proceedings of the Seventh Computer Security Applications Conference, San Antonio, TX, December 1991.

Kuhn, Jeffrey D. "Research Toward Intrusion Detection Through the Automated Abstraction of Audit Data." Proceedings of the Ninth National Computer Security Conference, Washington, DC, September 1986.

Kumar, Sandeep. "Classification and Detection of Computer Intrusions." Ph.D. thesis, Purdue University Department of Computer Sciences, W. Lafayette, IN, 1995.

——— and E. Spafford. "A Pattern Matching Model for Misuse Intrusion Detection." Proceedings of the Seventeenth National Computer Security Conference, Baltimore, MD, October 1994.

——— and E. Spafford. "A Software Architecture to Support Misuse Intrusion Detection." CSD-TR-95–009, Department of Computer Sciences, Purdue University, W. Lafayette, IN, 1995.

Lane, Terran and C. Brodley. "An Application of Machine Learning to Anomaly Detection." Proceedings of the Twentieth National Information System Security Conference, Baltimore, MD, October 1997.

Lankewicz, Linda and M. Benard. "A Nonparametric Pattern Recognition Approach to Intrusion Detection." Technical report TUTR 90–106, Tulane University Department of Computer Science, New Orleans, LA, October 1990.

———— and M. Benard. "Real-Time Anomaly Detection Using a Nonparametric Pattern Recognition Approach." Proceedings of the Seventh Computer Security Applications Conference, San Antonio, TX, December 1991.

Lee, Wenke and S. J. Stolfo. "Combining Knowledge Discovery and Knowledge Engineering to Build IDSs." Proceedings of the Second International Workshop on Recent Advances in Intrusion Detection, W. Lafayette, IN, September 1999.

————, S. J. Stolfo, and K. W. Mok. "A Data Mining Framework for Building Intrusion Detection Models." Proceedings of the Twentieth IEEE Symposium on Security and Privacy, Oakland, CA, 1999.

Levitt, Karl, ed. "Proceedings of Workshop on Future Directions in Computer Misuse and Anomaly Detection." University of California, Davis, CA, April 1992.

Lichtman, Zavdi and John Kimmins. "An Audit Trail Reduction Paradigm Based on Trusted Processes." Proceedings of the Thirteenth National Computer Security Conference, Washington, DC, October 1990.

Liepins, Gunar E. and H. S. Vaccaro. "Anomaly Detection: Purpose and Framework." Proceedings of the Twelfth National Computer Security Conference, Washington, DC, October 1989.

———— and H. S. Vaccaro. "Intrusion Detection: Its Role and Validation." *Computers and Security,* v 11, Oxford, UK: Elsevier Science Publishers, Ltd, 1992: 347–355.

Lindqvist, Ulf, E. Jonsson, and P. Kaijser. "The Remedy Dimension of Vulnerability Analysis." Proceedings of Twenty-First National Information System Security Conference, Crystal City, VA, October 1998.

Lundin, Emilie and E. Jonsson. "Privacy versus Intrusion Detection Analysis." Proceedings of the Second International Workshop on Recent Advances in Intrusion Detection, W. Lafayette, IN, September 1999.

Lunt, Teresa. "Automated Audit Trail Analysis and Intrusion Detection: A Survey." Proceedings of the Eleventh National Computer Security Conference, Washington, DC, October 1988.

————. "Real-Time Intrusion Detection." Proceedings of COMPCON Spring '89, San Francisco, CA, February 1989.

———— and R. Jagannathan. "A Prototype Real-Time Intrusion Detection Expert System." Proceedings of the 1988 IEEE Symposium on Security and Privacy, Oakland, CA, April 1988.

————, R. Jagannathan, R. Lee, S. Listgarten, D. L. Edwards, P. G. Neumann, H. S. Javitz, and A. Valdez. "IDES: The Enhanced Prototype." Computer Science Lab, SRI International, Menlo Park, CA, October 1988.

————, et al. "Knowledge-Based Intrusion Detection." Proceedings of the AI Systems in Government Conference, Washington, DC, March 1989.

————, et al. "A Real-Time Intrusion Detection Expert System (IDES)." Computer Science Lab, SRI International, Menlo Park, CA, May 1990.

————, et al. "IDES: A Progress Report." Proceedings of the Sixth Annual Computer Security Applications Conference, Tucson, AZ, December 1990.

McAuliffe, Noelle, D. Wolcott, L. Schaefer, N. Kelem, B. Hubbard, and T. Haley. "Is Your Computer Being Misused? A Survey of Current Intrusion Detection Technology." Proceedings of the Sixth Annual Computer Security Applications Conference, Tucson, AZ, December 1990.

McConnell, Jesse, D. A. Frincke, D. Tobin, J. Marconi, and D. Polla. "A Framework for Cooperative Intrusion Detection." Proceedings of Twenty-First National Information System Security Conference, Crystal City, VA, October 1998.

McKosky, Robert. "An Aposteriori Computer Security System to Identify Computer Viruses." PhD Thesis, University of Alabama in Huntsville, Huntsville, AL, 1989.

Mandanaris, Stefanos, M. Christensen, D. Zerkle, and K. Hermis. "A Data Mining Analysis of RTID Alarms." Proceedings of the Second International Workshop on Recent Advances in Intrusion Detection, W. Lafayette, IN, September 1999.

Mansfield, Glenn, K. Ohta, Y. Takei, N. Kato, and Y. Nemoto. "Towards Trapping Wily Intruders in the Large." Proceedings of the Second International Workshop on Recent Advances in Intrusion Detection, W. Lafayette, IN, September 1999.

Mé, Ludovic. "Security Audit Trail Analysis Using Genetic Algorithms." Proceedings of the Twelfth International Conference on Computer Safety, Reliability, and Security, Poznan, Poland, October 1993.

————. "GASSATA, a Genetic Algorithm as an Alternative Tool for Security Audit Trails Analysis." First International Workshop on the Recent Advances in Intrusion Detection, Louvain-la-Neuve, Belgium, September 1998.

Mell, Peter and M. McLarnon. "Mobile Agent Attack Resistant Distributed Hierarchical Intrusion Detection Systems." Proceedings of the Second International Workshop on Recent Advances in Intrusion Detection, W. Lafayette, IN, September 1999.

Moitra, Abba. "Real-Time Audit Log Viewer and Analyzer." Proceedings of the Fourth Workshop on Computer Security Incident Handling, Denver, CO, August 1992.

Mounji, A. "Languages and Tools for Rule-Based Distributed Intrusion Detection." Thesis, Faculte's Universitaires Notre-Dame de la Paix, Namur, Belgium, September 1997.

Mukherjee, Biswanath, L. T. Heberlein, and K. N. Levitt. "Network Intrusion Detection." *IEEE Network* 8, no. 3 (May–June 1994): 26–41.

Mutaf, Pars. "Defending Against a Denial-of-Service Attack on TCP." Proceedings of the Second International Workshop on Recent Advances in Intrusion Detection, W. Lafayette, IN, September 1999.

National Computer Security Center. "DoD Trusted Computer System Evaluation Criteria." DoD 5200.28–STD, December 1985.

———. "A Guide to Understanding Audit in Trusted Systems." NCSC-TG-001, v 2, June 1988.

Neumann, Peter G. and D. B. Parker. "A Summary of Computer Misuse Techniques." Proceedings of the Twelfth National Computer Security Conference, October 1989.

———, and P. A. Porras. "Experience with EMERALD to Date." First USENIX Workshop on Intrusion Detection and Network Monitoring, Santa Clara, CA, April 1999.

O'Brien, David. "Recognizing and Recovering from Rootkit Attacks." *Sys Admin* 5, no. 11, November 1996.

Ong, T. H., C. P. Tan, Y. T. Tan, C. K. Chew, and C. Ting. "SNMS—Shadow Network Management System." Proceedings of the Second International Workshop on Recent Advances in Intrusion Detection, W. Lafayette, IN, September 1999.

Paxson, Vern. "Bro: A System for Detecting Network Intruders in Real Time." Seventh USENIX Security Symposium, San Antonio, TX, January 1998.

——— and M. Handley. "Defending Against Network IDS Evasion." Proceedings of the Second International Workshop on Recent Advances in Intrusion Detection, W. Lafayette, IN, September 1999.

Piccioto, Jeffrey. "The Design of an Effective Auditing Subsystem." Proceedings of the 1987 IEEE Symposium on Security and Privacy, Oakland, CA, April 1987.

Porras, Phillip. "STAT, a State Transition Analysis Tool for Intrusion Detection." Master thesis, Computer Science Department, University of California, Santa Barbara, CA, July 1992.

——— and R. A. Kemmerer. "Penetration State Transition Analysis: A Rule-Based Intrusion Detection Approach." Proceedings of the Eighth Annual Computer Security Applications Conference, San Antonio, TX, November 1992.

———, and Peter Neumann. "EMERALD: Event Monitoring Enabling Responses to Anomalous Live Disturbances." Proceedings of Twentieth National Information System Security Conference, Baltimore, MD, October 1997.

Price, Katherine E. "Host-Based Misuse Detection and Conventional Operating Systems' Audit Data Collection." Master thesis, Purdue University, W. Lafayette, IN, December 1997.

Ptacek, Thomas H. and T. Newsham. "Insertions, Evasion, and Denial of Service: Eluding Network Intrusion Detection." January 1998. Available from http://www.nai.com/nai_labs/asp_set/advisory.asp.

Puketza, Nick, M. Chung, R. A. Olsson, and B. Mukherjee. "A Software Platform for Testing Intrusion Detection Systems." *IEEE Software* 14, no. 5 (1997): 43–51.

———, B. Mukherjee, R. A. Olsson, and K. Zhang. "Testing Intrusion Detection Systems: Design Methodologies and Results from an Early Prototype." Proceedings of the Seventeenth National Computer Security Conference, Baltimore, MD, October 1994.

———, K. Zhang, M. Chung, B. Mukherjee, and R. A. Olsson. "A Methodology for Testing Intrusion Detection Systems." *IEEE Transactions on Software Engineering* 22, no. 10: 719–729, October 1996.

Rao, K. N. "Security Audit for Embedded Avionics Systems." Proceedings of the Fifth Annual Computer Security Applications Conference, Tucson, AZ, December 1989.

Saltzer, Jerome H. and Michael D. Schroeder. "The Protection of Information in Computer Systems." *Proceedings of the IEEE,* 63, no. 9: 1278–1308, September 1975.

Schaefer, Marvin, B. Hubbard, D. Sterne, T. K. Haley, J. N. McAuliffe, and D. Woolcott. "Auditing: A Relevant Contribution To Trusted Database Management Systems." Proceedings of the Fifth Annual Computer Security Applications Conference, Tucson, AZ, December 1989.

Schaen, Samuel I. and B. McKenney. "Network Auditing: Issues and Recommendations." Proceedings of the Seventh Computer Security Applications Conference, San Antonio, TX, December 1991.

Schneier, Bruce and J. Kelsey. "Cryptographic Support for Secure Logs on Untrusted Machines." Proceedings of Seventh USENIX Security Symposium San Antonio, TX: 53–62, January 1998.

—— and J. Kelsey. "Secure Audit Logs to Support Computer Forensics." *ACM Transactions on Information and System Security* 1, no. 3 (1999), to appear.

Sebring, Michael M., E. Shellhouse, M. E. Hanna, and R. A. Whitehurst. "Expert Systems in Intrusion Detection: A Case Study." Proceedings of the Eleventh National Computer Security Conference, Washington, DC, October 1988.

Seiden, Kenneth F. and J. P. Melanson. "The Auditing Facility for a VMM Security Kernel." Proceedings of the 1990 IEEE Symposium on Research in Security and Privacy, Oakland, CA, May 1990.

Seleznyov, Alexandr and S. Puuronen. "Anomaly Intrusion Detection Systems: Handling Temporal Relations Between Events." Proceedings of the Second International Workshop on Recent Advances in Intrusion Detection, W. Lafayette, IN, September 1999.

Shieh, S. W. and V. D. Gligor. "Auditing the Use of Covert Storage Channels in Secure Systems." Proceedings of the 1990 IEEE Symposium on Research in Security and Privacy, Oakland, CA, May 1990.

—— and V. D. Gligor. "A Pattern-Oriented Intrusion Detection Model and Its Applications." Proceedings of the 1991 IEEE Symposium on Research in Security and Privacy, Oakland, CA, May 1991.

Shostack, Adam and Scott Blake. "Towards a Taxonomy of Network Security Assessment Techniques." Proceedings of 1999 Black Hat Briefings, Las Vegas, NV, July 1999.

Sibert, W. Olin. "Auditing in a Distributed System: SunOS MLS Audit Trails." Proceedings of the Eleventh National Computer Security Conference, Washington, DC, October 1988.

——. "Malicious Data and Computer Security." Proceedings of Nineteenth National Information System Security Conference, Baltimore, MD, October 1996.

Simonian, Richard, et al. "A Neural Network Approach Towards Intrusion Detection." Proceedings of the Thirteenth National Computer Security Conference, Washington, DC, October 1990.

Smaha, Stephen E. "Haystack: An Intrusion Detection System." Proceedings of the IEEE Fourth Aerospace Computer Security Applications Conference, Orlando, FL, December 1988.

———— and S. Snapp. "Method and System for Detecting Intrusion into and Misuse of a Data Processing System." US555742, U.S. Patent Office, September 17, 1996.

————, and J. Winslow. "Misuse Detection Tools." *Computer Security Journal* 10, no. 1, Spring 1994.

Smith, C. Fred. "Some Unintended Legal Consequences of Intentional Technological Disasters." Second Pacific Institute of Computer Security Workshop, San Diego, CA, February 1999.

———— and Erin Kenneally. "The Ties That Bind and Set Them Pleaing—Testimony from the Envisioned Trial of Kevin Mitnick." Second Pacific Institute of Computer Security Workshop, San Diego, CA, February 1999.

Snapp, Steven R., J. Brentano, G. Dias, T. Goan, T. Grance, T. Heberlein, C. Ho, K. Levitt, B. Mukherjee, D. Mansur, K. Pon, and S. Smaha. "A System for Distributed Intrusion Detection." Proceedings of COMPCON Spring '91, San Francisco, CA, February 1991.

————, J. Brentano, G. Dias, T. Goan, T. Heberlein, C. Ho, K. Levitt, B. Mukherjee, S. Smaha, T. Grance, D. Teal, and D. Mansur. "DIDS (Distributed Intrusion Detection System) Motivation, Architecture, and an Early Prototype." Proceedings of the Fourteenth National Computer Security Conference, Washington, DC, October 1991.

————, B. Mukherjee, and K. N. Levitt. "Detecting Intrusions Through Attack Signature Analysis." Proceedings of the Third Workshop on Computer Security Incident Handling. Herndon, VA, August 1991.

Sobirey, M., B. Richter, and H. Konig. "The Intrusion Detection System AID: Architecture, and Experiences in Automated Audit Analysis." Proceedings of the IFIPTC6/TC11 International Conference on Communications and Multimedia Security, Essen, Germany, September 1996.

Sommer, Peter. "Intrusion Detection Systems as Evidence." First International Workshop on the Recent Advances in Intrusion Detection, Louvain-la-Neuve, Belgium, September 1998.

Spafford, Eugene H. The Internet Worm: Crisis and Aftermath; Communications of the ACM; 32(6): 678–687, June 1989.

Staniford-Chen, Stuart, S. Cheung, R. Crawford, M. Dilger, J. Frank, J. Hoagland, K. Levitt, C. Wee, R. Yip, and D. Zerkle. "GrIDS—A Graph-Based Intrusion Detection System for Large Networks." Nineteenth National Information Systems Security Conference, Baltimore, MD, October 1996.

————, and L. Todd Heberlein. "Holding Intruders Accountable on the Internet." Proceedings of the 1995 IEEE Symposium on Security and Privacy, Oakland, CA, May 1995.

Sundaram, Aurobindo. "An Introduction to Intrusion Detection." *Crossroads: The ACM Student Magazine* 2, no. 4 (April 1996) available at `www.acm.org/crossroads/xrds2-4/intrus.html`.

Sytek, Inc. "Analysis of Computer System Audit Trails." Sytek technical reports 85009, 85018,86005, 86007, Mountain View, CA, 1985–1986.

Tener, William T. "Discovery: An Expert System in the Commercial Data Security Environment." Proceedings of the IFIP Security Conference, Monte Carlo, 1986.

————. "AI and 4GL: Automated Detection and Investigation and Detection Tools." Proceedings of the IFIP Security Conference, Sydney, Australia, 1988.

Teng, H. S., K. Chen, and S. C. Y. Lu. "Adaptive Real-Time Anomaly Detection Using Inductively Generated Sequential Patterns." Proceedings of the 1990 IEEE Symposium on Research in Security and Privacy, Oakland, CA, May 1990.

Ting, Christopher, T. H. Ong, Y. T. Tan, and P. Y. Ng. "Intrusion Detection, Internet Law Enforcement, and Insurance Coverage to Accelerate the Proliferation of Internet Business." Proceedings of the Second International Workshop on Recent Advances in Intrusion Detection, W. Lafayette, IN, September 1999.

TRW Defense Systems Group. "Intrusion Detection Expert System Feasibility Study." Final report 46761, 1986.

Tsudik, G. and R. Summers. "AudES—An Expert System for Security Auditing." Proceedings of the AAAI Conference on Innovative Applications in AI, San Jose, CA, May 1990, reprinted in *Computer Security Journal* 6, no. 1 (1990): 89–93.

United Nations Committee on Crime Prevention and Control. "International Review of Criminal Policy—United Nations Manual on the Prevention and Control of Computer-Related Crime." Revisions 43 and 44, New York, NY, 1999.

Vaccaro, Henry S. and G. E. Liepins. "Detection of Anomalous Computer Session Activity." Proceedings of the 1989 IEEE Symposium on Security and Privacy, Oakland, CA, May 1989.

Valcarce, E. M., G. W. Hoglund, L. Jansen, and L. Baillie. "ESSENSE: An Experiment in Knowledge-Based Security Monitoring and Control." Proceedings of the Third USENIX Unix Security Symposium, Baltimore, MD, September 1992.

Vert, Greg, D. A. Frincke, and J. McConnell. "A Visual Mathematical Model for Intrusion Detection." Proceedings of Twenty-First National Information System Security Conference, Crystal City, VA, October 1998.

Warrender, C., S. Forrest, and B. Pearlmutter. "Detecting Intrusions Using System Calls: Alternative Data Models." Proceedings of Twenty-Fifth IEEE Symposium on Security and Privacy, Oakland, CA, May 1999.

Wasserman, Joseph J. "The Vanishing Trail." *Bell Telephone Magazine* 47, no. 4, July–August 1968: 12–15.

Wee, Christopher. "LAFS: A Logging and Auditing File System." Proceedings of the Eleventh Computer Security Applications Conference, New Orleans, LA, December 1995.

————. "Policy-Directed Auditing and Logging." Ph.D. thesis, University of California, Davis, CA, April 1996.

Weiss, Winfried R. E. and A. Baur. "Analysis of Audit and Protocol Data Using Methods from Artificial Intelligence." Proceedings of the Thirteenth National Computer Security Conference, Washington, DC, October 1990.

Wetmore, Brad. "Audit Browsing." Master thesis, University of California, Davis, CA, 1993.

White, Greg, E. A. Fisch, and U. W. Pooch. "Cooperating Security Managers: A Peer-Based Intrusion Detection System." *IEEE Network* 10, no. 1: 20–23, January–February 1996.

————, and Udo Pooch. "Cooperating Security Managers: Distributed Intrusion Detection Systems." Oxford, UK: Elsevier Science Publishers, Ltd, *Computers and Security*, v 15, no. 5: 441–450, September/October 1996.

Winkler, J. R. "A UNIX Prototype for Intrusion and Anomaly Detection in Secure Networks." Proceedings of the Thirteenth National Computer Security Conference, Washington, DC, October 1990.

———— and W. J. Page. "Intrusion and Anomaly Detection in Trusted Systems." Proceedings of the Fifth Annual Computer Security Applications Conference, Tucson, AZ, December 1989.

Wood, Mark. "Intrusion Detection Exchange Format Requirements." Internet draft, Internet Engineering Task Force, June 1999.

Yip, Raymond and K. Levitt. "Data Level Inference Detection in Database Systems." Proceedings of the Eleventh IEEE Computer Security Foundations Workshop, Rockport, MA, June 1998.

———— and K. Levitt. "The Design and Implementation of a Data Level Database Inference Detection System." Proceedings of the Twelfth Annual IFIP WG 11.3 Working Conference on Database Security, Chalkidiki, Greece, July 1998.

Yuill, Jim, S. F. Wu, F. Gong, and M-Y. Huang. "Intrusion Detection for an Ongoing Attack." Proceedings of the Second International Workshop on Recent Advances in Intrusion Detection, W. Lafayette, IN, September 1999.

Zamboni, Diego M. "SAINT: A Security Analysis Integration Tool." Systems Administration, Networking and Security (SANS) Conference, Washington, DC, May 1996.

———— and E. H. Spafford. "New Directions for the AAFID Architecture." Proceedings of the Second International Workshop on Recent Advances in Intrusion Detection, W. Lafayette, IN, September 1999.

Zerkle, Dan and K. Levitt. "NetKuang—A Multi-Host Configuration Vulnerability Checker." Proceedings of the Sixth USENIX Security Symposium, San Jose, CA, July 1996.

APPENDIX

C

Resources

The quantity of resources available for those interested in intrusion detection and network security is truly mind-boggling. Here are the resources I use and recommend most often to customers and colleagues.

Books

Given the complexity of both security technology and the environments protected, a well-stocked bookshelf is a necessity. Included here are books from intrusion detection, other security technologies, and related areas.

Intrusion Detection and Associated Technologies

Amoroso, Edward G. *Intrusion Detection: An Introduction to Internet Surveillance, Correlation, Trace Back, Traps, and Response.* Intrusion.net, 1999.

Escamilla, Terry. *Intrusion Detection: Network Security Beyond the Firewall.* John Wiley and Sons, 1998

Freiss, Martin and R. Bach. *Protecting Networks with Satan.* O'Reilly and Associates, 1998.

Murray, James D. and D. Russell (ed.). *Windows NT Event Logging.* O'Reilly and Associates, 1998.

Northcutt, Stephen. *Network Intrusion Detection: An Analyst's Handbook.* New Riders Press, 1999.

Security References and Textbooks

Atkins, Derek. *Internet Security: Professional Reference.* New Riders Press, 1997.

Garfinkel, Simson and E. H. Spafford. *Practical UNIX and Internet Security.* O'Reilly and Associates, 1996.

Jumes, James and Coopers and Lybrand. *Microsoft Windows NT 4.0 Security, Audit, and Control.* Microsoft Press, 1998.

Kaufman, Charlie, R. Perlman, and M. Speciner. *Network Security: Private Communication in a Public World.* Prentice Hall, 1995.

Pfleeger, Charles P. *Security in Computing.* Prentice Hall, 1996.

Pooch, Udo and Gregory White. *Computer System and Network Security.* CRC Press, 1995.

Russell, Deborah. *Computer Security Basics.* O'Reilly and Associates, 1991.

Information Warfare, Critical Systems, and National Policy

Denning, Dorothy E. *Information Warfare and Security.* Addison-Wesley, 1998.

Neumann, Peter G. *Computer-Related Risks.* Addison-Wesley, 1995.

Schneider, Fred B. et al. *Trust in Cyberspace.* National Academy Press, 1999.

Introduction to Computer and Network Security

Kabay, Michel E. *The NCSA Guide to Enterprise Security: Protecting Information Assets.* McGraw Hill, 1996.

McCarthy, Linda. *Intranet Security: Stories from the Trenches.* Prentice Hall, 1997.

Cryptography

Garfinkel, Simson. *PGP: Pretty Good Privacy.* O'Reilly and Associates, 1995.

Schneier, Bruce. *Applied Cryptography: Protocols, Algorithms, and Source Code in C.* John Wiley and Sons, 1995.

Stallings, William. *Cryptography and Network Security: Principles and Practice.* Prentice Hall, 1998.

Firewalls

Chapman, D. Brent and E. Zwicky. *Building Internet Firewalls.* O'Reilly and Associates, 1995.

Cheswick, William R. and S. Bellovin, *Firewalls and Internet Security: Repelling the Wily Hacker.* Addison-Wesley, 1994.

War Stories

Freedman, David and C. Mann. *@Large: The Strange Case of the World's Biggest Internet Invasion*. Simon and Schuster, 1997.

Shimomura, Tsutomu and J. Markoff. *Takedown*. Hyperion Press, 1995.

Slatala, Michelle. and J. Quittner. *Masters of Deception: The Gang That Ruled Cyberspace*. HarperPerennial, 1996.

Stoll, Clifford. *The Cuckoo's Egg*. Doubleday, 1989.

Specific Application Venues

Garfinkel, Simson and E. H. Spafford. *Web Security and Commerce*. O'Reilly and Associates, 1997.

Ghosh, Anup K. *E-Commerce Security: Weak Links, Best Defenses*. John Wiley and Sons, 1998.

McGraw, Gary and E. Felten. *Securing Java: Getting Down to Business with Mobile Code*. John Wiley and Sons, 1999.

Cybercrime and Law Enforcement

Icove, David. *Computer Crime: A Crimefighter's Handbook*. O'Reilly and Associates, 1995.

Parker, Donn. *Fighting Computer Crime: A New Framework for Protecting Information*. John Wiley and Sons, 1998.

For Fun

This book, a gift from Gene Spafford long ago, describes an intrusion detection system that is still a *wee* bit beyond our current capabilities! It's a fun read for intrusion detection groupies.

Varley, John. *Press Enter*. published as a Tor Science Fiction Double with Robert Silverberg's Hawksbill Station, Tor SF Double, Number 26.

WWW Resources

Although books are my preferred source of information for fundamentals of any area, in security you must be prepared to deal with threats that materialize in "Internet time." Furthermore, many research papers have not been published in book form. To meet these needs, the World Wide Web is a fabulous resource.

This section focuses more on intrusion detection sites and those site providing information critical to the intrusion detection process. Many of the sites, especially the portals, provide pointers to resources for other security technologies.

Security Portals

Center for Education and Research in Information Assurance and Security, Purdue University: `http://www.cerias.purdue.edu/`

EnGarde System's Secure Zone: `http://www.securezone.com/`

Information Systems Security Resource at Algonquin College: `http://members.xoom.com/_XOOM/InfoSysSec/index.html`

National Institute of Standards and Technology Computer Security Resource Clearinghouse: `http://csrc.nist.gov`

Vulnerability Information Sources

CERT Coordination Center, Carnegie Mellon University: `http://www.cert.org`

Geek Girl (Intrusion Detection and other forum archives): `http://www.geek-girl.com`

Internet Security Systems's Xforce vulnerability database: `http://xforce.iss.net/`

L0pht Heavy Industries: `http://www.l0pht.com`

Computer Security News Daily: `http://www.mountainwave.com/`

NT-Bugtraq: `http://www.ntbugtraq.com`

Rootshell Vulnerability News: `http://www.rootshell.org`

Security Focus (Bugtraq and other security forum archives): `http://www.securityfocus.com/`

Organizations

International Information Systems Security Association (ISSA): `http://www.issa-intl.org/`

Information Systems Audit and Control Association (ISACA): `http://www.isaca.org/`

Advanced Computing Systems Association: `http://www.usenix.org/`

International Information Systems Security Certification Consortium (ISC2): `http://www.isc2.org/`

Computer Security Institute: http://www.gocsi.com/

System Administration, Networking, and Security Institute: http://www.sans.org/

Internet Society: http://www.isoc.org/

Internet Engineering Task Force: http://www.ietf.org

Intrusion Detection Working Group of IETF:
http://www.ietf.org/html.charters/idwg-charter.html

Institute of Electrical and Electronic Engineers: http://www.ieee.org

Association for Computing Machinery: http://www.acm.org

Government Sites

FBI National Infrastructure Protection Center: http://www.fbi.gov/nipc

Network Research Group, Lawrence Berkeley Laboratory: http://ee.lbl.gov/

U.S. Department of Justice Computer Crime and Intellectual Property Section:
http://www.usdoj.gov/criminal/cybercrime/index.html

Academic Sites

George Mason University: http://www.isse.gmu.edu/~csis/

Iowa State University: http://www.issl.org/

James Madison University: http://www.infosec.jmu.edu/programinfo/

Purdue University: http://www.cs.purdue.edu

University of California, Davis: http://seclab.cs.ucdavis.edu

University of California, Santa Barbara: http://cs.ucsb.edu

University of Cambridge: http://www.cl.cam.ac.uk/

University of Idaho: http://www.cs.uidaho.edu

University of Wollongong: http://www.uow.edu.au/

Commercial Products, Services, and Research

Arca Systems: http://www.arca.com/

Axent Technologies: http://www.axent.com

Bindview Development: http://www.bindview.com

Cybersafe: `http://www.cybersafe.com`

Counterpane Systems: `http://www.counterpane.com`

EnGarde Systems: `http://www.engarde.com`

Hyperon Consulting: `http://www.hyperon.com`

Internet Security Systems: `http://www.iss.net`

Network Security Wizards: `http://securitywizards.com`

Network Associates: `http://www.nai.com`

Security Dynamics: `http://www.securitydynamics.com`

SRI International: `http://www.csl.sri.com/sri-csl-security.html`

Tripwire Security Systems: `http://www.tripwiresecurity.com`

Miscellaneous Intrusion Detection References

Dan Farmer's security pages: `http://www.fish.com`

ICSA Intrusion Detection Consortium:
`http://www.icsa.net/services/consortia/intrusion/`

IDS FAQ: `http://www.robertgraham.com/pubs/network-intrusion-detection.html`

Lachlan Cranswick's home page: `http://www.ccp14.ac.uk/people/lachlan/`

Michael Sobirey's intrusion detection reference page:
`http://www-rnks.informatik.tu-cottbus.de/~sobirey/ids.html`

Checklist

When you're looking at a particular intrusion detection system, it's sometimes helpful to note the features and then compare them to your needs. The features listed here are covered in Chapter 2, "Concepts and Definitions."

Features	Your Information
Platforms Supported:	*Platforms Supported:*
Host hardware	
Software	
Target hardware	
Software	
Monitoring Approach:	*Monitoring Approach:*
Application-based	
Applications supported	
Target-based	
Host-based	
Network-based	
Analysis Type:	*Analysis Type:*
Anomaly detection	
Algorithm type	
Misuse detection	
Detection strategy	
Source of detection patterns	

continues

Features	Your Information
Sampling Frequency:	*Sampling Frequency:*
Batch- or interval-based	
Length of interval between runs	
Real time	
Delay from collection to detection	
Intrusion Detection Goal:	*Intrusion Detection Goal:*
Establish accountability	
Host accountability?	
User accountability?	
Detect and respond	
Lapse between detection and response	
Control Strategy:	*Control Strategy:*
Centralized control	
Integrated with Network Management Package	
Which packages?	
Stand-alone host-level controls	

Index

Symbols

* wild card, 80
? wild card, 80

A

AAFID (Autonomous Agents
 for Intrusion Detection),
 113-115
absence of security
 management, 179
abuse statutes, 198
access
 control, 34
 legal evidence, 196-197
 networks constraints,
  219-220
 systems (credentialed
  approaches), 141-143
accountability
 analysis, 81
 goals, 41
 ID analysis, 81
accreditation, 219
acquisitions, 250. *See also*
 corporate transitions
actions
 active responses, 125-129
 immediate responses, 132

long-term
 global responses, 133
 local responses, 132-133
 timely responses, 132
active approaches,
 vulnerability analysis,
 141-143
active responses, 125-129
 additional data, 128
 environment, 127-128
activity
 logs, 74-75
 monitoring
  case studies, 208-214
  laws, 207-214
 logs, 74-75
 rules, 14
adapters, ethernet
 networks, 70
addresses, IP structures,
 69-73
administering security
 systems, 248
Advanced Research Products
 Agency. *See* ARPA
advice to users, 124-125
agent-based detection,
 112-113
 AAFID, 113-115
 EMERALD, 115

AI (artificial intelligence), 165
Air Force Standard Base Level
 Computers. *See* SBLC
alarms
 display screens, 129
 false, 130-131
 passive responses, 129
 plug-ins, 129
 remote notification, 129
 responses, 41, 122-125
  active, 125-128
  advice to users, 124-125
  *operational
   environment, 123*
  passive, 128-129
  priorities/purposes, 123
  *regulatory
   requirements, 124*
  statutory requirements, 124
  types, 125-129
 SMNP traps, 129
alerts. *See* alarms
algorithms, genetic, 111-112
amending system
 environments, 127-128
analysis, 79
 accountability, 81
 batch mode, 40, 99-100
 credentialed techniques,
  151-152

The *Technology Series* is a comprehensive and authoritative set of guides to the most important computing standards of today. Each title in this series brings computing professionals closer to the scientists and engineers behind the technological implementations that will lead tomorrow's innovations in computing.

The following titles are currently available in the *Technology Series*:

Understanding Public-Key Infrastructure

by Carlisle Adams and Steve Lloyd
(ISBN: 1-57870-166-x)

Public-Key Infrastructure (PKI) is a technology critical for securing data and communication in both enterprise and Internet environments. *Understanding Public-Key Infrastructure* provides network architects and implementers with essential information for deploying and enhancing critical business services. The authors, Carlisle Adams and Steve Lloyd, have been extensively involved with the design of PKIs and the standardization of their underlying technologies. *Understanding Public-Key Infrastructure* presents unique expertise on PKI technology not available in any other source.

Directory Enabled Networks

by John Strassner
(ISBN: 1-57870-140-6)

Directory Enabled Networks (DEN) is a rapidly developing industry and standards effort in the Desktop Management Task Force (DMTF). DEN allows network architects and engineers to manage their networks through centralized control and provisioning, which yields significant reductions in cost of ownership. DEN is also a fundamental technology for policy-based networking. The author, John Strassner, is the creator of the DEN specification, as well as the chair of the DMTF DEN working group. *Directory Enabled Networks* is a critical resource for network architects and engineers who are considering how to optimally utilize this technology in their networking environments.

Supporting Service Level Agreements on IP Networks

by Dinesh Verma
(ISBN: 1-57870-146-5)

Service level agreements (SLAs), which allow providers of network services to contract with their customers for different levels of quality of service, are becoming increasingly popular. *Supporting Service Level Agreements on IP Networks* describes methods and techniques that can be used to ensure that the requirements of SLAs are met. This essential guide covers SLA support on traditional best-effort IP networks, as well as support of SLAs using the latest service differentiation techniques under discussion in the IETF and other standards organizations. *Supporting Service Level Agreements on IP Networks* provides information services managers and engineers with critical practical insight into the procedures required to fulfill their SLAs.

Differentiated Services for the Internet

by Kalevi Kilkki
(ISBN: 1-57870-132-5)

One of the few technologies that will enable networks to handle traffic to meet the demands of particular applications, Differentiated Services is currently being standardized by the IETF. *Differentiated Services for the Internet* offers network architects, engineers, and managers of Internet and other packet networks critical insight into this new technology.

Gigabit Ethernet Networking

by David G. Cunningham, Ph.D. and William G. Lane, Ph.D.
(ISBN: 1-57870-062-0)

Written by key contributors to the Gigabit Ethernet standard, *Gigabit Ethernet Networking* provides network engineers and architects both the necessary context of the technology and advanced knowledge of its deployment. This book offers critical information to enable readers to make cost-effective decisions about how to design and implement their particular network to meet current traffic loads and to ensure scalability with future growth.

DSL: Simulation Techniques and Standards Development for Digital Subscriber Line Systems

by Dr. Walter Chen
(ISBN: 1-57870-017-5)

The only book on the market that deals with xDSL technologies at this level, *DSL: Simulation Techniques and Standards Development for Digital Subscriber Line Systems*, is ideal for computing professionals who are looking for new high-speed communications technology, who must understand the dynamics of xDSL communications to create compliant applications, or who simply want to understand this new wave of technology.

ADSL/VDSL Principles: A Practical and Precise Study of Asymmetric Digital Subscriber Lines and Very High Speed Digital Subscriber Lines

by Dr. Dennis J. Rauschmayer
(ISBN: 1-57870-015-9)

ADSL/VDSL Principles provides the communications and networking engineer with practical explanations, technical detail, and in-depth insight needed to fully implement ADSL and VDSL. Topics that are essential to the successful implementation of these technologies are covered.

LDAP: Programming Directory-Enabled Applications with Lightweight Directory Access Protocol

by Tim Howes, Ph.D. and Mark Smith
(ISBN: 1-57870-000-0)

This book is the essential resource for programmers, software engineers, and network administrators who need to understand and implement LDAP to keep software applications compliant. If you design or program software for network computing or are interested in directory services, *LDAP: Programming Directory-Enabled Applications with Lightweight Directory Access Protocol* is an essential resource to help you understand the LDAP API; learn how to write LDAP programs; understand how to LDAP enable an existing application; and learn how to use a set of command-line LDAP tools to search and update directory information.

The *Network Architecture and Development Series* is a comprehensive set of guides that provide computing professionals with the unique insight of leading experts in today's networking technologies. Each volume explores a technology or set of technologies that is needed to build and maintain the optimal network environment for any particular organization or situation.

The following titles are currently available in the *Network Architecture and Development Series:*

The DHCP Handbook,
by Ralph Droms and Ted Lemon
(ISBN: 1-57870-137-6)

The DHCP Handbook provides network architects and administrators with an authoritative overview of the Dynamic Host Configuration Protocol (DHCP), as well as expert information on how to set up and manage a DHCP server. This book gives networking professionals already working with DHCP systems guidance on how to take full advantage of the technology to solve their management and address assignment problems. An essential resource, *The DHCP Handbook* provides the reader with critical information and expertise from author Ralph Droms, the chair of the IETF Dynamic Host Configuration (DHC) working group on automated network configuration, and author Ted Lemon, who wrote the ISC DHCP server code.

Designing Routing and Switching Architectures for Enterprise Networks,
by Howard C. Berkowitz
(ISBN: 1-57870-060-4)

A critical resource for network architects and engineers, *Designing Routing and Switching Architectures for Enterprise Networks* shows readers how to select the optimal switches and routers for their network environment and offers guidance on their effective deployment. This book provides the unique insight and experience of real-world network design from Howard Berkowitz, an experienced network designer, developer, and contributor to the standards process.

Wide Area High Speed Networks,
by Dr. Sidnie Feit
(ISBN: 1-57870-114-7)

Conventional telephony, ISDN networks, ATM networks, packet-switched networks, and Internet data technologies currently coexist in a complex tapestry. This book clearly explains each technology, describes how the technologies interoperate, and puts their various uses and advantages into perspective. *Wide Area High Speed Networks* is an authoritative resource that enables networking designers and implementers to determine which technologies to use in their networks and for which roles.

Switched, Fast, and Gigabit Ethernet, Third Edition
by Sean Riley and Robert A. Breyer
(ISBN: 1-57870-073-6)

Switched, Fast, and Gigabit Ethernet, Third Edition is the one and only solution needed to understand and fully implement this entire range of Ethernet innovations. Acting both as an overview of current technologies and hardware requirements as well as a hands-on, comprehensive tutorial for deploying and managing Switched, Fast, and Gigabit Ethernets, this guide covers the most prominent present and future challenges network administrators face.

Understanding and Deploying LDAP Directory Services,
by Tim Howes, Mark Smith, and Gordon Goode
(ISBN: 1-57870-070-1)

This comprehensive tutorial provides the reader with a thorough treatment of LDAP directory services. Designed to meet multiple needs, the first part of the book presents a general overview of the subject. The next three sections cover detailed instructions for design, deployment, and integration of directory services. The text is full of practical implementation advice and real-world deployment examples to help the reader choose the path that makes the most sense for the specific organization.

Designing Addressing Architectures for Routing and Switching,
by Howard C. Berkowitz
(ISBN: 1-57870-059-0)

Designing Addressing Architectures for Routing and Switching provides a systematic methodology for planning the wide area and local area network streets on which users and servers live. It guides the network designer in developing rational systems that are flexible and maintain a high level of service. Intended for people who are—or want to be—responsible for building large networks, this book offers a system and taxonomy for building networks that meet user requirements. It includes practical examples, configuration guides, case studies, tips, and warnings.

Wireless LANs: Implementing Interoperable Networks,
by Jim Geier
(ISBN: 1-57870-081-7)

This book provides both a context for understanding how an enterprise can benefit from the application of wireless technology, and the proven tools for efficiently implementing a wireless LAN. Based on the most recent developments in the field, *Wireless LANs: Implementing Interoperable Networks* gives network engineers vital information on planning, configuring, and supporting wireless networks.

Network Intrusion Detection:
An Analyst's Handbook

Written by Stephen Northcutt

Network
Intrusion
Detection:
An Analyst's
Handbook

- **AUTHORITATIVE:** Written by Stephen Northcutt, original developer of the Shadow intrusion detection system and Co-chair of the annual SANS conference.

- **TIMELY:** As networks grow, there are more types and numbers of attacks. Learn from the experts how to protect your information.

- **QUALITY ASSURED:** Peer reviewed by six of the top names in network security.

Unparalleled Technical Content

Network intrusion detection is one of the hottest growing areas in networking. As the number of corporate, government, and educational networks grow and as they become more interconnected through the Internet, there is a correlating increase in the types and numbers of attacks to penetrate those networks. Network intrusion detection specialists, security analysts, and consultants responsible for setting up and maintaining an effective defense against network security attacks will find all the information they need in this book.

Experience & Expertise

You want answers and solutions from someone who's been in the trenches. Someone who understands what it is you really need to know. *Network Intrusion Detection* from Stephen Northcutt is the answer. This book is a training aid and reference for those in the network security field. What sets this book apart is Stephens's approach and depth of experience. Stephen Northcutt is a name you know and trust. He is the author of *Incident Handling Step-by-Step* and *Intrusion Detection,* both published by the SANS Institute. He was the original developer of the Shadow intrusion detection system and served as the leader of the DOD Shadow Intrusion Detection Team for two years. He is currently the Chief Information Warfare Officer for the Ballistic Missile Defence Organization at the Department of Defense.

Trustworthy Advice

The *Landmark* series from New Riders targets the distinct needs of the working computer professional by providing detailed and solutions-oriented information on core technologies. We begin by partnering with authors who have unique depth of experience and the ability to speak to the needs of the practicing professional. Each book is then carefully reviewed at all stages to ensure it covers the most essential subjects in substantial depth, with great accuracy, and with ease of use in mind. These books speak to the practitioner – accurate information and trustworthy advice, at the right depth, at an attractive value.

For More Information

The book is in bookstores and computer stores nationwide. For more information, visit us online at **www.newriders.com**.

New Riders

www.newriders.com